AF598787

AVIATION

Boeing YC-14

US Air Force Experimental STOL Aircraft

JOHN K. WIMPRESS

Library of Congress Control Number: 2022944480

Type set in Impact/Minion Pro/Universe

ISBN: 978-0-7643-6653-6
Printed in India

Published by Schiffer Publishing, Ltd.
4880 Lower Valley Road
Atglen, PA 19310
Phone: (610) 593-1777; Fax: (610) 593-2002
Email: Info@schifferbooks.com
Web: www.schifferbooks.com

Acknowledgments

Information on details related to both the original AIAA case study and the re-write book was given to the authors from many sources. The contributors to the AIAA document deserving special recognition include:

Prof. Conrad Newberry, who initiated the idea of writing a case study on the YC-14, and co-authored with John Wimpress the resulting document that was published by the American Institute of Aeronautics and Astronautics (AIAA) in 1998. He added many interesting paragraphs and obtained the copyright approval from many different sources.

Al Bahrenburg, who was responsible at Boeing for developing the Tactical Airlift Military Requirements, prepared much of the section on the activities of the Air Force and Department of Defense (DoD) prior to the prototype development.

Lt. Col. Henry Van Gieson, Ret., who was the Advanced Medium STOL Transport (AMST) project officer for the Tactical Air Command (TAC), added some specific details about the early background of the AMST development.

Ken Hurley supplied most of the information in the section on the flight testing at Edwards Air Force Base and the deployment to Europe.

Ray McPherson, the Boeing project pilot, describes his viewpoint on flying the airplane and its contribution to STOL technology.

Maj. David Bittenbinder, the Air Force project pilot, has provided his observations on both the airplane and the overall program.

Maj. Gen. Alexander Kent Davidson, USAF, Ret., prepared his observations which is the viewpoint of an evaluator and potential operational user of the airplane.

James Hutton provided the impressions of a working level engineer on the program.

To this list must be added the specific contributors to this book: Mike Lombardi, Corporate Historian, who gave us complete access to the Boeing Company Archives and guided our pursuit of information on specific issues and personalities. James Stemm and Jennings Heilig, Pima Air Museum, generously facilitated access to the YC-14 Airplane One for purposes of research and photography. Marlene Taylor Houtchens, retired Boeing, for her tenacious efforts during the endless hours of organizing, editing, and typing the different versions of this book as we gradually forced the text into its final form. Special recognition must be given to Capt. Dan Dornseif, aviation writer, who proposed that the AIAA publication could be modernized and made less technical, thereby making it attractive to a broader readership. He helped edit and simplify many complex paragraphs and was our facilitator in dealings with the publisher. In addition, I owe a debt of gratitude to the following people: Bob Carver, Cover Photo, by permission; Alexander Dornseif; W. T. "Buddy" Fincher (USMC, Ret.); John Fredrickson (Boeing); Gary McGavran (Ret. Boeing); Peter Morton (Ret. Boeing); John Roundhill (Ret. Boeing); Loa Schneewind (Ret. Boeing); and Kevin Severe (USAF). Throughout the story, mention is made of various individuals and their contributions to the program. In making these observations, the author recognizes that important contributions by many people will not have received the notice they deserve. Hopefully any reader that was involved in the program and feels some neglect will be sympathetic to my limitations of space, time, and memory. It must be emphasized that this story does indeed represent the viewpoint of the author and in no way represents the positions of the US Air Force (USAF), the Boeing Company, or the Naval Post Graduate School.

Contents

Foreword

The YC-14 was an experimental aircraft developed by the Boeing Company and sponsored by the US Air Force. Its basic mission was to carry large, bulky payloads into and out of short, rough dirt fields. It was meant to replace the Lockheed C-130 Hercules for the Tactical Air Command (TAC) with an airplane that had considerably more capability. The YC-14 was developed over a period of six years, from 1971 to 1977, in response to an Air Force request for proposal (RFP) based on requirements by the Tactical Air Command. Basically, it was planned as a technology demonstrator, one of a number of such demonstrators that were being developed at that time throughout the Department of Defense (DoD) (another being the lightweight fighter, which eventually became the General Dynamics F-16 Falcon). The YC-14 had a high wing configuration with a large T tail. It was powered by two turbofan engines of approximately 50,000 pounds of thrust each, mounted above and ahead of the wing. The aircraft had a very large fuselage meant to carry the largest tanks, trucks, and vans in use by the US Army at that time. A unique aspect of the configuration was its high-lift system, needed to meet the field length requirements for takeoff and landing. For this high-lift system, the flow from the turbofan engines was exhausted over the top of the wing and passed over the upper surface of the deflected flaps. The flow was turned by the flaps and deflected in such a way as to augment the aerodynamic lift of the configuration. This high-lift system was designated as upper surface blowing (USB) and was the most efficient powered-lift system ever developed. The performance of the airplane included the capability to operate from rough dirt fields just 2,000 feet in length, even if an engine failed at the most critical time during takeoff or landing. It had a high-altitude cruise speed of about 370 knots with ferry range from the West Coast to Hawaii, which meant it could be delivered anywhere in the world. It was flight-tested for one year during 1976 and 1977 and met all the technical goals of the original RFP. After completion of the flight test, a proposal for a production program was made to the US Air Force both by Boeing and a competing team from McDonnell Douglas, who had flown their experimental airplane, the YC-15. The production program was canceled, however, before the evaluation of the two proposals was completed, as the Air Force's interest shifted to a more strategic-type airplane rather than a tactical aircraft. The two YC-14 prototype airplanes are now located near Tucson, Arizona, one of them in the Pima Air Museum and the other at Davis-Monthan Air Force Base.

This YC-14 book describes the conception, design, construction, and the testing of this unique prototype airplane. It all began with Prof. Conrad Newberry at the US Naval Post Graduate School in Monterey, California, where he taught senior military officers in their course of aeronautical engineering. He felt that the course was too science oriented, and he was looking for a way to introduce the entire process of airplane design. Prof. Louis Schmitt, a mutual friend and fellow aerodynamicist, told Prof. Newberry, of my relationship with the YC-14, and he contacted me about joining him in writing a book describing the program. He felt my viewpoint was particularly valuable since, I was the only engineer that participated in the entire program from the pre-proposal studies clear through observing the last flight of the airplane to storage.

The technical document created by Prof. Newberry and me was written as a case study. It showed how a specific aircraft really was designed, built, and tested, while describing the decisions that determined the airplane's configuration and characteristics. The YC-14 was selected for a case study because it incorporated several features that were at the leading edge of applied technology, thereby contributing to airplane design progress even though it was strictly a prototype airplane with no direct production follow-on. Our document titled "The YC-14 STOL Prototype: Its Design, Development and Flight Test," was published in 1998 by the American Institute of Aeronautics and Astronautics (AIAA), and it forms the core of the present book of which I am the sole author.

After the AIAA document had been in print for about twenty years, there entered a very important personality in the history of this present writing, Captain Dan Dornseif, a 737 pilot with a major US airline, who had written three outstanding books about Boeing transport airplanes. He had read the AIAA published document about the YC-14 and felt the story could be modernized and simplified technically, and thereby made attractive to a broader readership. He suggested contacting Schiffer Publishing, Ltd., who had published his books as well as other books on military and commercial aircraft. He agreed to guide me through the publishing process, an offer I gratefully accepted.

Also, I received a great idea from a fellow Boeing retiree, Peter Morton, who had been a flight deck engineer, and was used to explaining complicated processes and situations to others. He suggested that the basic story of the airplane's development be the main part of the book and then put the more technical aspects into applicable appendices. This approach enabled the basic airplane story to be told in a way understandable to the casual reader and yet make the more technical aspects available to those with deeper technical interests and capability. He continually added his encouragement to re-write this book saying "the history of the YC-14 will be told only once. Therefore, the recording should be accurate and as complete as possible".

The story related in this re-write book primarily is one of technological development, and a concerted effort is made to explain the design processes that were followed to arrive at the various design decisions. However, many of the decisions of the program were not purely technical but involved the politics of Boeing, the Air Force, the Department of Defense (DoD), and Congress. These political and other non-technical influences had large impacts on the program and illustrate the way a new vehicle design can be affected by factors over which the designer has essentially no control.

The contributions of individual personalities involved in the program are discussed also to show how emotions and personal opinions get into designs, thereby making the description a little less sterile than a purely technical recital would be. Throughout the narrative a first-person description of many of the events is made by the author. This technique is used to emphasize that many of the opinions expressed are strictly personal ones and to convey the emotional involvement that occurs when one's activities are devoted completely to a challenging development program. It may appear to the reader that this program was fraught with an unusual number of problems, because much of the document is devoted to describing how they happened and how they were solved. The YC-14 included technology that was on the leading edge of applied knowledge in several areas, so the development did produce more new problems than would occur on a more conventional design. One must recognize also that much of the design went rather routinely, but the problems that occurred required most of the attention of the engineering manager whose viewpoint is represented by this writing.

This story is based on the research and recollections of the author. Since some of these events took place many years ago, these recollections may not be completely accurate. The author's memory was helped by a rather complete set of diary notes made during much of the development of this airplane. These notes, when coordinated with the papers written for technical societies, such as The Society of Automotive Engineers (SAE) and The American Institute of Aeronautics and Astronautics (AIAA), done during the design period, have helped to make the series of events related here reasonably accurate.

CHAPTER 1

The United States Air Force Need for a New Airlifter

Background

By the 1970s, Boeing had a demonstrated record of experience in the design, manufacture, and operation of military transport aircraft. This expertise was enhanced by their pioneering efforts in the design of multi-engine jet transport aircraft.

Boeing's Military Transport Interest

It was only natural that Boeing should enter into the competition for a military short takeoff and landing (STOL) transport design. Boeing had been developing military transport airplanes since the end of World War II. That war demonstrated the utility of carrying goods of all kinds by air. Boeing spent the war years building B-17s and B-29s but, immediately after the war, developed a large four-engine airplane that incorporated the wings and tail of the B-29. This airplane became the Boeing 377 Stratocruiser, for commercial service, and the C-97 and KC-97 for the USAF. Nearly 900 of these airplanes were built for use as freighters and aerial tankers, respectively.

The Boeing 377 was the airliner version of the C/KC-97, built for the USAF. The design was based on the Boeing B-29 bomber from World War II. *Courtesy of the Boeing Company*

In 1954, the Boeing 367-80 (commonly known as the "Dash 80") flew for the first time, an aircraft that became the basis both for the Boeing 707 jetliner and the KC-135. Developed in 1956, the KC-135 was used primarily as a tanker to refuel the B-52 but was also as a freighter throughout the world. Over seven hundred C- and KC-135s were built and, along with the C- and KC-97, put Boeing firmly into the military transport business. Boeing also entered the competitions for the C-141 and the C-5. Both of these were lost by Boeing to Lockheed.

The Boeing KC-97 was an important aircraft that normalized aerial refueling and continued the use of the modern-style refueling boom that was developed for the KB-29. *Courtesy of the Boeing Company*

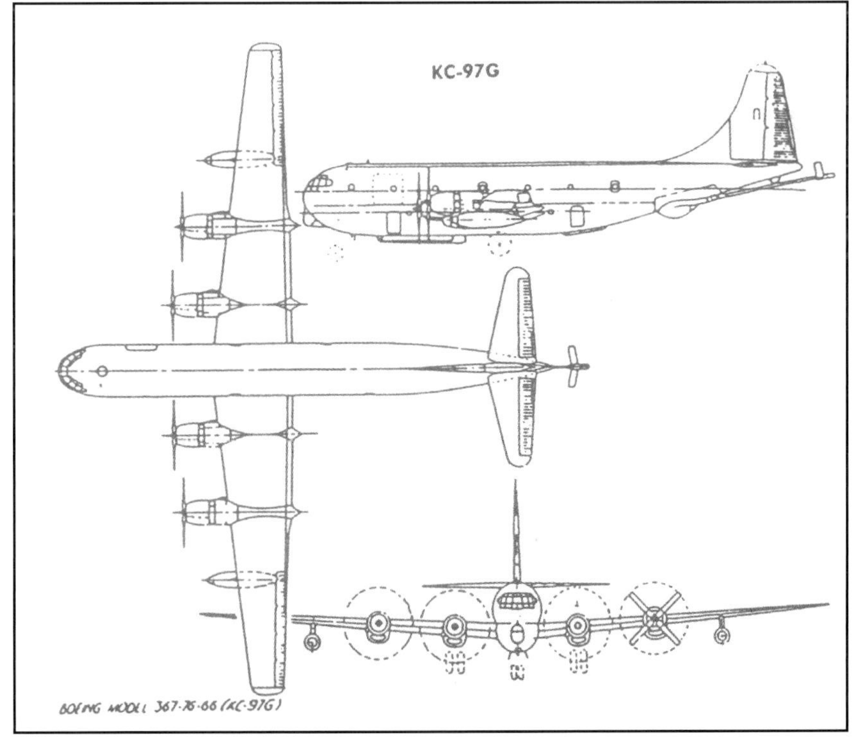

The Boeing 367-80, known informally as the "Dash 80," was the test aircraft that led to both the KC-135 jet tanker and the famous Boeing 707 series of jetliners. *Courtesy of the Boeing Company*

However, not being victorious in a competition is not always a bad result. The loss of the C-5 competition to Lockheed enabled Boeing to develop the 747, which was a large factor in placing the company in a dominant position in the jetliner business. With thirty years of military transport experience, it was entirely logical that Boeing entered the competition to develop a STOL military transport in 1972.

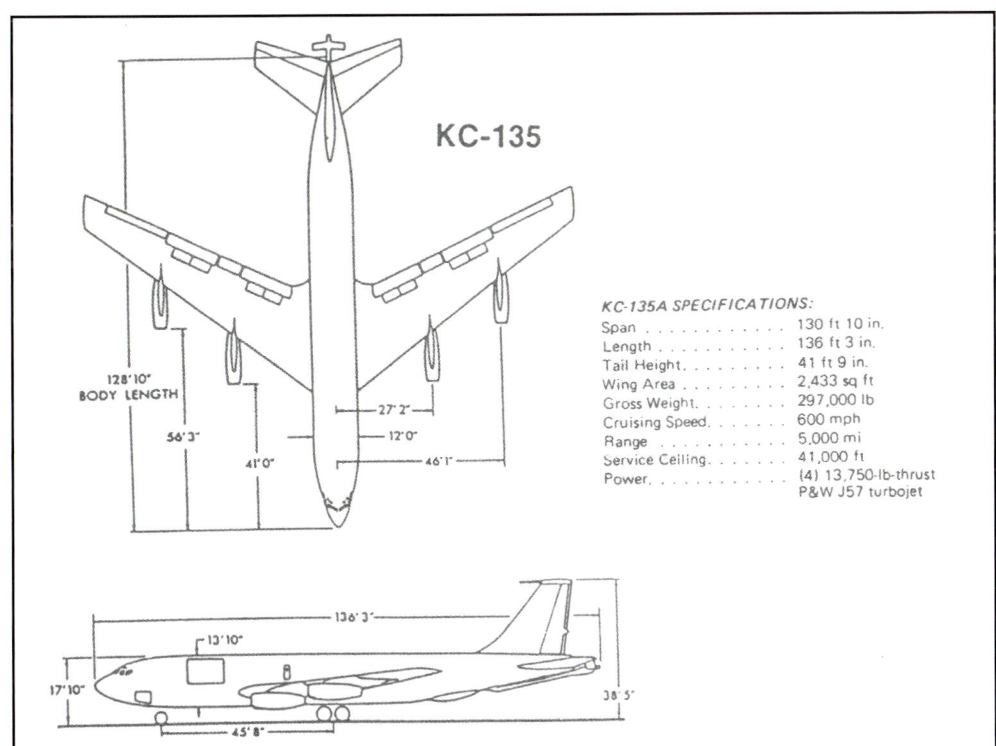

The Boeing KC-135 built upon the progress made with the KC-97 and added jet speed to the tanker operation. *Courtesy of the Boeing Company*

The Boeing 727 was the most successful jetliner of its time and truly brought air travel to the masses. *Courtesy of the Boeing Company*

Boeing's STOL Interest

Boeing also had appreciable experience in the development of airplanes exhibiting short takeoff and landing distances. However, the high-lift system for the 707 was relatively rudimentary. Early 707s had no leading-edge, high-lift devices. Its trailing-edge flaps, although providing reasonable takeoff characteristics, were primarily designed for landing. On landing approach, a fairly high-drag configuration was needed so that higher thrust could be maintained by the engines. At these higher thrust values, the engines had better acceleration and deceleration response characteristics, thereby aiding approach path control and rapid go-around initiation. Leading-edge flaps were added to the 707 design later on to provide lower drag during takeoff. When the Boeing 727 jetliner development began, there was a distinct requirement for a more sophisticated high-lift system. One of the requirements specified by Eastern Airlines for the 727 was the ability to operate out of New York's La Guardia Airport. At that time, La Guardia's runways had not yet been extended onto piers over Flushing Bay. It had a short runway that was a very challenging requirement for a jet transport. There was also the requirement by United Airlines that the airplane must operate from Denver, a high-altitude airport with hot summer temperatures. This requirement meant that the airplane had to have flaps with very low aerodynamic drag in the takeoff configuration. These two requirements led to the development of the 727's triple-slotted flaps, having a great deal of Fowler (aft-articulating) motion for takeoff and a large angle deflection with three slots for landing. The same flap concept was carried on to the 737, Boeing's entry into the short-range jet transport market. The success of these high-lift systems led Boeing to continue research and development into more-exotic high-lift systems for slow flight. The Dash 80 was modified to include sophisticated leading-edge devices as well as boundary layer control (BLC) both on leading-edge and trailing-edge flaps (see appendix 2, figure A-12). These research efforts gave Boeing a great appreciation for the benefits of slow flight capability. They also gave Boeing practical experience in the difficulties involved with building high-lift systems, particularly those that required large quantities of hot, high-pressure air for use in boundary layer control systems. While exceedingly useful, extracting large volumes of bleed air from a jet engine can reduce engine efficiency and performance to the point that there is no net improvement from the BLC system.

During this period, Boeing was monitoring American and European development of the concept of using jet exhaust to augment aerodynamic lift. English aerodynamicist I. M. Davidson wrote his pioneering paper titled "The Jet Flap" in 1956, around the same time that NASA was doing experimental work on this concept. Most of NASA's work concentrated on configurations having the jet sheet coming directly from the trailing edge of the wing (internally blown jet flap). However, they also studied a jet flap in which the flow from a podded jet engine impinged on the trailing-edge flap and spread out to form a jet sheet or jet flap behind the wing (externally blown flap). The possible use of an externally blown flap on a 707 was examined by Boeing to enhance takeoff and landing performance. The 707, however, typically was runway limited on takeoff rather than on landing, and, unfortunately, for takeoff the jet flap proved to have no advantage.

In 1959, George Schairer, Boeing vice president of research and development, presented a paper (unpublished) at Langley Field, Virginia, titled "A Designer Looks at V/STOL." In this paper, he examined the power requirements to fly very slowly. He showed that nearly as much thrust is required to fly slowly in descent as is required to fly slowly while climbing (please see appendix 2, figure A-02). In 1961, in a paper titled "Looking Ahead in V/STOL," which was presented to a joint meeting of the Institute of Aeronautical Sciences and The Royal Aeronautical Society in London, England, Mr. Schairer went on to show that to descend, the thrust must be deflected to a greater angle relative to the airframe than is required for takeoff. Thus, the landing became the more challenging problem, because nearly as much thrust is needed and it has to be deflected farther. In 1965, I wrote a paper for the Advisory Group for Aeronautical Research and Development (AGARD) titled "Shortening the Takeoff and Landing Distances of High-Speed Aircraft." In this paper, I showed that for the type of wing loading needed for high-speed, high-altitude performance, thrust deflection of some kind was needed to obtain takeoff and landing field lengths much less than about 2,000 feet. Aerodynamics alone could not support the airplane at the low speeds required for such a short field length, and some measure of thrust deflection must be used to help hold the airplane aloft. Even if the aerodynamic technology advanced to the point where extremely high lift coefficients could be obtained, the power required to overcome the induced drag of such a high lift became prohibitive, and it was more efficient to utilize engine thrust to produce part of the lift (please see appendix 2, figure A-03).

In the early 1960s, Boeing submitted its competitive proposal for the C-5 logistic transport, which had requirements for short and rough fields. To meet these requirements, Boeing proposed an externally blown flap system where high-bypass-ratio turbofan engines exhausted against the flap to form a jet flap. Although this system was effective for the C-5, it was recognized that large thrust losses resulted from the jet impinging on the slotted trailing-edge flaps (see appendix 2, figure A-04). Also, the jet flow could not be turned far enough to allow high thrust to be used to create lift and still descend along the approach path. This problem is described in detail in a paper I wrote for the New York Academy of Sciences in 1968, titled "Aerodynamic Technology Applied to Takeoff and Landing."

The high-lift systems on the 727 were complex, but effective. Boeing engineers used to jokingly refer to the 727 flap extension and retraction as the disassembly and reassembly of the wing. *Courtesy of the Boeing Company*

During this period of the late 1960s, there was a great deal of interest in STOL in the United States (both in the military and at NASA for commercial application) as well as in Europe. To keep abreast of these developments, Boeing was involved in studies of many kinds trying to ascertain the particular advantages for each STOL system, while at the same time trying to put a sense of reality into the configurations being studied. Concepts that at first glance looked very promising gave way to rather mediocre performance when the realities of the installation were considered. Items such as weight, complexity, and losses in the net propulsive effort due to air bled for boundary layer control detracted from theoretical performance levels. Although there had been successful applications of boundary layer control on several Navy and Air Force fighter airplanes, no true STOL airplane had been developed that had practical performance, including high-speed performance.

About this time the DoD, at the urging of the Defense Science Board, instigated a series of technology demonstration projects. The idea behind these demonstration projects was to show what technology was available for practical application to new weapons systems. This demonstration effort included projects from infantry rifles to fighter aircraft. One of the concepts that was selected was that of a STOL transport; that is, to demonstrate the technology required to produce a successful STOL transport. In mid-1970, the Air Force contracted with Boeing, McDonnell Douglas, Fairchild, and another company or two to study various types of tactical aircraft transports. This study was called the Tactical Aircraft Investigation (TAI). It was strictly a paper design study to come up with different concepts of airplanes that might make good tactical transports. Boeing looked at a great number of powered-lift systems for these airplanes, including boundary layer control, the ejector flap, and the externally blown flap (EBF).

The basic problem of designing a STOL airplane is shown in appendix 1, figure A-01. This kind of plot was used to select the proper wing loadings for the various thrust deflection methods that were considered in the TAI studies. At the same time, rather detailed drawings were made of the inboard profiles of the aircraft, in particular how the engine installations were arranged to augment the aerodynamic lift. These studies went on for about a year into the middle of 1971. None of the configurations looked particularly attractive to Boeing. None of them gave the really good results that they felt were needed.

To summarize, studies made over several years showed that any practical STOL airplane designed to operate from runways shorter than 2,000 feet must utilize deflected thrust. Aerodynamic lift alone would not be sufficient. Naturally, high thrust is required at takeoff due to the need for acceleration and climb. Therefore, the wing flaps are set at a small angle, and the thrust vector is directed to be more in line with the wing chord plane. The climbing, nose-up angle will supply the small thrust deflection needed. During a STOL approach, highly deflected thrust is still needed to help support the airplane because airspeed and resulting aerodynamic lift are relatively low. The thrust must be directed far from the wing chord plane (essentially pointing toward the ground), and the flaps must be in high-drag position to keep the airplane from accelerating down the glide path. Thus, the landing is the more difficult technical problem—the thrust required is nearly as much as during takeoff, and it must be deflected to a far-greater angle. Also, it is evident that the thrust level during approach is much higher than that for a conventional airplane. The culmination of these studies led to the use of the upper surface blowing (USB) concept, involving trailing-edge flaps used in conjunction with jet efflux to create additional lift for the YC-14.

The US Air Force and the Desire for a STOL Transport

From the standpoint of the United States government, there were two basic goals associated with the Advanced Medium STOL Transport (AMST) program. The first was to satisfy the USAF need for airlift that was designed specifically to support operational troops on the ground. The second was the Department of Defense (DoD) desire to reduce risks in major weapon system development and to simplify acquisitions on the basis of studies conducted in 1969.

The Vietnam conflict highlighted the USAF's airlift dilemma. Lockheed's C-141 Starlifter and C-5A Galaxy jet transports had good payloads, range, and speeds but required elaborate and complex facilities to operate effectively. At the other extreme, helicopters were independent of air bases but were slow and vulnerable and could move heavy cargo only over short distances. Between these two extremes were several fixed-wing airplanes, including the de Havilland C-7 Caribou, Fairchild C-123 Provider, and Lockheed C-130 Hercules. These aircraft were less dependent on paved runways when carrying light loads but were limited by payload weight and volume, speed, and range. There was no aircraft type that could interface effectively with the heavy logistics transports and carry the men and materiel (including large vehicles) to a point where they could be used directly by the operational troops or picked up and delivered efficiently by helicopters.

During the 1960s, the USAF spent considerable effort developing the Light Intra-Theater Transport to meet this need. This airplane was to have vertical takeoff and landing (VTOL) capability and was meant to replace the C-7 and the C-123. However, Gen. Spike Momyer had become the commanding officer of the Tactical Air Command just after being in charge of air operations in Vietnam. He was convinced that a larger airplane was needed to be a true C-130 replacement. In a memo written in December 1969, he correctly assessed that VTOL was going to be too expensive and that a 2,000-foot takeoff and landing capability would be sufficient. He went on to indicate that the cargo box volume of the C-130 was insufficient and that the replacement should be turbojet powered.

The USAF recognized that the key technology elements needed to make a breakthrough in airlift capability were becoming available. Large turbofan engines that were efficient and quiet were well proven, with many thousands of hours in commercial service. Further, the ability for these high-technology engines to support powered lift in low-speed flight had been proven, both in the wind tunnel and during full-scale testing. This capability, combined with high-flotation landing-gear systems and state-of-the-art flight

Boeing's 367-80 was used, among other things, to test high-lift systems. Here, the aircraft is being fitted with stationary leading-edge slats to test their potential effectiveness. *Courtesy of the Boeing Company*

control technologies, meant the aircraft could be produced while keeping reasonably low production costs.

With this background, the USAF embarked on a series of trade studies to formalize a required operational capability (ROC) defining a single transport aircraft type, exhibiting no undue economic or performance compromises. These trade studies examined how the following parameters affected airplane cost: runway length, roughness, and bearing strength, along with payload weight, cargo box size, and mission radius. Operational capability, including interface with ground forces and logistics systems, also was an important factor that was considered.

The results of these studies helped define the ROC that was released in June 1970 (and later revised in December 1975). There were five elements of the ROC that most influenced the AMST airplane:

Range and Payload: The airplane needed to be capable of inter-theater deployment with an unrefueled range of 2,600 miles while carrying a payload of 38,000 pounds (the payload weight requirement was reduced to zero for the prototype airplanes). Tactical mobility for the aircraft in an intra-theater environment was to be shown by achieving a radius of 400 nautical miles unrefueled, with a payload of 27,000 pounds carried each way. From the standpoint of intra-theater logistics, the aircraft needed to be capable of carrying 62,000 pounds of payload over a distance of 1,000 nautical miles without refueling.

Runway: The aircraft needed to be capable of safe operations into and out of relatively soft, semi-improved landing fields no larger than 2,000 feet in length and 60 feet in width, while carrying a 27,000-pound payload at an ambient temperature of 103° Fahrenheit.

Propulsion Systems: This aircraft was required to be operated on soft fields with a minimum of ground support equipment. This environment pushed forth the requirement for the aircraft to be able to back up a 3% grade at typical STOL operating weights using reverse thrust.

Landing Gear: The undercarriage was required to be robust enough to endure the semi-improved runway environment required for frontline support. To this end, the landing gear and tires were required to be capable of running over 4-inch smooth rocks on a relatively hard surface without doing damage to the aircraft or tires at typical STOL operating weights.

Cargo Compartment: The USAF had a very specific requirement for the internal volume of the cargo compartment. These measurements were to be no less than 47 feet in length, 11.7 feet wide, and 11.3 feet in height.

The Lockheed C-141 Starlifter first flew on December 17, 1963. The type served with the USAF until May 2006. *Public domain*

The Lockheed C-5 Galaxy was first introduced into USAF service in June 1970. The updated C-5M model remains in service today as a strategic airlifter. This aircraft (c/n 500-0051) resides today at the Museum of Aviation, Robins AFB, Georgia. *Public domain*

These requirements summarized what the USAF needed: a multimission airplane that could be deployed over long distances at jet speeds while carrying heavy, bulky payloads into short, austere fields (while retaining good ground mobility). Such an aircraft would need to interface with and augment the strategic airlift fleet as well as the organic transportation systems of ground forces near the combat zone.

In 1969, the DoD initiated a series of studies aimed at simplifying weapons systems acquisition and reducing risk. One of the policies that emerged from these DoD studies was the increased use of competitive prototypes in keeping with a plan to "fly before you buy." In July 1969, the Defense Science Board issued a report titled "The Use of Prototypes in DoD Research and Development." This document reiterated the need for new aircraft to be tested using production prototype aircraft so that the DoD could be sure that the equipment would meet design objectives. The report made a further point that, prior to this, many new aircraft programs missed this critical element of research and development activity for military equipment. Another point highlighted in the Defense Science Board (DSB) report was the distinct difference between a "development prototype" and a "production prototype." A development prototype is intended to be as simple as possible, while having the capability to obtain the required engineering data on the craft's unique features. A production prototype, on the other hand, should provide an accurate representation of the machine that later would be deployed into military service and combat. This distinction between these two types would go on to haunt Boeing during the design and demonstration of the YC-14, as described later in this story.

The DSB was not alone in this line of thinking. In July 1970, a blue-ribbon defense panel urged the increased use of competitive prototypes to test new technology while relying less upon paper studies. This was further supported by the DSB in August 1970, which formed a panel with the intent to simplify weapon systems in order to cut expenses for new equipment. The DoD board determined that competitive prototyping should be employed as a rule, except when financial or other government constraints made this approach impractical. Soon thereafter, in March 1971, Deputy Secretary of Defense David Packard appeared before the House Subcommittee of DoD Appropriations and strongly supported the prototyping approach. He testified that he believed that the most effective way of controlling the cost of a new program was to make practical trade-offs between operating requirements and engineering design. Additionally, the "fly before you buy" mentality required less dependence on paper studies and more emphasis on actual flyable prototypes. This policy, more specifically, indicated that the development of a new weapons system, when it involves technical uncertainties, should be completed before a substantial commitment is made to production, thus limiting governmental fiscal risks.

In June 1971, a USAF ad hoc committee met to define the characteristics of a good prototype development program and identify suitable candidates. This group decided the proper candidate for prototyping should support or satisfy an anticipated military need and significantly reduce uncertainty. Also, it should provide new and feasible operational or technological options and have a reasonable chance of success. Timeliness was also important, requiring the new equipment to be testable within approximately twenty-four months while remaining cost effective.

All told, forty-four different development concepts were identified as candidates for new military procurement programs. Of these, only six were supported by Congress in the fourth quarter of 1971, two of which were the AMST program (in which the YC-14 participated) and the lightweight fighter, which eventually lead to the highly successful General Dynamics F-16 Falcon fighter jet. For the AMST, Congress further stipulated two manufacturers be involved, and that a competitive flyoff be conducted before committing to full-scale production.

As far as the AMST prototype program itself was concerned, the following three general requirements were established:

- Prove the feasibility of an aircraft that incorporates safe short-field performance without undue degradation of conventional jet transport characteristics such as speed, range, and payload
- Demonstrate acquisition techniques having lower costs while minimizing risks
- Significantly contribute to design-to-cost practices

Boeing's Preparation for the Request for Proposal (RFP)

It had become apparent nearing the end of 1971 the Air Force was preparing to issue an RFP to design, build, and flight test a technology demonstrator for STOL transport. By October 1971, a USAF team working on the Tactical Aircraft Investigation (TAI) study visited Seattle to see how the Boeing group was doing. They were quite surprised that Boeing had not yet chosen a specific high-lift system for their proposal. The USAF was hoping that each contractor would pick a different type of high-lift system, and thereby they would get results from at least two and possibly three different configurations. Boeing told them that it was not satisfied with any of the existing systems, and that none were particularly promising when compared to the others. Boeing really had not made up its mind with respect to which high-lift system would be proposed, even if the RFP came suddenly.

Design for Safety

During the period of the TAI studies, an important personality entered the Boeing AMST program. His name was William H. "Bill" Cook. He had been director of technology for the Commercial Airplane Company and had moved in the corporate organization to become director of technology for the Advanced STOL Program in the Military Airplane Systems Division. Cook had worked on every airplane Boeing had built since the B-29, was head of aerodynamics for the B-47, and was responsible for putting much of the high technology into the 727 and 737. Because he flew his own twin-engine amphibian airplane, he understood the problems of accurate piloting and the need for good controllability, particularly during final approach. He laid down a series of simple requirements in a Boeing internal document, titled "Design for Safety," which proved to be the essence of good STOL airplane design. These requirements were:

- The airplane had to have very precise control of the flight path during final approach. It should be possible to modulate the flight path without changing engine thrust.
- The landing gear should have the capability to absorb the landing shock with no flight path flare prior to touchdown. That is, the airplane should be able to continue the approach path right to touchdown, much like is done by an airplane landing on an aircraft carrier.
- Some built-in visual aid should be provided to help the pilot make an accurate approach to an unprepared field.
- The airplane should have plenty of excess power to get out of unexpected emergencies.

An airplane meeting these requirements could conduct a very precise approach at constant speed to a predetermined spot on the arrival end of the runway, make a touchdown without using up distance making a flare, and get firmly on the runway, where strong braking and reverse thrust could produce a short ground roll. At the same time, plenty of power would be available to make a go-around or to climb quickly away from the field after takeoff.

Two Engines versus Four

From discussions with the USAF, it was very evident that cost was going to be an important criterion for selecting the STOL design winner. They did not want to risk losing a very expensive airplane in tactical situations. This requirement was to have a large influence on the YC-14 design. These cost constraints made a twin-engine airplane look very favorable, because two large engines are less expensive than four smaller ones. Additionally, operational costs

William "Bill" Cook's thirty-six-year career at Boeing included leadership positions on projects such as the B-29, B-47, 707, 720, 727, and B-2707 Supersonic Transport. The YC-14 was his last major project prior to retirement. *Courtesy of the Boeing Company*

generally are up to 6% less for an aircraft with two or three engines as compared to those having four engines. These advantages are evident in Boeing's engine choice for the smaller aircraft in its commercial fleet: three engines on the 727 and two on the 737.

Furthermore, the twin jet had the advantage of having more power available for that 99.99% of the time that all engines were operating. The reason for this advantage in excess power is that both two- and four-engine designs are made to withstand the failure of a single power plant at liftoff. When all engines are running, the four-engine airplane has four-thirds the required minimum power, whereas its twin-engine counterpart has twice the required minimum power. Thus, for the vast majority of the time, a twin-engine airplane has appreciably more power to use for maneuvering or to escape a hostile situation when compared to a four-engine airplane. Another advantage of the twin is that the engine controls and fuel system are simplified, which generally provides better reliability. Also, there are fewer dials and gauges for the crew to monitor and fewer levers to control, making the twin easier to operate.

Boeing knew that its twin-engine jetliner had the best safety record of its entire fleet, even though these airplanes were used widely in the less developed areas of the world, where maintenance and training were minimal. Statistics from the Vietnam War showed that even when combat damage was considered, engine failure was not a large factor in the losses of either two- or four-engine airplanes. Boeing became convinced that a twin-engine airplane would be cheaper, would have much-better all-engine characteristics, and actually would be safer than a corresponding four-engine airplane. This concept was a very difficult one to put across to the potential USAF customers and probably served as a detriment to the configuration throughout the program. However, the basis for the twin configuration certainly has been justified by the current use of twin-engine large commercial transports flying across the world's oceans while enjoying outstanding safety records.

George Schairer was largely responsible for bringing swept-wing technology to Boeing after studying German aerodynamic research immediately following World War II. *Courtesy of the Boeing Company*

Powered-Lift Concept

By this point, program leadership was convinced that the twin-engine, high-bypass engine platform showed the most promise, both in cost and performance. The question was what method was to be used to achieve the requisite slow flight performance and control. The extensive use of boundary layer control (BLC) came at a significant cost. The newer high-bypass engines required for the twin-engine airplane could not produce the massive amounts of bleed air needed for effective surface blowing without severely restricting the maximum thrust available. Some thought was given to developing a three-stream engine. This engine would have a flow path that was strictly for high-pressure boundary layer control air, in addition to the usual separate flows through the fan and engine core. However, this approach meant the development of an entirely new kind of engine, possible from an existing core, but by any measure, a large engine development program with attendant costs and risks.

These constraints made it evident that the high-lift system had to include turning the whole flow of the main engine exhaust, and an externally blown flap configuration was chosen as the best course of action. During single-engine flight, such a system would produce significant yawing (nose side to side) and rolling (bank) forces, which would become more pronounced the farther away from the fuselage the engines were installed. Mounting the engines under the wing but close to the fuselage would result in aerodynamic interference between the fuselage and the engine nacelles, particularly at relatively high Mach numbers, leading to high cruising drag and decreased range. What was needed was a new concept for deflecting the jet flow behind a high-bypass ratio engine. Such a process became visible to Boeing through a fortuitous series of events.

George Schairer had shown me data from some old NASA tests that indicated blowing the jet flow over the top of a deflected flap might produce more efficient turning than did the externally blown flap. He was curious as to whether or not NASA was doing any further work with this system. (A jet flowing across the upper surface of a deflected flap is turned by its tendency to adhere to the adjacent physical surface, even though the surface curves away from the jet's original direction. This characteristic is called the "Coandă effect," named after Prof. Henri Coandă, the first person to investigate its application to aerodynamic design.) For more information on the Coandă effect and Boeing's STOL efforts, please see appendix 2, figures A-05 through A-08, and A-13.

In November 1971, I visited the NASA laboratories at Langley Field for a conference on STOL aerodynamics. At NASA, I inquired as to whether or not any further work was being conducted using this concept. Someone indicated that Joe Johnson, a NASA research aerodynamicist, was doing some work of this nature in the wind tunnel. I visited Joe Johnson the day after the conference and found that he had just completed a test having exactly the data Boeing needed. The test was being done in a small tunnel situated under the diffuser of the 30-by-60-foot wind tunnel. This small tunnel actually was scheduled for retirement, but Johnson had bootlegged these tests of a very high-bypass-ratio engine exhausting over the top of a wing with a highly deflected flap. These data indicated lift coefficients (as a function of thrust coefficient) as high as for any system I had ever seen, which was very exciting. Johnson told me he could not give me the data because it was not yet officially available for release. This key piece of data was of significant importance. However, he was willing to let me make a tracing of some of it, which I did, and brought the information back to Seattle.

This information was fundamental in making the twin-engine configuration fall into place. Because the engines were located on top of the wing, they could be placed close to the centerline of the airplane without causing significant aerodynamic interference with the fuselage. Boeing immediately began building wind tunnel models to verify the NASA data in a realistic configuration representing the lower-bypass-ratio engines that Boeing actually was considering for use at the time. During this period, the Boeing group started to make more-detailed drawings of the engine and airplane integration. These configuration studies were carried on at the same time Boeing was continuing the design of four-engine airplanes, on which they had adequate wind tunnel data to develop the configurations and performance. Prior to the AMST RFP release, the Boeing Commercial Airplane Division had been studying engines mounted ahead and above the wing, with the

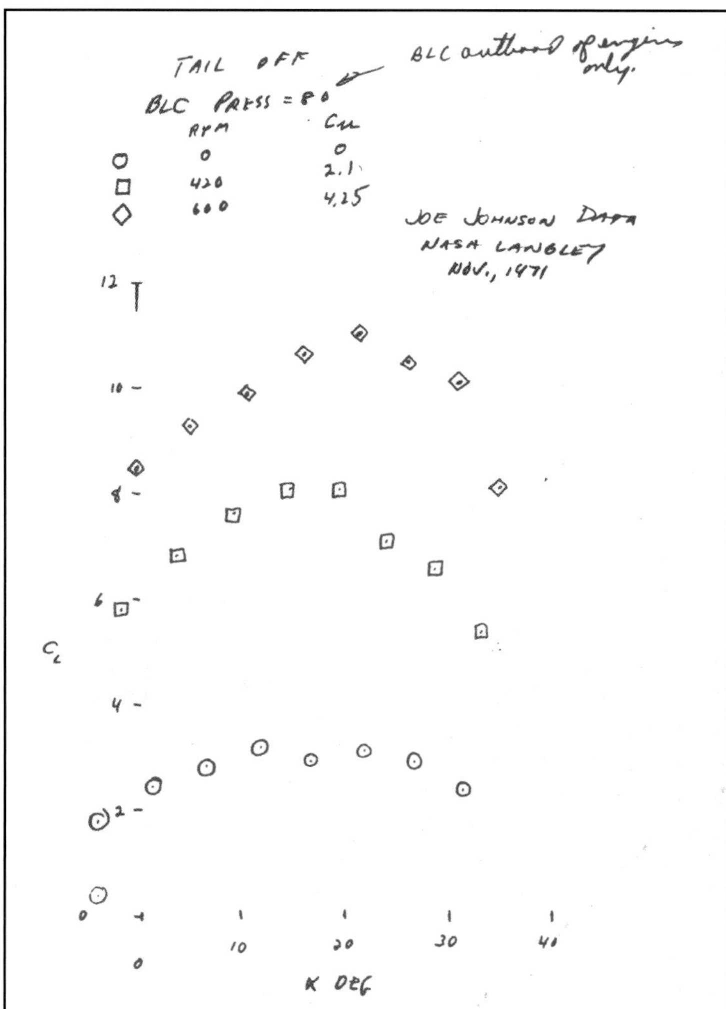

The NASA data on USB. These data were shown just as I traced them from the plots at the NASA Langley Laboratory. They launched Boeing on the path to the YC-14 configuration. *Author's collection*

exhaust flowing over the wing upper surface in an effort to reduce the noise heard on the ground from airplanes passing overhead. These studies indicated that the engines could be placed in this configuration with minimal drag penalties at cruise speed.

The availability of a suitable engine had a large influence on the YC-14's configuration. For a twin, modern engines were available. These included the CF6 series from General Electric and the JT9 series from Pratt & Whitney. For the four-engine airplane, however, the situation was different. The only engine of the proper output was the JT8D produced by Pratt & Whitney. This engine was an old design, and Boeing thought it probably was going to be out of production by the time the advanced

The General Electric CF6-50 turbofan engine. *Dan Dornseif collection*

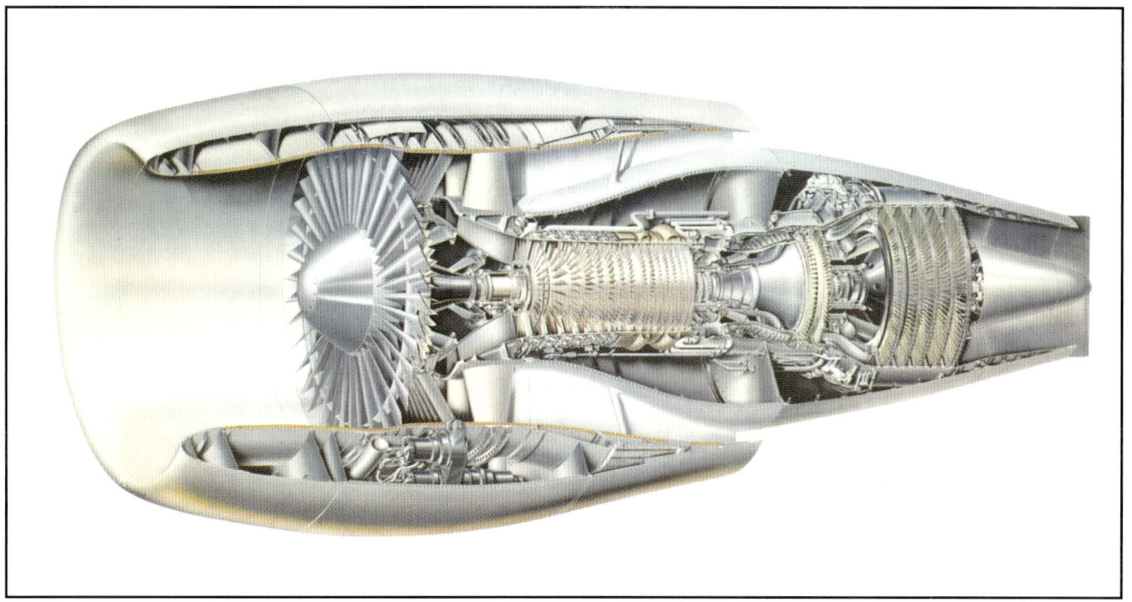

medium STOL transport came into production. Concurrently, there was considerable promotion within the USAF technical community to develop a new engine for the STOL transport, along with other possible applications. However, there were others within the same community who were not anxious to support a new engine at that time. General Electric and SNECMA of France had just begun negotiations on a cooperative venture to build the CFM56 high-bypass turbofan. This engine would be approximately the right size for a four-engine airplane, but even if it came into existence (which was questionable at the time), it was thought that the price would be very high. Thus, the four-engine airplane configuration was stuck with the aging JT8D for a prototype application, and there still would not be a suitable modern engine to put on a production machine. By the end of 1971, Boeing knew a good propulsive high-lift system had been conceived, but data on this concept were sparse, and more could be obtained only through extensive wind tunnel tests. The twin-engine airplane looked like it had a distinct advantage in terms of cost because of having less expensive engines, but Boeing had not yet achieved a configuration that appeared satisfactory from the standpoint of both performance and controllability. The four-engine designs looked easy to build and quite straightforward but would lack a modern production engine. At that time, it appeared that the US government's RFP likely would arrive in January 1972, which was approaching rapidly. Boeing was extremely busy establishing the technological base for a proposal configuration.

The RFP and Proposal

Early Tests on the Twin

By the end of 1971, the Boeing AMST group was trying hard to make a twin-engine configuration workable. They were continuing activity on four-engine configurations as well but recognized that the twin offered certain advantages that warranted continued investigation. Because of this, and the unresolved technical challenges involved, most of the attention was given to the twin configuration. By mid-December, Boeing had started wind tunnel tests both on the high- and low-speed twin configurations. The low-speed tests were done in Boeing's wind tunnel at Vertol, which has a 12-by-15-foot test section and the ability to represent engine thrust using compressed airflow. The high-speed tests were being done at Boeing's transonic wind tunnel in an 8-by-12-foot test section. Additionally, Boeing was running low-speed tests in the University of Washington Aeronautical Laboratory (UWAL) wind tunnel, which also had an 8-by-12-foot cross section. At UWAL, the aerodynamicists were trying to optimize the distribution and quantity of air used in the boundary-layer control (BLC) system that they were planning to use on the wing leading edge.

Engine Choice

In the meantime, the USAF Aeronautical Propulsion Laboratory in Dayton, Ohio, had gone to the extent of sponsoring a new engine design targeted for the 25,000-pound thrust range for use on an AMST aircraft. Waiting for this new engine to emerge could cause delays in the AMST program. Boeing was anxious to get its twin-engine configuration exposed to the USAF and show it could proceed quickly while utilizing an existing modern engine. McDonnell Douglas took a simplified approach to the competition by using four underslung, podded engines. The integration of newer power plants later in the program would be simplified by this configuration, but it was a compromise to the eventual performance of the aircraft. Boeing had three modern engines of the right size and type available: the Pratt & Whitney JT9D (employed on the 747-100 and -200), the Rolls-Royce RB211 (the only option on the L-1011), and the General Electric CF6 (being used on the McDonnell Douglas DC-10 and Airbus A300). Boeing had a lot of experience with the JT9D during certification and early revenue operation of the 747. The early versions of this engine had a propensity for compressor stalls, particularly during slam accelerations with strong crosswinds distorting the inlet flow. A compressor stall is caused by the aerodynamic stall of the individual blades in the compressor rotor. This action causes the air flowing through the compressor to stop or even reverse, resulting in a dramatic loss of thrust, and normally producing an impressively loud bang with visible burning exhaust exiting out the tailpipe, inlet, or both. Given the harsh environments into which the YC-14 would be deployed, the sensitivity of the JT9D to such conditions was seen as a detriment. The RB211 was considered quite novel in that it used a three-spool design, whereas two was considered "industry standard." The engine had a limited in-service track record, and, largely because of this, as well as labor problems at Rolls-Royce at the time, it was not seriously considered. General Electric, on the other hand, offered the use of CF6-50 engines that had been used for DC-10 certification and could be repurposed for the YC-14. Additionally, the CF6 had favorable compressor stall margins, mitigating the risk that would be assumed through the use of the JT9Ds. Additionally, General Electric had a reputation for excellent support, which later became a major benefit during the YC-14's flight testing.

Cargo Box Size

During the early AMST studies, prior to the emergence of the official RFP, speculations about the cargo box size requirements circulated around the industry. The USAF had unofficially indicated that it needed a cargo box with both a height and width of 12 feet. Contradictory information was also put forth that the C-130 box dimensions of 8 by 10 feet were all that was required. Many within Boeing suspected that this rumor was likely put out by Lockheed to "muddy the waters" and confuse the initial studies made both by McDonnell Douglas and Boeing. These exterior activities made Boeing wonder when the RFP would be released and what form of aircraft would be requested. By this time, Congress had put $264 million in the budget for an AMST prototype program. Boeing felt that this amount was enough money to build and test two aircraft from each contractor. This was just the program Boeing wanted to pursue.

First-Try Studies

One day prior to the 1971 Christmas holidays, the Boeing AMST group gathered to examine the results of their first studies comparing the twin-engine airplane to a four-engine configuration. These studies were relatively shallow—on the basis of the data that could be obtained from outside sources, since their own tests were not yet finished. The AMST program at Boeing was directed by the Aeronautical and Information Systems Division, part of the Aerospace Company, which was dominated by people who had grown up in the space and missile business. I felt they knew little about airplanes and had no appreciation for the amount of study needed to complete a solid airplane configuration. Therefore, the number of people who could be assigned to these studies was relatively small, approximately one hundred for the entire engineering effort. The USAF, on the other hand, looked at an airplane proposal as a description of absolutely how the airplane was to be built. They would evaluate the proposal on the basis of their analysis of the described airplane and their analysis of the validity of the data and studies that were submitted as part of the proposal. Thus, the USAF felt that the machine should be built as described, while the Boeing Aerospace Company thought it should be redesigned on contract money after the competition was won. The true situation, of course, lay somewhere between these two extremes. However, the proposal at least had to be based on enough analyses and test data to assure Boeing management that the airplane could do the task for which it was being designed.

In order to understand Boeing's reluctance to invest heavily in this program, one must recognize the financial condition of the company during this period. It had just gone through a severe cash-flow problem with the 747 program costing much more than expected. At the same time, Boeing had a number of program cancellations, including the supersonic transport. The company had gone through a traumatic period of layoffs, shrinking its workforce in Seattle from over 100,000 down to about 33,000. This reduction included about half the engineering staff. The company was in a position of making very little money while having tremendous cash demands. Concurrently, it was bidding the lightweight fighter and had other commercial research programs going on that were costly. For this reason, the studies performed for the AMST could not be as extensive as those working on the program might have liked.

The twin-engine configuration, at this time, had the engines mounted on the body ahead and forward of the wing, exhausting over the top of the wings and inboard trailing-edge flaps. The analysis indicated that it was going to be very hard to control the loss of an engine, particularly in roll. It also indicated that a great deal of boundary layer control was going to be needed on the wing leading edge to help solve this roll problem. This necessary amount of boundary layer control airflow required large ducts through the wing, and the designers struggled with how to route them around the structure. The four-engine airplane still looked relatively straightforward. It could fly a final approach with a lift coefficient of about 4.4 versus only 3.5 for the twin. Also, the twin weighed about 4% more than the four-engine airplane in terms of operating empty weight to do the same job. It really was difficult to say that the twin would be the better airplane when considering all the variables. On the other hand, the cost analysis indicated that using only two engines could save over 20% of the costs of engines, maintenance, and spare parts.

Refining Potential Configurations

When the AMST group returned to work after the 1971 Christmas holidays, they began to analyze the first data from the various wind tunnel tests. The tests from the Vertol tunnel were quite encouraging. They showed that a USB system would have extremely high thrust recovery. The studies showed values of 90% thrust recovery at deflections as much as 70°, which was far superior to a conventional externally blown flap. Because of this efficiency, the airplane was able to achieve approach lift coefficients between 4.5 and 5 with one engine out while properly trimmed in roll. The high-speed tests showed that the nacelle installation did not cause excessive drag, and by using a relatively large horizontal tail, any high-speed pitch instabilities at high attitude could be overcome satisfactorily. The test on the leading-edge BLC system showed less effectiveness than we had hoped. However, the aerodynamicists did feel that a relatively satisfactory BLC system could be made using the bleed air from a General Electric CF6 engine operating through an ejector to augment the mass flow.

With these new data, the designers began another series of studies to be completed by the end of January, which included both two- and four-engine configurations. Work was done to establish the proper wing sweepback that would result in a good airplane at cruise Mach numbers as well as at low speeds, and to establish a proper wing aspect ratio from the standpoint of lift-to-drag ratio, weight, and fuel volume. Horizontal tail considerations included whether it should be positioned on top of the fin or on the body, its size, the rate it should move to overcome large pitch changes in ground effect, and how it would be influenced by engine wake. Studies continued on the operational characteristics on soft, semi-improved fields, and on the influence of various cargo compartment sizes. These efforts were aimed at making some fairly firm configuration decisions by the end of January 1972.

CHAPTER 2

The Request for Proposal and Boeing's Response

The Request for Proposal (RFP)

The RFP arrived during an unusually snowy day on Monday, January 20, 1972. The details stated in the RFP were defined as goals rather than absolute requirements. These objectives included operation into and out of a 2,000-foot, semi-prepared field at the midpoint of a 500-nautical-mile mission while carrying a 27,000-pound payload both ways. This mission was to be done with a hot day temperature of 103° Fahrenheit and was to include the effects of an engine failure at any time. The cargo box size was defined as 12-by-12-foot cross section and 47 feet long with a flat floor. The semi-prepared field was defined as having a California Bearing Ratio of 6.0 (a moderately soft, fine-grained soil), and the airplane needed to be able to make four hundred passes on that terrain. The ferry range goal was 2,600 miles, which would permit flying from the West Coast of the United States to Hawaii. With this ferry range, the airplane could deploy to any spot in the world. The big new input that Boeing was not expecting in the new RFP was the requirement for production cost, stated as a requirement, not a goal. The requirement was that the production cost of the three hundredth unit should be $5 million, including engines, in 1972 dollars.

Another very interesting requirement was that the basic proposal must be only fifty pages long. The page size, print size, and number of foldout pages and attached drawings were defined. This novel approach to a proposal was very refreshing to me, since I had been through both the C-5A and the B-1 proposals at Boeing. These previous document submissions had included literally tens of thousands of pages going into extreme detail on every aspect of the proposal. No one could possibly assimilate everything that was in those documents. When the C-5A proposal was submitted, it took an entire C-130 just to carry the documents back to Dayton! With this shortened AMST proposal, as it turned out, one could read it from beginning to end in a couple of hours and have an extremely good idea of what the airplane was, what it could do, and what data it was based on. It ended up being an excellent proposal form. The proposal was due on March 31, 1972, which gave Boeing only ten weeks to respond. Within a week of the RFP's arrival, most of the major configuration decisions had been made to define the YC-14, on the basis of the parametric studies that were initiated earlier in the month. These decisions were made by a relatively small group of people.

The Traditional Boeing Design Approach: Technical Staff and Design Project Teams

The YC-14 development program employed an engineering organizational structure that had been used by Boeing to produce an uninterrupted thirty-year stream of extremely successful commercial and military airplanes. The YC-14 engineering team, therefore, had two coequal organizations who worked together to develop, design, and validate the aircraft as follows:

1. The Technical Staff Group, led by the chief engineer of the Technical Staff, had these primary responsibilities:
   a. To define the airplane requirements in areas such as safety, mission performance, handling qualities, etc. In order to accomplish this task, a Design Requirements and Objectives document was prepared and distributed widely to the program team.
   b. To lead the trade studies, which resulted in the firm configuration milestone being met prior to the start of detailed design. "Firm configuration" is defined as the point where all requirements are firm and documented, the airplane geometry is known, the systems architectures are firm, and space allocations are made to support the detail design.
   c. To support the data analysis needs of the project designers.
   d. To validate the design through flight test and analysis.
2. The Design Project Group, led by the chief project engineer, specified the detailed design that led to the construction of the airplane. This group participated in all phases of the program. It became the majority of the program engineering team after firm configuration was reached, and the manpower was increased to develop and release the design drawings to the Manufacturing Department.

Although the management of the YC-14 program was assigned to the Boeing Aerospace Company, essentially all of the engineering manpower came from the Boeing Commercial Airplane Company. This relationship encouraged the powerful technical organization to provide guidance regarding company technical history; company, industry, and regulatory standards; and corporate technical philosophy. Also, it gave the YC-14 Engineering Department an independent route to the top airplane-oriented technical management of the Boeing Company, in case it felt the YC-14 program was going astray technically.

Defining the Proposal Configuration

Following the Boeing philosophy, the AMST parametric studies were guided by the Technical Staff, which also was in charge of the wind tunnel and propulsion tests that were being done concurrently. The results of the studies and tests were presented to the program management along with recommendations regarding decisions related to the configuration. The people involved in these decisions, made in the first week after the proposal arrived, were Maynard Pennell, vice president in charge of the AMST program, who had been the principal designer of the 707; Bill Cook, chief engineer of the Technical Staff; Omar Bygland, chief project designer; Bob Person, chief preliminary designer; Jim Foody, assistant program manager; Dave Norton, chief aerodynamicist on the program; and me (John Wimpress, assistant chief engineer, Technical Staff).

Cook, as head of the Technical Staff, was concerned mostly with the basic philosophy of the program, and I handled the management of the studies and the test program. Therefore, I made most of the presentations to this group in preparation for making decisions. Most of the time, the data were such that a consensus was fairly evident. In some cases, however, there would be conflicts, and the decision would escalate to the appropriate level.

By the end of the week, it had been decided to propose a twin-engine airplane based on the satisfactory test results obtained in Boeing's most recent tests. For the horizontal tail, it was decided to go with a T-tail configuration. A horizontal stabilizer on the body was considered, but it would have had to be larger than the T tail and also would have needed a very rapid motion capability to account for the changes in the wing downwash as the airplane approached the ground. The T tail was a worry in that it could lead to pitch-up problems when flown at extremely slow airspeeds, but the control engineers felt that those could be handled by careful design.

The boundary-layer control (BLC) system was chosen to be located only on the leading edge of the wing, utilizing pressurized air that could be bled from the CF6 engines and then augmented by an ejector. The wing aspect ratio was chosen to be 9.5 on the basis of having superior cruise and low-speed performance. Boeing data on the effects of aspect ratio were not too complete, but all of those involved felt they would like a fairly high aspect ratio. The wing-sweep decision, however, was more difficult. Some of the group wanted to hold a higher cruise speed, which Boeing traditionally had done, but it conflicted with the requirement to have very high lift, which was enhanced by a straight wing. The

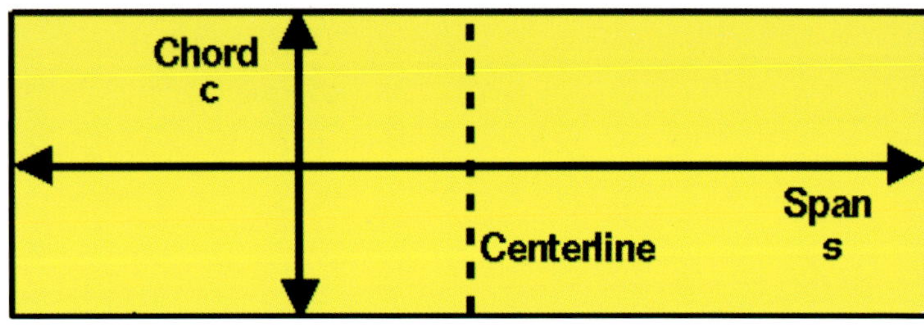

The aspect ratio of a wing is calculated by dividing the wingspan by the average wing chord. Aspect ratio has significant effects on wing performance. The aspect ratio concept was also used by engineers to define the shape of the YC-14 engines' exhaust nozzles (width divided by average nozzle opening height in that instance). *Courtesy of NASA*

decision eventually was made to go with a wing that had a straight rear spar, which allowed about 10° of leading-edge sweep. This shape kept the wing uncomplicated and less costly and would permit using a simple hinge for the trailing-edge flaps since the flap brackets would align properly with the airstream. Also, the decision was that we would use the -50 version of the CF6, which had been developed for the heavier versions of the McDonnell Douglas DC-10. At the same time, the control engineers developed their criteria for establishing satisfactory handling of the airplane after an engine failure on final approach. The criteria stated that the pilot must be able to do one of two things at all times: the pilot must either be able to make a go-around, or if the altitude is too low for that, proceed to the landing and hit the runway without exceeding maximum design loads on the landing gear. Such a criterion permits a failure to occur at any time in the flight path, and the corresponding result will be satisfactory.

USAF Contacts

Having selected a twin-engine configuration, Boeing now faced an unusual quandary. The USAF knew very little about Boeing's work on this new configuration, although much time and forethought was expended in its establishment. Boeing also knew that the USAF did not like surprises in their proposals. Instead, they preferred to evaluate a configuration that they had already studied before the RFP is issued. With respect to the AMST, Boeing was going to submit a configuration about which the USAF knew nothing. Boeing engineers also knew that the USAF evaluators were not well versed in the techniques of STOL flight. Boeing and other contractors had worked diligently over the prior year or so

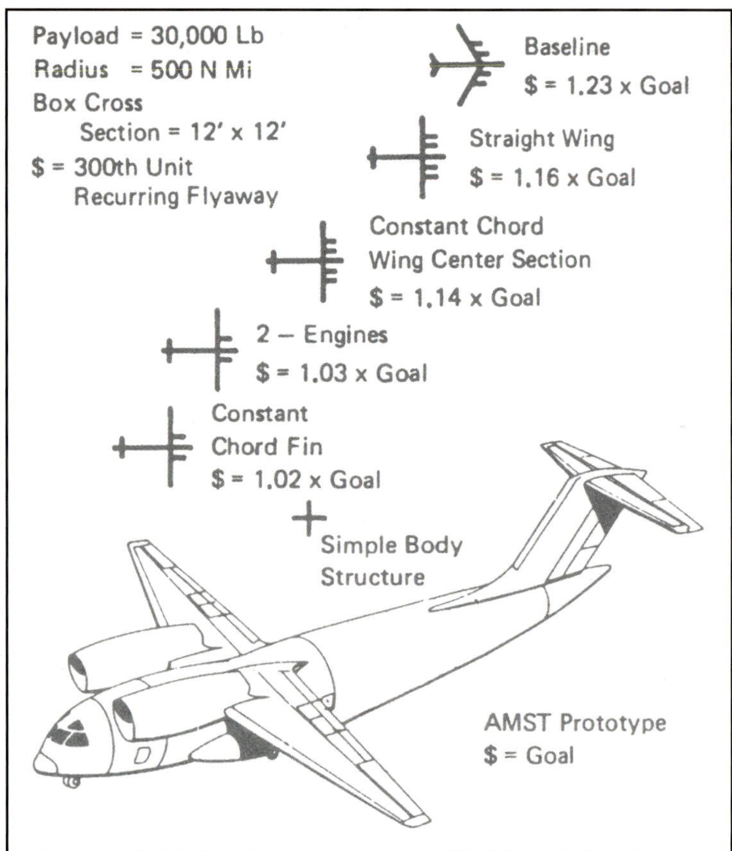

The AMST design progression. The YC-14 configuration was influenced greatly by the estimate of the cost of the production version of the airplane. In order to meet the cost goal, all elements of the airplane had to be made as simple as possible. *Reprinted with permission from SAE paper 730365 © 1973 Society of Automotive Engineers, Inc.*

trying to introduce and familiarize the USAF with the philosophy and details of very slow flight, but the actual evaluators might still be somewhat unfamiliar with various concepts. Boeing had hoped they would be able to talk with the USAF during the proposal period and give them some feeling about the salient features of Boeing's configuration. Unfortunately, instructions from the USAF indicated that contractors could have absolutely no contact within the conceivable USAF evaluation community during the proposal period. This constraint certainly caused some unusual challenges for Boeing.

At the bidders' briefing that followed receipt of the RFP, Boeing obtained additional information. The total amount of money available for the program, including two contractors, was only $165 million (compared with the $264 million initially approved by Congress), with $2 million of that being allotted to Edwards Air Force Base for flight test support. If one contractor bid more than half of that amount, the other contractor would have to bid less because the total was only the $165 million. The USAF indicated that it did not expect the prototype to demonstrate any cargo handling or air drops. The contractors were strongly urged to meet the production goal of $5 million per aircraft (for the three hundredth production airplane). Many at Boeing thought that such a low amount was almost impossible to achieve, but the USAF was adamant that they wanted the low production price to be met.

On February 10 and 11, aerodynamicist Fred May and I visited NASA Langley to show them the Boeing data on the USB design and to explain to them the twin-engine configuration. We met with Dick Kuhn, Dudley Hammond, Jim Hassell, and others associated with the NASA STOL program. The NASA personnel were extremely interested in the Boeing data and were quite surprised that Boeing had adapted the USB concept to their AMST configuration. NASA felt that Boeing's aerodynamicists had enough data to convince both NASA and themselves that the Boeing twin was a workable configuration. We also talked to people doing high-speed research, showing them how Boeing had very successfully solved the high-speed drag problem of the overwing nacelle. NASA was planning to do a relatively extensive program on USB within the next year and a half. They felt, however, that the work Boeing was preparing to do would cover most of the areas they were planning to investigate, so that they were very anxious to see any data from Boeing's final series of tests before the Boeing proposal was submitted.

The Tactical Air Command also was based at Langley Field, Virginia, and from our contact there we learned that Dick Kuhn would be the principal NASA participant on the AMST evaluation committee. This information encouraged me to believe that Boeing could get their data into the system, via NASA, that would be considered in the proposal evaluation. If Boeing could verify their data during their last series of tests, they would get NASA Langley to support the contention that Boeing did, in fact, have a viable configuration.

Proposal Configuration Improvements

By mid-February 1972, the AMST group had selected the lateral control system. It consisted of an aileron at the outboard end of the wing, assisted by flaperon just inboard (a flaperon is a flap that could also be moved rapidly and automatically for roll control).

YC-14 Flight Control Surfaces

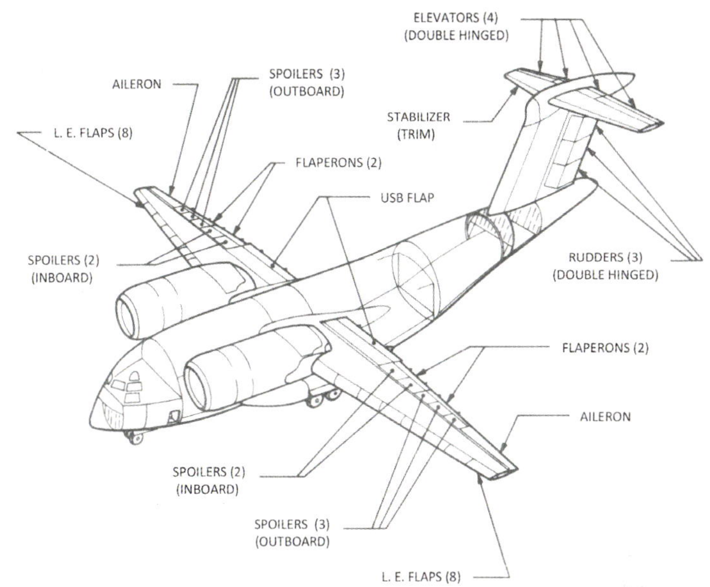

Courtesy of the Boeing Company

Additionally, a segment of pure flap, directly behind the engine, would be installed. The system would include spoilers just outboard of the engine for high-speed control as well as increased control during low-speed maneuvering. The system concept was that the aileron and flaperon would be used to trim out the loss of lift caused by a failed engine, and the spoilers, which cause high drag, would be used only when needed for maneuvering. This system had a large number of components, both aerodynamically and mechanically, but they were all "known quantities" at Boeing from previous aircraft projects.

By this time, Boeing also had selected other details of the configuration. Jim Foody thought he had a feel for the political atmosphere of the project and wanted to make the airplane as compact as possible while still meeting the requirements. Maynard Pennell, on the other hand, wanted a slightly larger aircraft, asserting that such an airplane would be more versatile and actually would be easier to build. In the end, the larger airplane won out. A body diameter of 220 inches was chosen, along with a wing area of approximately 1,750 square feet, which gave the airplane a gross weight at the midmission point of 160,000 pounds. With this wing area, the approach speed was low enough that the airplane would meet the field length requirement during landing, even without the use of thrust reversers.

The directional control system was selected to be a double-hinged rudder, with the first segment locked out when the flaps were up (see diagram on page 25). By this time, the engine mount had been changed to connect to the wing rather than to the body, as was originally conceived. The reason for this change was that carrying the engine weight loads through to the body and back out on the wing resulted in a long load path, which added extra weight both to the wing and body. Having the engine mounted directly to the wing provided bending-moment relief to the wing, thereby reducing structural weight. The inboard engine mount was lined up with the side-of-body rib of the wing for better structural efficiency, while minimizing engine-out rolling tendencies.

By early March 1972, the second series of high-speed and low-speed wind tunnel tests had been completed. The low-speed model used compressed air to represent the jet. The nozzles had to be modified after the tests began to make the flow turn properly around the upper surface blown flap (Note: the resulting data can be reviewed in appendix 2, figures A-05 through A-08). High-speed tests were relatively few but largely concentrated on obtaining proper stability and the ideal shape of the aft body. Because the program was emphasizing low-speed performance and there were few criteria for cruise performance, testing in this regime was minimal, strictly for lack of time. At the time the proposal was submitted, Boeing had completed about four hundred hours of wind tunnel testing, less than one-tenth of that usually required to complete a typical airplane design.

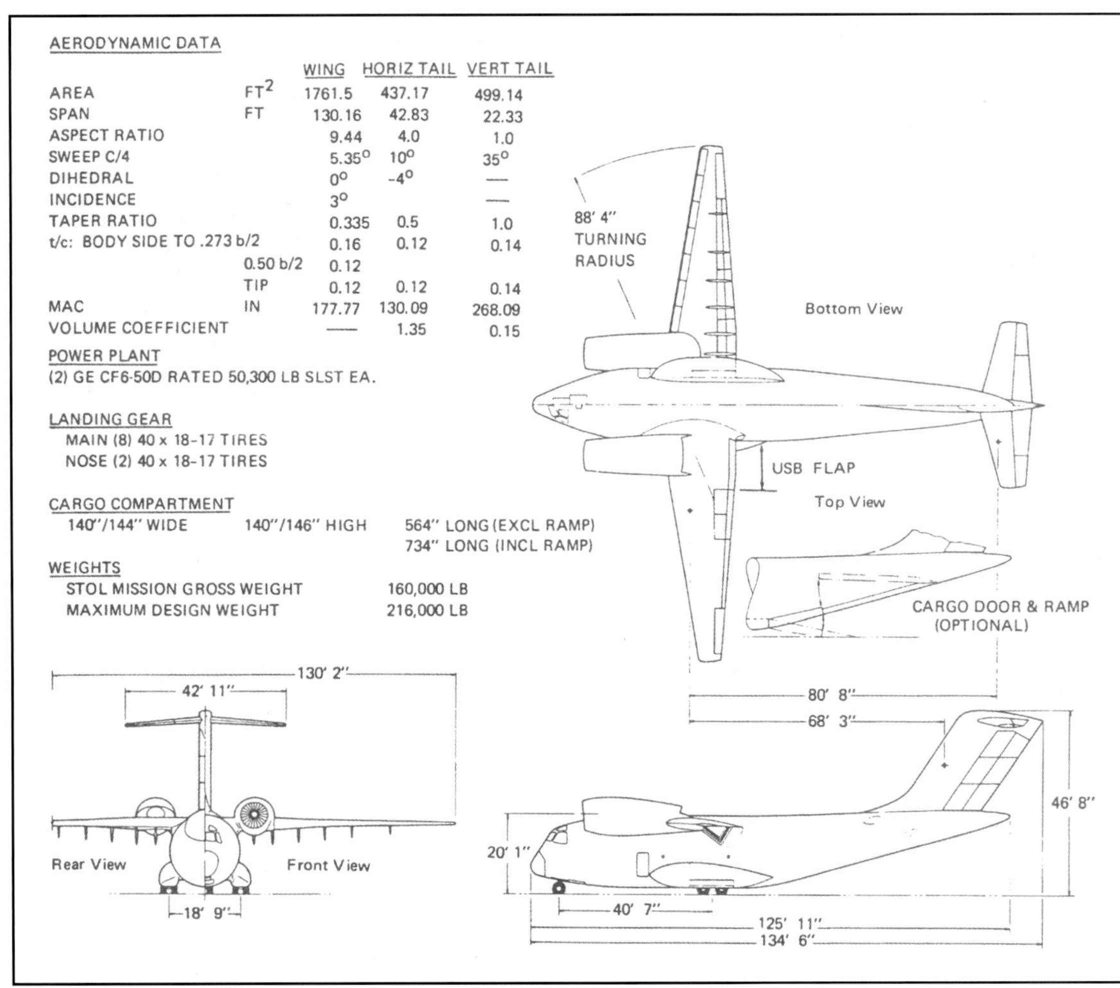

The AMST configuration as submitted in the proposal of March 31, 1972. *Courtesy of the Boeing Company*

Submitting the Proposal

The proposal was submitted on March 31, 1972, as required by the RFP. The last week was a frantic period squeezing the proposal into exactly fifty pages, because each contractor had been told that if their proposal exceeded that amount, it would be eliminated from consideration. Proposals were also submitted by McDonnell Douglas, Lockheed-Georgia, Fairchild Industries, and Bell Aerospace. Although certainly Boeing felt that the proposal configuration could be built and meet the specified performance, the proposal did include a number of inconsistencies in its data due to the engine installation and exhaust nozzle configuration.

Due to the time-compressed preparations for the RFP, the exhaust nozzles were not properly calibrated for the CF6 thrust level due to small last-minute changes required to make the USB flap configuration work properly. Also, it was found that during single-engine flight, the exhaust flow for the operating engine would cling to the fuselage and wrap around the aircraft body, causing large yawing forces. The plan, given further development, was to add flow deflectors along the fuselage side to prevent this unwanted characteristic. Further, the engine nozzles used on the low-speed wind tunnel model did not accurately represent what could realistically be built on a full-size airframe. Additional high-speed wind tunnel time would be required, using compressed air to represent jet thrust in order to estimate thrust losses due to the engine jet stream flowing along the wing and body. Last, the low-speed model represented engine nacelles that were not placed in exactly the correct position on the wing. The Boeing AMST team did not feel that these differences were unusual for a design at this point in its development. These issues merely meant that there were some areas that would require refinement before the design could be committed to production.

Boeing applied for, and received, a US patent on the proposal configuration, with the people considered most responsible listed as inventors. Patents also were filed covering many of the airplane's components, such as the engine installation and the USB flap. Unfortunately, no filing was made for international patents, and so the configuration was copied, in concept, by non-US manufacturers without consequence (see the Soviet Antonov An-72 and An-74 on page 105).

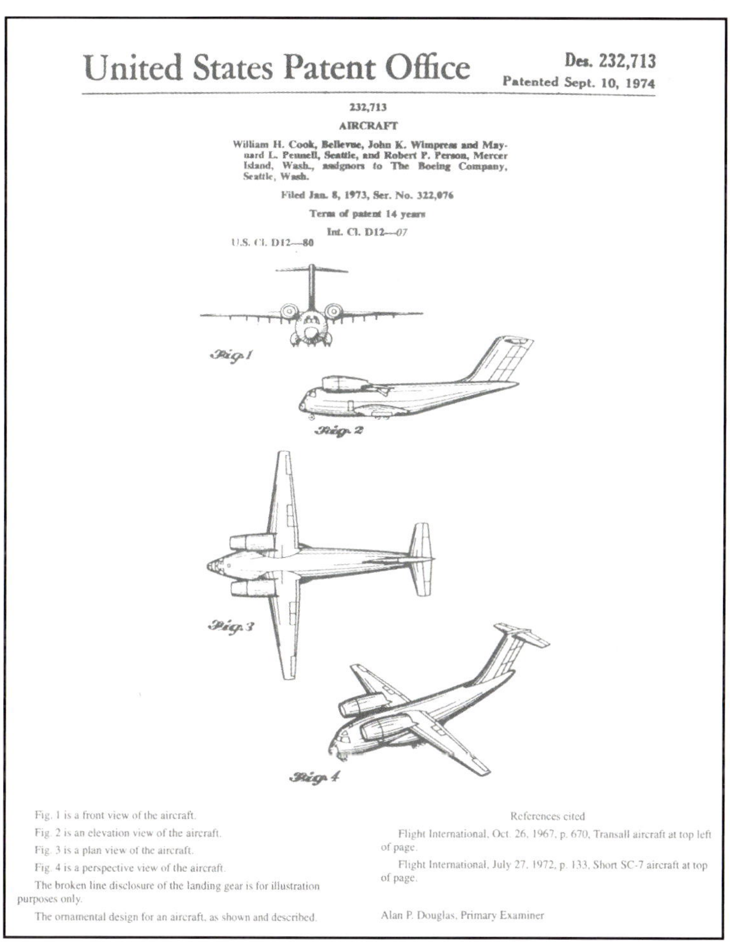

United States Patent Office — Des. 232,713 — Patented Sept. 10, 1974

232,713

AIRCRAFT

William H. Cook, Bellevue, John K. Wimpress and Maynard L. Pennell, Seattle, and Robert P. Person, Mercer Island, Wash., assignors to The Boeing Company, Seattle, Wash.

Filed Jan. 8, 1973, Ser. No. 322,076

Term of patent 14 years

Int. Cl. D12—07

U.S. Cl. D12—80

Fig. 1 is a front view of the aircraft.

Fig. 2 is an elevation view of the aircraft.

Fig. 3 is a plan view of the aircraft.

Fig. 4 is a perspective view of the aircraft.

The broken line disclosure of the landing gear is for illustration purposes only.

The ornamental design for an aircraft, as shown and described.

References cited

Flight International, Oct. 26, 1967, p. 670, Transall aircraft at top left of page.

Flight International, July 27, 1972, p. 133, Short SC-7 aircraft at top of page.

Alan P. Douglas, Primary Examiner

US patent for the YC-14 configuration. *Author's collection*

Informing NASA

Because Boeing knew that NASA was going to be heavily involved in the proposal evaluations, they wanted NASA to understand their latest data. Therefore, immediately after the proposal was submitted, I left on a trip to visit all of the NASA laboratories to show them what Boeing had done. I visited the Ames Laboratory, the Edwards Flight Test Center, the Langley Laboratory, and finally the Lewis Laboratory, where the NASA aircraft engine work was done. The USAF never had said Boeing could contact NASA. On the other hand, they never indicated that Boeing could not, so I just went out and did it. I had gone to Washington, DC, with a plan to talk with NASA headquarters about the Boeing data, when the USAF finally found out what I was doing. As I came into the hotel the night before my scheduled meetings, I was told that the USAF had declared that I could not continue my NASA activities. By that time, I felt I really had talked to the people who were important in the Boeing evaluation, and had given them a good view of the depth of Boeing's background in the airplane that was being proposed. The one piece of data that all the laboratories felt was missing was that of a full-scale demonstration that USB would work; that is, that the flow really would turn across the upper surface of the deflected flap behind a real operating engine.

The Waiting Period

While the proposal was being evaluated by the USAF, the Boeing AMST team was drastically reduced in size because of the financial burden of keeping the team together. Boeing continued to be concerned that their proposal evaluation might suffer because no data from full-scale blowing tests had been submitted.

Full-Scale and Model Tests

At the time of the proposal release, the contractors were told the evaluation would take place within sixty days. Boeing was very anxious that the missing full-scale data be provided to the USAF somehow, so that the evaluators would know that Boeing's system really would work. In order to get the data, AMST propulsion engineers used a Pratt & Whitney JT9D engine mounted on a Boeing test rig. The fan and primary exhaust flow from this engine were directed into a separate collector and nozzle placed over a wing and leading to a curved sheet of metal representing the full-scale USB flap. To prevent the ground under the rig from affecting the exhaust flow, the stationary rig was oriented upside down to get accurate airflow data. Water was sprayed into the jet flow where it vaporized into steam, allowing the flow to be visualized. Also, steel straps were placed in the exhaust stream on hinges so they could be used as high-temperature tufts. These tests showed dramatically that the flow would turn at full scale. Also, pressures taken along the surface of the wing and flap agreed

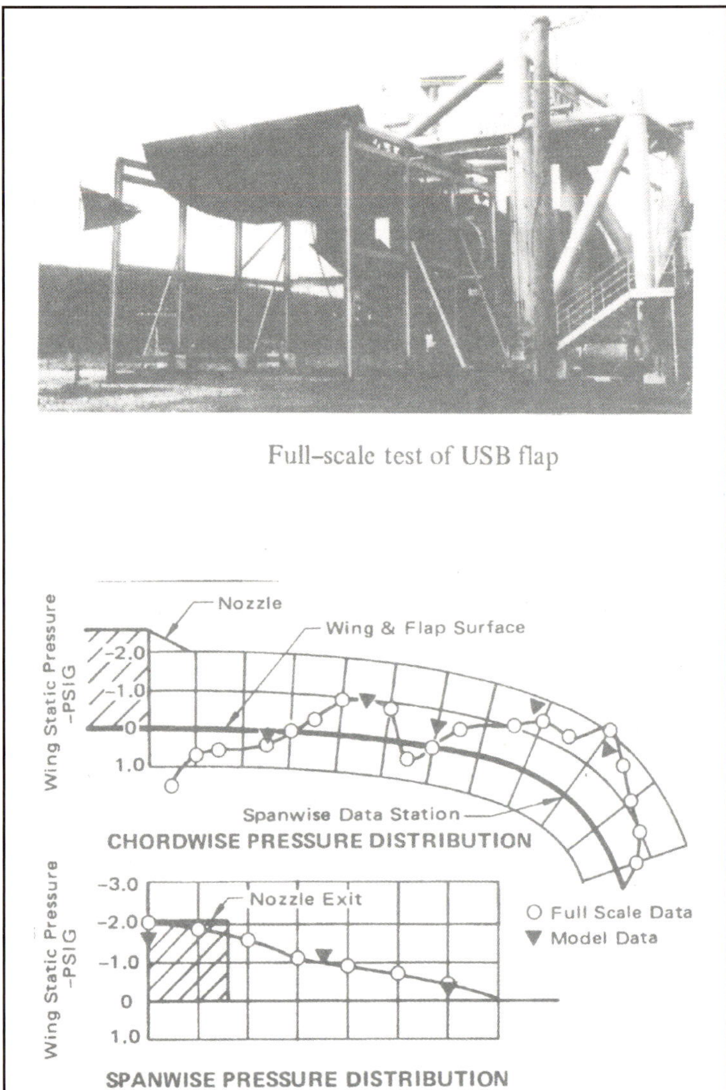

Full-scale USB tests, using a Pratt & Whitney JT9D engine wing and flap inverted to deflect flow away from the ground, confirmed the model test pressure distribution results with high precision. Note the hinged metal "tufts" being blown upward aft of the flap and the flag pointing toward the wing because of the air entrained by the deflected jet. *Courtesy of the Boeing Company*

very closely with those measured in small-scale tests, giving Boeing high assurance that their small-scale data on the airplane were satisfactory. Although Boeing could not give this data directly to the USAF (no contact on technical subjects was allowed once the proposal was submitted), they let it be known through the engine companies and NASA that the tests had been accomplished satisfactorily. Boeing was confident that the results got to the evaluators one way or another.

It soon became evident that the USAF was not going to meet its sixty-day response schedule. The engineering team working on the AMST was reduced to only about twenty people, enough to answer specific questions from the USAF, but not enough to do any profitable work. Thus, not much design work was done through the summer of 1972. There were some interesting tests run with a very small-scale model of the nozzle and USB flap, using a vacuum cleaner motor as a power source. This little model was built by one of the engineers in the project Propulsion Group, and some surprisingly good data were obtained on the effects of different nozzle shapes. The AMST aerodynamicists wished to do some wind tunnel testing to start cleaning up some of the vacancies in the data they knew existed, but Boeing was unwilling to spend money on further testing.

USAF Reaction

Throughout the summer there were some contacts between the upper management of the AMST program at Boeing and USAF management at Wright-Patterson Air Force Base in Dayton, Ohio. Discussions were held with Gen. Stewart, head of the USAF Systems Command, and with Col. Lyle Cameron, head of the USAF's Prototype Office. Through these contacts, Boeing management became convinced the program was going to start sooner or later, and authorized an increase in activity for an eight-month period of "design refinement." During this phase of design, the configuration was to be analyzed more thoroughly. An in-depth analysis would be done of weights and performance, with the configuration being refined to the point where the components would be ready to go into detailed design. Additionally, the flexibility of the aircraft structure and how it would respond to air loads in flight (aeroelasticity) would be scrutinized to ensure the YC-14 would have no bad habits and would resist the onset of aerodynamic flutter at high speeds.

NASA 716 was a de Havilland Canada Buffalo modified with the augmentor wing for STOL research. The aircraft is seen here at Navy Crow's Landing, California, in May 1973. *Public domain*

The question of a new engine for the AMST was still alive, and there were debates among the USAF, the Pentagon, and Congress about the need for a new engine for this airplane. The USAF actually asked for resubmittals of the March proposals on the basis of the use of engines that were in the existing inventory. Boeing merely replied that their original proposal still stood because it was based on such an engine. It was during these debates that the first inclination from Congress came that they were looking at this program not as one for prototypes but as the beginning of a major production program.

The waters were muddied further by the fact that NASA was considering a contract for building a high-performance STOL airplane called QUESTOL (Quiet Experimental STOL Transport). Elements of the government were anxious for the QUESTOL program to be incorporated into the AMST program, potentially minimizing costs. In the end, however, NASA held out for an airplane that was more sophisticated and aimed at even-slower flight than the AMST. They wanted an experimental airplane that would push the boundaries of technology further than the USAF would be willing to do on a production airplane.

Identifying the Risks

By September 1972, Boeing had identified additional risk areas on the airplane. It was found that the calibration of the blowing nacelles used to determine low-speed performance was in error. The thrust values created were about 8% greater than had been used in the performance calculations, thereby making all of these calculations considerably optimistic. Boeing did feel, however, that the USB nozzle could be improved to meet the performance levels used in the proposal, but these values did indicate that there was substantial work ahead in refining this nozzle. Also, more-detailed analysis of the pitching moments and ground effects indicated that the horizontal tail used in the proposal was appreciably too small. The airplane was going to need a larger horizontal stabilizer (or perhaps even an all-moving one) in order to obtain the requisite control authority. By the end of September, Boeing had completed the first iteration of the configuration in the design refinement phase.

The NASA Quiet Short-Haul Aircraft (QSRA) was a modified de Havilland Canada C-8A Buffalo. This aircraft, NASA 715, made use of upper surface blowing effects, similar to the YC-14. *Public domain*

In early November, I visited NASA Langley again to see what they were doing in USB development. I found that tests were being run there by both Joe Johnson and Dudley Hammond. In both cases they were getting data that verified the high-lift data that Boeing had submitted in their proposal, and they were launching a very extensive and systematic study of various USB configurations, nozzle shapes, and so forth. They reported to us that Boeing's lead in USB was being lost rapidly as other contractors began to pick up the idea from the Langley Field investigations and started incorporating USB into designs of their own.

Winners Announced

On November 10, 1972, the announcement was made that Boeing and McDonnell Douglas had been selected as contractors to work on the AMST prototypes. The official announcement to Boeing was from Col. Cameron of the Prototype Office to T. Wilson, Boeing's chairman of the board. Wilson made the announcement over the company's public-address system for all to hear. Those on the program at Boeing had waited for so long, through so many false starts, that when the announcement finally came, it was received very calmly. After work, there was a party for all the proposal participants in the cafeteria, where T. Wilson spoke and congratulated them for winning this contract. It was a relatively subdued party that broke up about 6:30 in the evening. This win was the first one for Boeing of an airplane based on a paper competition since the B-52 was won twenty-four years earlier. On Monday, November 13, the Boeing AMST team began to work under contract.

Configuration Development

The initial contracted work focused on trade studies aimed at lowering the production cost of the airplane. Shortly thereafter, the year-long design refinement period began that defined, in detail, the configuration that actually was built.

Trade Studies

Under the contract, the first month or so was to be spent doing additional trade studies, attempting to reduce the size of the aircraft to a point where everyone could agree that the three hundredth production unit could be built for the $5 million goal. Although there was support for the airplane program within the USAF, there were elements within the DoD who felt that the airplane could never be built at the projected cost if it remained the size that met the requirements of the proposal work statement. Gen. Stewart, who headed the USAF Systems Command, was anxious to have the studies done by early December so that the results could be reported to the secretary of the USAF, Robert Seamens, prior to the end of the year. Boeing could proceed to work on the details of the design that were not dependent on size, so that wind tunnel models could be built, tests could be started, and data could be gathered under the contract. The USAF was willing to examine the possibility of reducing the requirements in terms of payload or field length to drive the cost down at least 10%.

The trade studies lasted only a month, allowing Gen. Stewart to report to the USAF and the DoD by year's end on what the program really would involve. In an effort to make the airplane smaller, Boeing examined the use of the CF6-6 engine, which had been used on the original DC-10, and also looked at four-engine versions based on the smaller Pratt & Whitney JT8D. However, because the USAF had defined the cargo box dimensions down to a tenth of a foot, along with the range of the mission, it was very difficult to reduce the aircraft's size. For instance, a 15% change in wing area results in only an 8% change in the wing cost because the number of parts remains essentially the same. Because the wing is only about 8% of the cost of the airplane, the 15% wing area change results in an airplane cost change of only 0.6%. Thus, it can be seen that after the mission and the engines are selected, it does not change the cost of the airplane much to vary such things as the wing area. The four-engine airplane continued to look superior for the case of one engine out, as the airplanes were driven down to a smaller size in an effort to reduce the cost. The smallest engine available for a twin was the CF6-6, and it required a certain-sized wing area just to control it in the case of an engine out. The four-engine airplane could use the JT8D in any of its several versions, which would allow it to become a smaller airplane. The disadvantage, of course, was that the JT8D was expected to be out of production by the time the AMST had started into production. Another suitable engine for a four-engine airplane was the General Electric F-101 being developed for the B-1 bomber. This engine could be used on the transport without an afterburner. General Electric, the builder of the engine, was offering it at a relatively low price, hoping to capture the business if the AMST airplane were to emerge as a four-engine configuration. Just before Christmas, Boeing's final presentations to the USAF indicated that they could build a somewhat smaller twin than they had proposed, based on the CF6-6 engine. If a good engine came along that was suitable for the transport, Boeing could adapt the configuration to a four-engine version for final production. The USAF appeared to be content with that position.

As it turned out, continuing small changes in the USAF requirements for the cargo compartment and amendments to the rules used to compute the critical design mission eventually forced the airplane up to a size essentially identical to that originally proposed. Although the mission had been reduced from 500 to 400 miles, the rules relative to fuel reserves and conservatism allowances had changed enough to make the actual fuel requirements about the same. However, Boeing felt that they had reduced the unit production cost to nearly the level the USAF wanted of $4.5 million (10% below the $5 million proposal requirement) by simplifying the construction of the airplane.

Contract Begins

The prototype contract was signed in early January 1973 at a price of $96.2 million for the design and construction of the two airplanes and one year's flight testing. The work statement had been changed to include an operable cargo door, but no allowance had been made for that in the price. This price was accepted in spite of the fact that Boeing's best analysis of the work statement indicated that the lowest possible cost would be about $130 million. The matter was a classic example of the USAF taking the position that there was only so much money to be spent, and the type of airplane they wanted had been determined. Does the contractor want to be in on the game or not? The contractor had the choice of either bidding much lower than it thought reasonable, or it could just give up on the entire program. As in the case of so many defense contracts, the contractor elected to take the risk. There may have been people in the top Boeing management who thought the proposal cost estimates were padded enough that the contract price could be met. I do not believe there was anybody close to the program who felt Boeing could do it. The AMST team felt that their cost analysis had been made very carefully and was affirmed by the people in the Commercial Airplane Company, who had thousands of airplanes in their background.

CHAPTER 3

Configuration Refinement

The YC-14 was designed to reliably operate from austere fields as short as 2,000 feet in length. *Courtesy of the Boeing Company*

In January 1973, Boeing started on the actual design of the airplane. They began with a more formal continuation of the configuration refinement started the previous August with Boeing funding. The airplane was defined in much greater detail than in the proposal and gradually was formed to where it would work well in all its different aspects. This design refinement period lasted roughly one year. Starting with the proposal configuration, the AMST team went through seven configuration iterations, gradually closing down to the final design.

Included in these seven iterations were two that included a complete aeroelastic cycle. An aeroelastic cycle is one wherein the aerodynamic loads and the weight distribution are estimated for the configuration. The corresponding aeroelastic deflections are calculated so that more accurate estimates can be made of the performance, the structural weight, and particularly the stability and control characteristics. These calculations are quite lengthy and could not be done quickly enough to be incorporated into each configuration change.

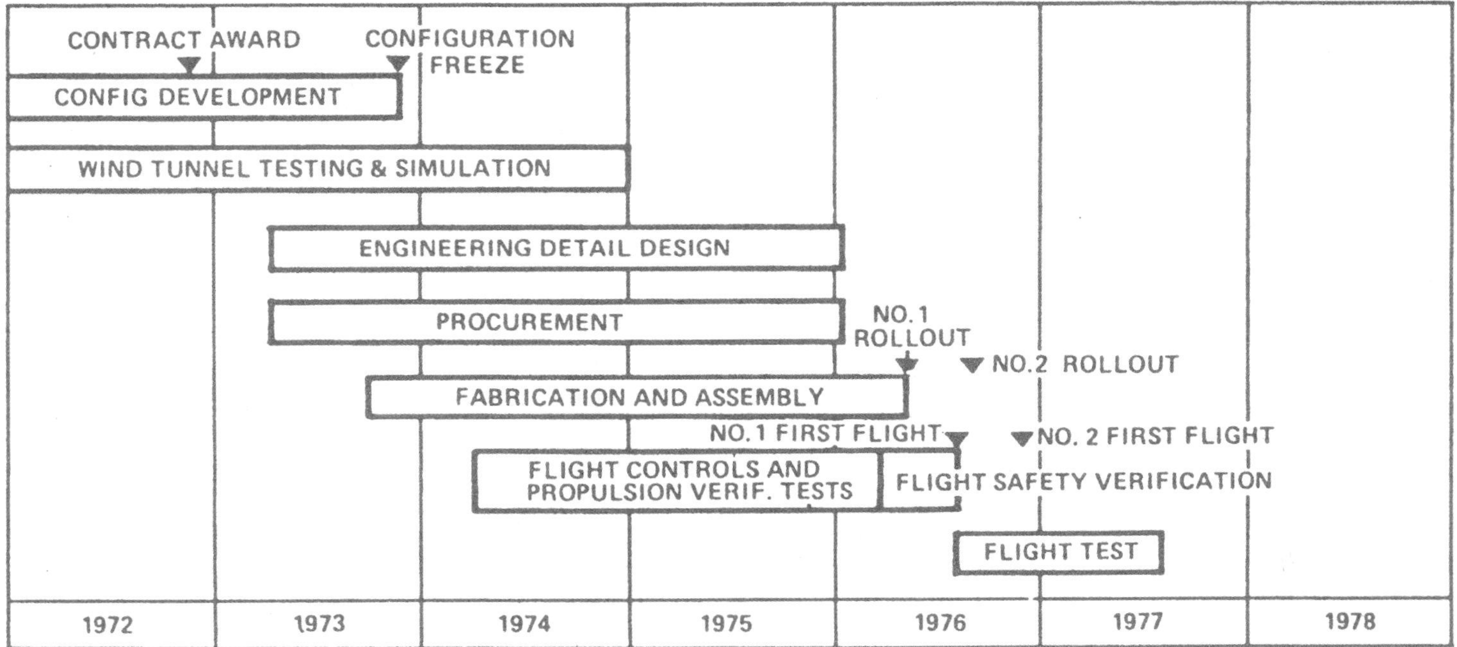

The YC-14 development program schedule. The entire program took four and a half years from the time of contract award to the end of flight testing. The large overlap of the periods for detail design and for fabrication and assembly was accomplished by designing the parts in the general sequence that they would be built and assembled. *Courtesy of the Boeing Company*

At each configuration step, the technical data that had been generated in the previous several months was incorporated into the design process to make necessary configuration decisions. The 1973 design schedule was laid out very carefully so that decisions would be made early in the year on those items requiring the longest lead time to manufacture. The ones requiring less manufacturing time were gradually firmed up later on (see schedule chart above). For instance, decisions on the planform of the wing were the earliest, closely followed by the decision on the thickness distribution across the span. The YC-14 airfoil was selected on the basis of Boeing's past experience and early AMST wind tunnel tests. However, the precise shape was defined in stages. The shape between the spars was defined first, since the spar caps, skin, and stringers were long-lead-time items for manufacturing. The leading- and trailing-edge contours were selected after further wind tunnel tests, but the dimensions and slopes at the front and rear spars had to mesh with those of the interspar structure determined earlier. Finally, at the very last, the leading-edge and trailing-edge flaps were defined to blend with the airfoil contours. The same general approach was used for design decisions on the tail, fuselage, and landing gear. Again, starting with items that required the longest manufacturing time and then gradually refining the details as time went on. While this series of changes was being made, there was heavy emphasis on cost, which had to be controlled from the beginning. It is well known at Boeing that about 80% of the aircraft cost is typically determined at the time the first drawing is released to manufacturing. In other words, most of the cost of the airplane is determined by its configuration. Small design details generally have a relatively small influence on cost.

As Boeing entered the configuration refinement phase of the design, the USAF indicated that they were going to monitor the team's progress with their own technical personnel. On other military programs, monitoring had resulted in appreciable interference. Special meetings had to be set aside to brief the USAF personnel, and considerable time was spent answering their specific questions. No budget had been allowed in the bid to take care of this kind of coordination, and thus it was decided that the AMST team would simply let the USAF sit in on their regular design review meetings. There was a certain amount of risk to this position, because the USAF would then be exposed to the team's internal problems and squabbles. Past experience had indicated that these observers had a way of amplifying problems far beyond their real worth and thereby creating more questions and additional problems. However, Boeing really had no choice. During the early meetings attended by USAF personnel, they were quite surprised by the process and the debates that occurred in trying to refine a design. They were used to highly sterilized presentations and thus had no idea what really went on behind the scenes. After one of these meetings, one of the USAF technical people came up to me and asked, "Is that really the way things happen all the time?" I told him it was the same on every program I had ever been on. It was quite some time before the USAF felt comfortable that the Boeing team members really knew what they were doing and were merely working through the challenges, and that eventually the design would work out well. They were surprised by how much the design had to be modified from the configuration that was in the original proposal. The USAF personnel always felt that the airplane would be built simply as proposed, and thus had little appreciation for the intense struggle required to formulate an airplane design.

During one of the USAF visits, some of their technical people questioned whether or not a pilot really could make a landing on a narrow, 2,000-foot field in an airplane with an approach speed of around 85 knots like Boeing had proposed. Because I was a

A cutaway drawing of the YC-14.
Courtesy of the Boeing Company

private pilot, I took them in a Cessna 182 to a small airport nestled among the trees near Seattle that very closely approximated the USAF RFP specification. There, I could demonstrate an 85-knot approach exactly as described in Boeing's proposal, and show how easily corrections could be made during the last few minutes and seconds before touchdown. Interestingly, later when the YC-14 was tested, it was found that it did indeed fly much like a light airplane on final approach.

A Closer Look at the YC-14's Unique Features

The following paragraphs will discuss the design and development of each of the major components of the YC-14 airplane, such as the wing, body, nacelles, tail, and control system. Each component will be followed through its development with the reasons provided for the various design choices that resulted in the final configuration.

Engine Nozzle and Upper-Surface-Blown Flap

The development of these two components of the airplane was by far the most time-consuming technical problem in the program. Their development completely paced the evolution of the entire configuration. At the time of the proposal, no wind tunnel tests had been made of the same configuration at both high and low speeds. In the low-speed testing, a fairly high-aspect-ratio nozzle with a rather rectangular shape was used. Conversely, high-speed testing used an idealized nozzle shape that was more semicircular. However, a nozzle had been tested statically (without wind tunnel airflow) that looked fairly realistic for both speeds, and it turned the jet flow over the USB flap satisfactorily. The propulsion engineers hypothesized that the dynamic pressure of the jet flow from the nozzle was so high (compared to the dynamic pressure of the free stream) that if the nozzle worked statically, it also would work in the free-stream flow. That is, the free-stream flow would not have enough energy to modify the flow of the basic engine. This assumption turned out to be a serious misconception.

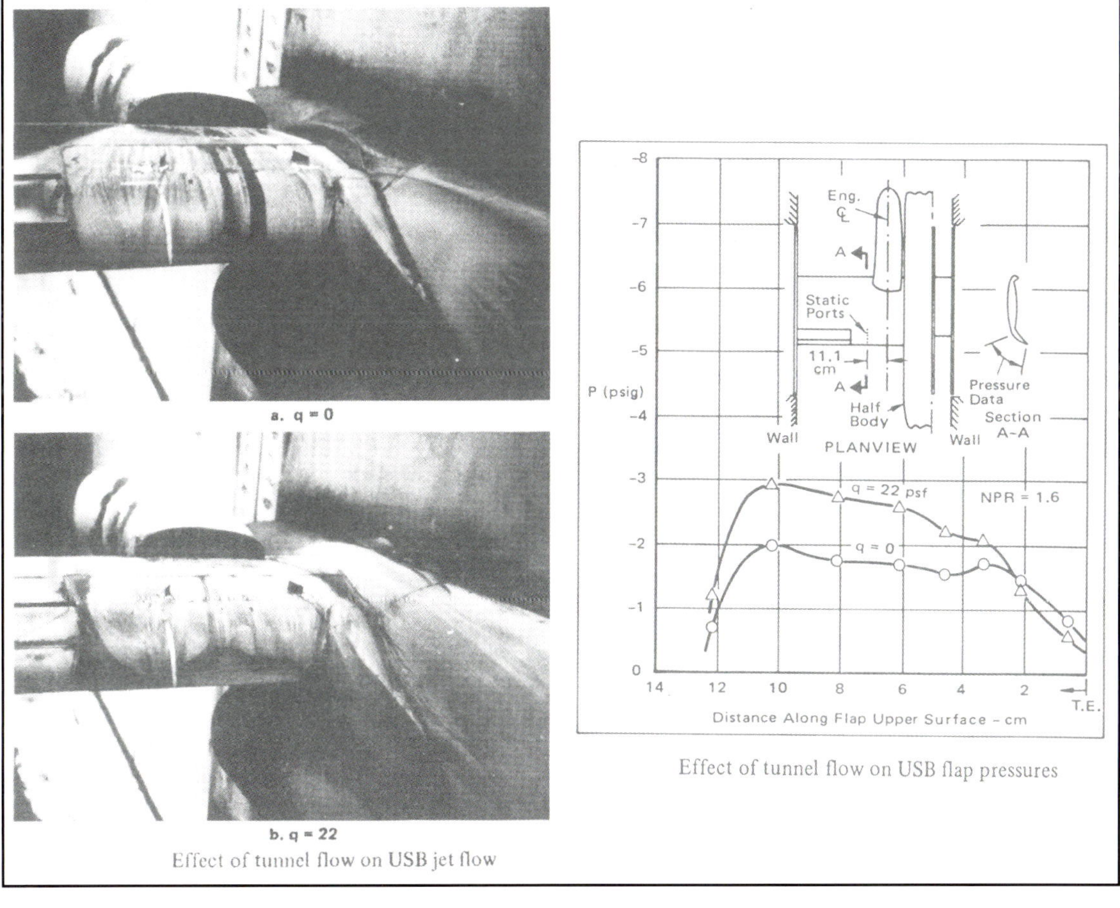

The first major technical surprise. The external flow past the airplane had a marked influence on the flow over the USB flap, reducing the jet spreading and causing separation ahead of the flap trailing edge. *Courtesy of the Boeing Company*

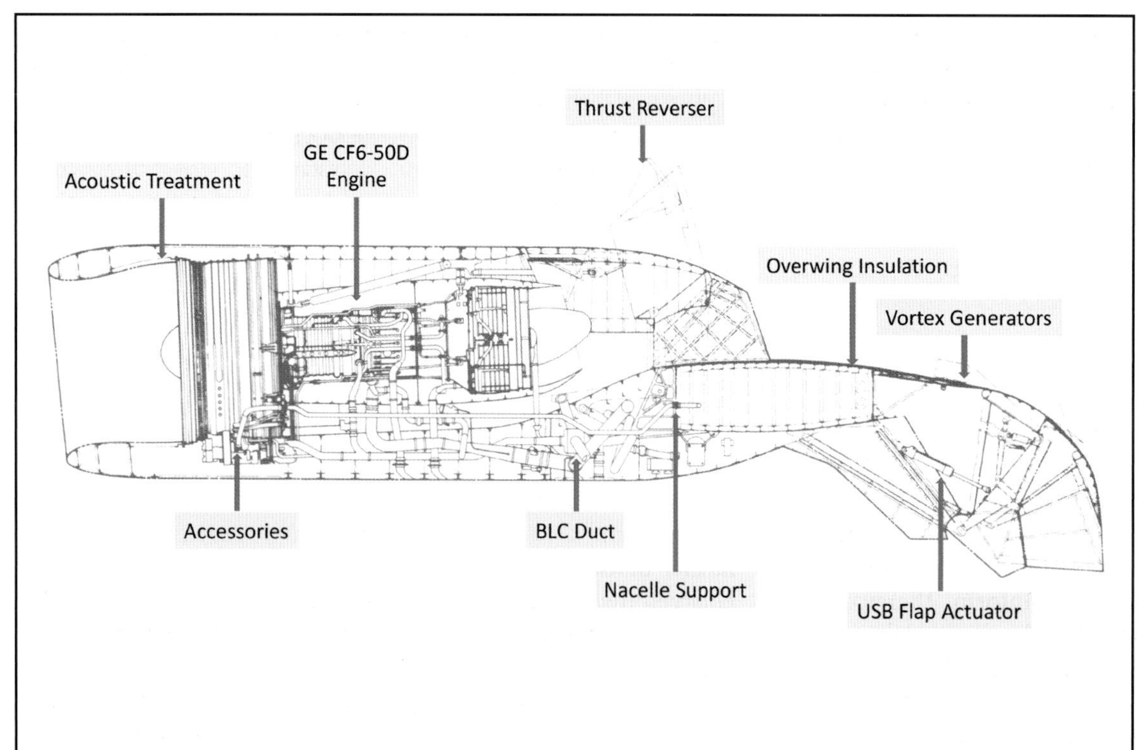

Engine and nacelle cross section. *Courtesy of the Boeing Company*

When the wind tunnel testing program actually began, it was found that the pressure gradient on the USB flap near the trailing edge was roughly doubled when the combined free-stream air and engine air were flowing, compared to the gradient existing when just the engine airflow was operational. This increase in pressure gradient resulted in separation of the flow from the USB flap when the test was being done with the wind tunnel air flowing, whereas there was no separation when the system was tested statically. This result was found in the very first test that was run during the design refinement period. A simple, single test in the summer of 1972 would have found this problem and given Boeing months of lead time to work on it. Instead, they were faced with trying to develop a nozzle at the same time they were trying to develop the rest of the configuration. In addition, calibration of the nozzles that were used in the low-speed testing of the proposal airplane configuration indicated that the thrust levels used during the proposal analyses were about 5 to 8 % optimistic. It was estimated that eventually the nozzle would perform that well, but the performance described in the proposal really was optimistic by about that amount.

The first high-speed tests were done in March 1973 with a fairly idealized nozzle. The external nacelle flow showed no unacceptable shock wave activity. The engine flow adhered to the wing behind the nozzle and created a slight jet flap effect even at cruise speeds. The engine jet flow did not touch the body appreciably, so no nonlinear effects occurred in the yawing moments due to the jet flow adhering to the body side. Such effects could have conceivably caused controllability issues during single-engine operations.

Low-speed tests were initiated in a 3-by-8-foot research tunnel at Boeing, using the same nozzles that were used in the Vertol tunnel, although with a simplified installation. These tests were started in April 1973, utilizing a nearly rectangular nozzle having an aspect ratio (width divided by height) of about 4.3. This nozzle shape really could not be built without a large number of moving parts, but it served as a starting point for low-speed testing.

The original proposal design had the thrust reverser made from the nozzle trailing edge rotating into the jet flow. As the nozzle development proceeded, it became evident that such a configuration could not be used. A strong arch across the nozzle trailing edge was needed to support the high-pressure loads produced by the engine flow, so the thrust reverser door was made as an independent part, slightly ahead of the nozzle in the final configuration.

The YC-14 engine installation produced far more coupling between the geometry and aerodynamics of the nozzle and of the wing and flap than on a conventional airplane. The nozzle influenced the wing, and the wing influenced the nozzle. To get proper consideration of these cross-coupling effects, the propulsion and aerodynamic teams working on the nozzle and wing were put under the direction of a single person, Howard Skavdahl. He had extensive experience in both areas and could see that the best design compromises were made to get optimal performance.

When the schedule for the configuration refinement period was established in January 1973, Boeing expected to have the nozzle fairly well defined around the following May. As it turned out, Skavdahl and his team were still trying desperately through September to get a nozzle that would work. It was not until October that they finally had a nozzle that looked practical to build and, at the same time, gave good performance at both high and low speeds. By mid-August, they had found that the flow would not turn adequately over the flap that fit into the basic wing planform. Therefore, the USB flap was extended approximately 10 inches beyond the trailing edge of the wing—a planform that remained throughout the airplane's development. Getting the jet flow to follow the flap contour when the flap was at the high deflection angles required for landing was a real challenge! Boeing wanted the flow to adhere to the flaps, so that the flaps could be modulated to control the thrust component of the jet flow and thereby change glide path without changing the basic engine thrust. This feature permitted the precise control critical for making good STOL landings. The control engineers felt that about 2° above and below the basic glide slope of 6° was needed to get the control characteristics they wanted.

The other major low-speed challenge was getting adequate climb capability with one engine out, both on takeoff and during a go-around. It was found to be necessary to provide an asymmetric setting of the USB flap to achieve good single-engine climb performance. With one engine out, the USB flap would be fully extended behind the inoperative engine and retracted slightly behind the operating engine. These minor variations in the flap deflection resulted in changes to the flaps-down drag coefficient, higher in fact than the entire drag coefficient of a 737 jetliner during a go-around! By the end of August, the team was of the opinion that no practical fixed-geometry nozzle would meet every requirement. An added complication was the fact that during cruise, the nozzle was influenced by the local pressures on the top of the wing. This influence does not matter for the case of an engine slung under the wing, where the local pressures are fairly close to free-stream static pressure. Above the wing the pressures are much lower than free-stream static. The nozzle is exhausting into this low-pressure field and therefore must be a smaller diameter than it would be under free-stream conditions. A nozzle was required that changed area, as well as shape, between the low- and high-speed flight configuration. During this desperate testing period in August and September 1973, the Boeing transonic wind tunnel had a major failure of its electrical system and was shut down for about eight weeks. During this period, high-speed testing was shifted to the tunnel at Cornell University. Fortunately, that tunnel had adequate balance systems and air supplies to provide the blowing of the simulated engines. These tests and their predecessors indicated how carefully the nozzle outer contours had to be shaped to keep them from causing high drag under cruise conditions. By the end of September, a nozzle configuration that looked like it would meet the required performance both for high- and low-speed flight was finally designed and tested. This nozzle configuration consisted of a basic elliptical exit with a small door on the outboard side that could open during takeoff and landing and allow the engine exhaust jet to spread farther outboard over the USB flap. At the same time, the door enlarged the effective exit area of the nozzle slightly. To make this nozzle work at very large flap deflections, retractable vortex generators were installed just forward of the USB flap to mix the high-energy engine exhaust flow with the local boundary layer. This persuaded the flow to go against the pressure gradients downstream of the flap corner. These vortex generators were extended only when the USB flap was deflected 30° or more and were retracted against the wing surface during cruise flight.

The final nozzle configuration that was chosen was adequate in all of its required flight regimes. It did not give quite the increase in glide slope that was wanted, only about 1½° compared to the 2° that was desired, but simulation of the approach path and go-around indicated that this smaller value would be satisfactory.

After all this work had been done on the nozzle and on the wing shape, the AMST team was dealt another technical blow. When the Boeing tunnel began operating again, it was found that all the previous tests on the YC-14 had been done with about a quarter of a degree of upward deflected airflow in the test section. This small up-flow resulted in all the drag values being artificially low by about 5%. Here again was an error in the Boeing data that had to be made up in the design or just swallowed in the airplane performance. It seemed that just about everything that could go wrong in the wind tunnel testing had gone wrong. It was very painful indeed to get to the point where the design was essentially committed, and then to find out that the foundation for the predicted performance was in error. It was really too late to do anything about it. A detailed description of the technical development of the nozzle, both low-speed and high-speed, is beyond the scope of this book. However, the story is covered well in SAE and AIAA publications.

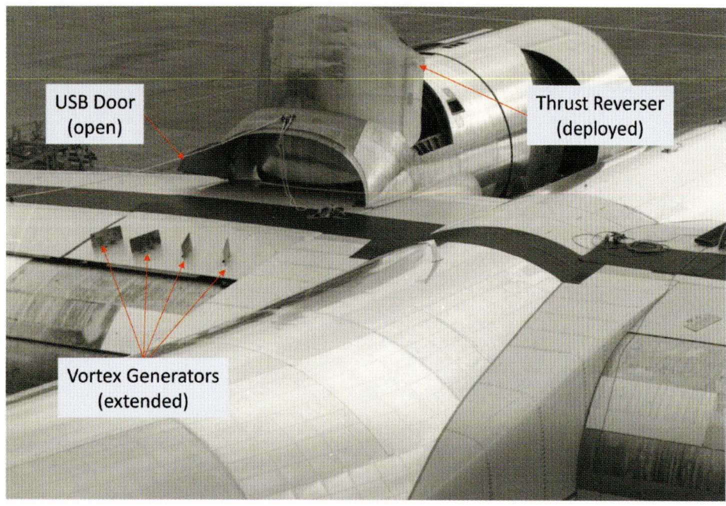

Nozzle and reverser. The USB nozzle door opened any time the flaps were extended, allowing the jet flow to spread over the USB flap. The vortex generators extended only for extreme flap deflection. The thrust reverser was a bucket type that was formed from the upper part of the nacelle and deflected the mixed flow from the engine. A short movable lip helped turn the flow forward. With an engine inoperative, the first segment of the USB flap rotated slightly, forming a double-slotted flap for superior aerodynamic performance. *Courtesy of the Boeing Company*

Wing

Most of the wing planform decisions were made prior to the submission of the proposal. During the preparation, the decision was made to make the wing with a straight rear wing spar and the wing dimensions were chosen. The area remained essentially the same (1,762 square feet) throughout the configuration refinement period. The big debate during this period was concerned with obtaining a proper trade between performance and production cost. It was considered desirable to keep the wing physical features that were displayed in the proposal—no joints throughout the length of the wing and a spanwise airfoil thickness distribution that permitted a constant center section between the outboard sides of the two nacelles. It also was preferable to prevent the need to preform any of the skins or stringers prior to installing them on the ribs and spars. To keep this characteristic, it was a manufacturing requirement that the skin or stringers could not be bent tighter than a 3,000-inch radius. With this very large radius, it would be possible to drape the stringers and skins onto the wing ribs without any preforming. This concept produced a very cost-effective wing, because it eliminated all the costly joints that involved fittings and fasteners. However, it did lead to an awkward spanwise airfoil thickness distribution. Previous Boeing jet airplanes had a constant center section wing through the fuselage, and then the outer panels of the wings were fastened to this center section. This arrangement permitted a spanwise thickness distribution that could be fairly constant on the outer part of the span and then increase rapidly toward the root, where the bending moments increased. There would then be a thickness distribution discontinuity at the joint between the wing outer panels and the wing center section. With a continuous wing structure, however, the thickness distribution had to have an S-shape, starting from the thickness of the outer panel moving continuously through an S-shape to the thickness of the center section. Boeing knew from previous experience that the high Mach number characteristics of the wing were largely determined by the airfoil maximum thickness ratio at approximately 40% span (as measured from the airplane centerline). Unfortunately, it was impossible to go from the desired thickness at 40% span to the desired thickness in the center section in only the distance between the 40% span point and the outboard edge of the nacelle and maintain the 3,000-inch radius bending limit (see page 41).

The program schedule called for making a decision on the inner spar structural shape by early July 1973. The decision was made to utilize the 3,000-inch-radius curve in fairing from the center section thickness at the outboard edge of the nacelle to the thickness of the outboard wing. Subsequent wind tunnel data, which arrived late, indicated that this resulted in about a 5% decrease in range. This penalty was caused by the increased thickness extending out well beyond the 40% span point where it should reach the proper thickness ratio for the outboard portion of the wing. The Manufacturing Department had indicated they really could not provide the radius of curvature that was shown in the proposal document. They wanted to hold the constant section out as far as the outboard side of the nacelle so that the fittings that attached the nacelle to the wing's spar structure would be identical in all four places. This was an obvious manufacturing cost savings but would be an aerodynamic compromise.

A month later (early August), the decision was made to move the transition point to the centerline of the engine rather than to its outboard side and to optimize the design as much as manufacturing could tolerate. The nacelle attachment fittings were essentially the same, with only slight modifications between inboard and outboard. The minimum radius ended up being 1,800 inches, but only in a small area, which Manufacturing was willing to accept. This shape did extend the higher thickness ratio out beyond the 40% span point, however, with an attendant cruise Mach number penalty. This choice was one example of performance being sacrificed in order to get the low cost required.

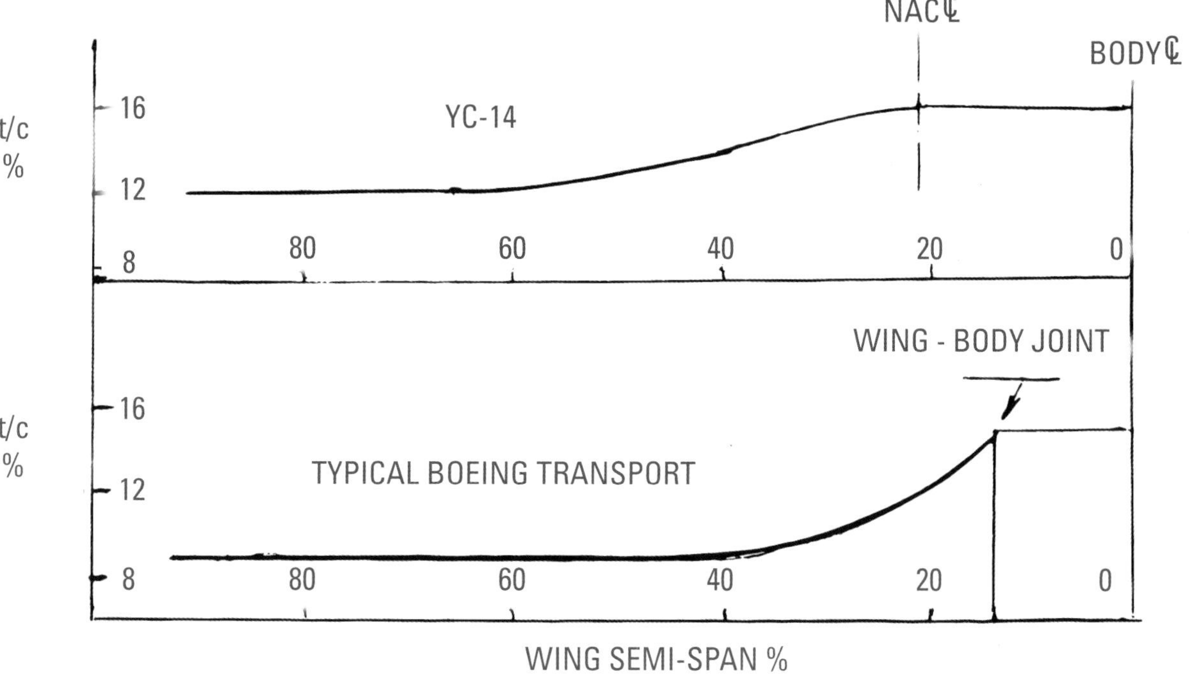

NOTE: t/c = Airfoil Max Thickness Divided by Airfoil Chord Length

The airfoil used on the airplane was a supercritical type, developed by Boeing aerodynamic research that had been carried on since the 747 had been designed. This wing design had a very low-drag rise with an increase in airspeed / Mach number. However, the leading edge was blunt compared with the 747 airfoil and had a fair amount of aft camber. This shape produced a center of lift that was quite a bit farther aft on the wing than was the case for airfoils more familiar to Boeing. It also had a constant thickness at the trailing edge. The wind tunnel data and theoretical analysis indicated that the trailing edge, over the inboard half span, probably should be about 1-inch thick for optimum performance. I felt reluctant to accept a thickness of that magnitude when Boeing had no previous experience with blunt trailing edges. As a compromise, the trailing-edge thickness was made 1/2 inch, which also reduced manufacturing costs.

Some of the older aerodynamicists at Boeing were reluctant to accept this airfoil only on the basis of analytical studies and wind tunnel tests, due to previous experiences, some of which dated back to World War II. Tests on these airfoils predicted long runs of laminar flow and very high performance. Yet in full scale, that performance benefit never was obtained. Fortunately, NASA was also working on supercritical airfoils that had shapes quite similar to the ones Boeing was using. They had run a flight test on a North American T-2C Buckeye naval trainer with a supercritical wing and had shown that, at least in their case, the airfoil worked the same in flight as it had in wind tunnel testing. Boeing learned a couple of years later, during their flight test program, that the wing performed essentially as predicted. Pressure distributions measured on the actual airplane in flight closely agreed with those measured in the wind tunnel test. This same approach to airfoil design was used on the next Boeing commercial airplanes developed—the 757 and 767.

YC-14 configuration details.
Courtesy of the Boeing Company

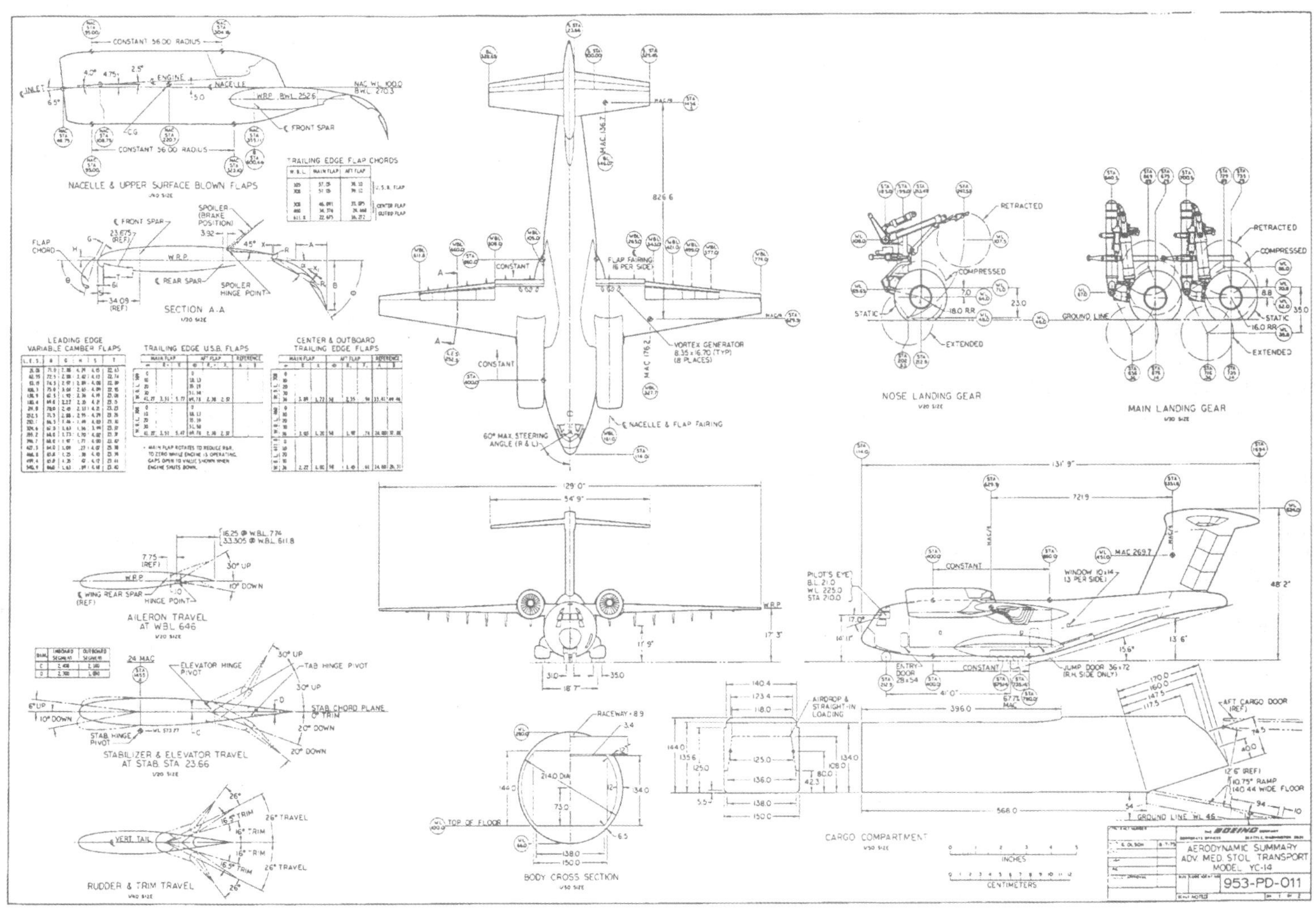

Because the engine exhaust jet flowed over the top of the wing, the wing structure had to be protected from the high gas temperatures involved. The engine exhaust nozzle was shaped in such a way that the cooler air from the fan section of the engine protected the wing from the very hot air coming from the core of the engine. Because of this feature, the real design requirement for heat protection was an accidental fuel fire on top of the wing. Such a fire could be caused by an abnormal engine start blowing fuel out the nozzle, where it could catch fire and burn. A 1-inch thick, polymide, honeycomb-type heat shield was used to protect the wing. The shield was then faired out to meet the wing surface so it caused no appreciable aerodynamic effect. This design passed the burning-fuel test quite readily and was one problem that was solved more easily than anticipated when the configuration was first developed.

Another design parameter that had to be monitored constantly during the wing development was that of adequate fuel volume. One of our goals was to have the ability to fly from the US West

Coast to Hawaii without external tanks, albeit without any payload—strictly a ferry mission. In the proposal, it was estimated that fuel tankage in the wing would be adequate if fuel extended from outboard of the engine nacelles to the inboard end of the aileron. As it turned out, it was necessary to put fuel in the wing center section above the body as well as in the region behind the engines. Because of unanticipated drag problems that were discovered later during flight tests, there was just barely enough fuel to meet the ferry mission requirement in the final analysis.

Body

The basic philosophy of the YC-14 body design was to make it extremely simple in order for it to be durable yet inexpensive to build. A constant section was held for the entire length of the flat-floor cargo compartment. The tail cone was a simple straight-line taper from the beginning of the cargo door back to the aft pressure bulkhead, which served also as a major support for the vertical fin. The proposal airplane had a cargo box with dimensions of 12 by 12 by 47 feet and a total body diameter of 220 inches, allowing the carriage of six pallets on the flat floor, plus another on the loading ramp. In the trade studies, considerable effort was put into making the body smaller, lighter, and less expensive. Through careful examination of the vehicles that the aircraft was expected to carry, the USAF reduced the box width requirement to only 11.7 feet, while keeping the requirements of 12 feet high and 47 feet long. Placing the personnel walkways slightly up on the sidewall in a wider portion of the cross section, a reduction of the body diameter to 214 inches was realized. This cargo compartment was big enough to carry all the US Army's large trucks, shop vans, and even a self-propelled howitzer in addition to 86% of the vehicle types used by a mechanized infantry division.

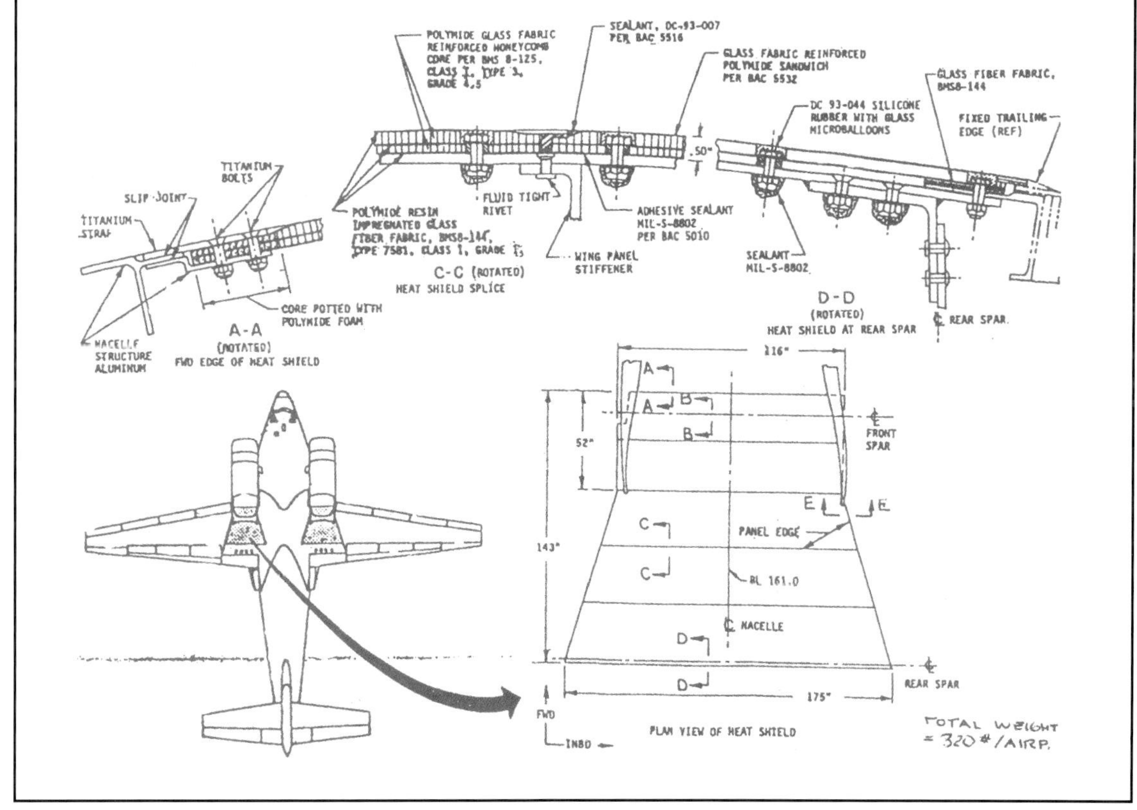

The wing heat shield protected the wing structure from hot jet gases and, more critically, from the heat of fuel burning on the surface as a result of a "hot" engine start or tailpipe fire. *Courtesy of the Boeing Company*

The outer body diameter could be reduced to 214 inches by placing the troop seats against the sidewall. *Courtesy of the Boeing Company*

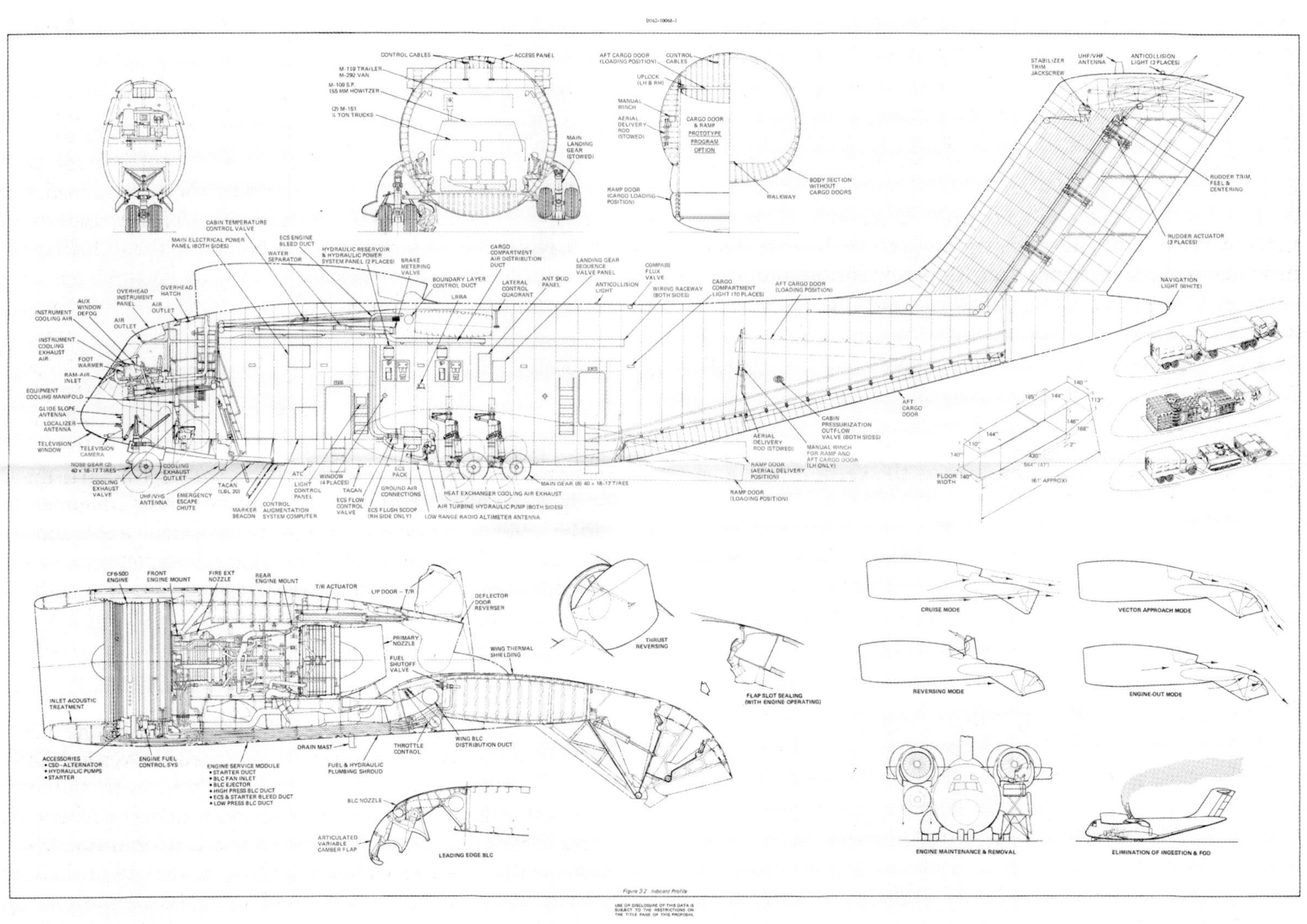

The forward fuselage shape, including the pilot's compartment, was selected fairly early in the design process, because it varied relatively little from the proposal configuration. As shown in the proposal, the pilots were placed close enough together so that only one set of throttles, as well as flap and landing-gear controls, was required, thereby simplifying the cockpit arrangement. Large windows were located to provide good visibility during approach and landing. An additional window below the normal windows was added to give a good view of the area used to signal the proper point to make aerial delivery drops. An eyebrow window was placed above the normal side window to improve visibility while doing tight maneuvering around the landing field. The eyebrow window was particularly important for a left-seat pilot flying a right-hand pattern. Also, by moving his head slightly from the normal flying position, the pilot could view his wingtip, which aided greatly in ground maneuvering. This pilot positioning resulted in an aircraft nose that was pinched into a fairly narrow configuration with rather flat sides to accommodate the large windows. These flat sides increased structural weight because the cabin was pressurized, but it was decided that the resulting good visibility warranted this compromise.

The aft body went through a number of configuration iterations. The proposal configuration had a relatively long tail cone tapering gradually from the ramp hinge line to the vertical fin support structure. It had a low upsweep angle and a flat upper profile. This configuration had relatively low drag for an airplane that permitted drive-in cargo capability. On the second iteration of the design, which occurred in mid-March 1973, the body was shortened 106 inches to save weight. However, this caused the body drag to be unacceptably high. A number of design studies were made having a short body but not quite as much upsweep of the aft fuselage. This shape was made feasible by creating a rather complex door design that achieved more clearance underneath the opened door structure for trucks to drive through than would be the case with just a simple hinged door. These efforts to create a short body with low upsweep angle continued until mid-year. About that time, a young engineer named Howard Levy, who worked in the Weight Staff (the group that estimated and kept track of the airplane weight), made an unsettling discovery. With the upsweep angles being examined, it was impossible for a standard Army loading vehicle to engage the airplane ramp without scraping on the bottom of the aft fuselage. It was estimated that all of the loaders in the US Army inventory could be modified to fit the airplane for less than the cost of one airplane. However, it was also recognized that those dollars came from different sources, and that it would be a distinct disadvantage to have the airplane unable to interface with existing Army equipment. The ramp could not be made longer, because its width would be greater than the width of the airplane as it tapered toward the tail. A bridge was considered that would go from the cargo ramp to the loader, but that meant another piece of heavy ground equipment would be required, to say nothing of making the loading operation appreciably more awkward. This interface with the Army loader was the final deciding factor that determined the upsweep of the aft body. The original observation was a classic example of how a bright young engineer, looking in areas completely outside his realm of responsibility, can make a unique contribution to a design and keep the program out of a lot of trouble!

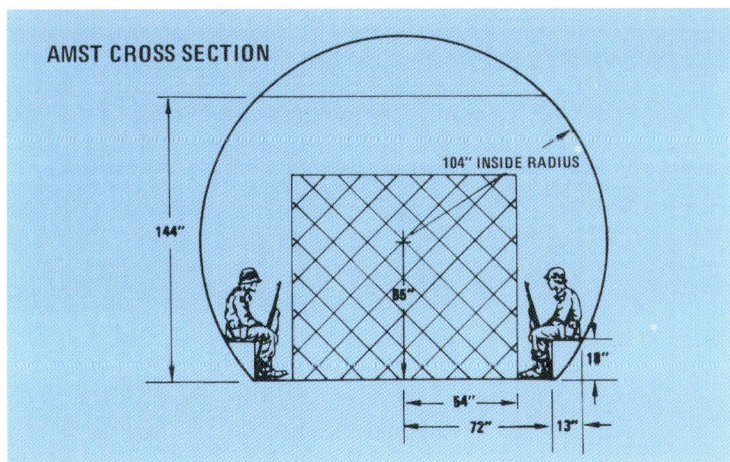

The YC-14 cargo compartment was long enough to carry seven 463L cargo pallets, including one on the 14-foot-long cargo ramp. At cargo densities from 10 to 14 pounds per cubic foot, payloads of up to 40,000–50,000 pounds could have been achieved with loads of both cargo and military passengers when operating in and out of conventional-length airfields. *Courtesy of the Boeing Company*

The very aft end of the airplane was a fiberglass tail cone that extended out beyond the structure that carried the vertical fin. This tail cone was drooped down markedly, since wind tunnel data indicated that such a shape recovered about one-quarter of the drag penalty paid for the basic body upsweep. Unfortunately, the drooped tail cone extended into the area allotted for body clearance during a high-attitude takeoff or landing. However, it was felt that if an extreme attitude occurred accidentally and the fiberglass cone was damaged, it could be replaced easily, and the normal clearance tolerance was maintained only for the basic body structure. These basic decisions on the body were finally made in mid-July 1973, over halfway through the configuration refinement period.

The YC-14 cockpit. Note the excellent visibility for both pilots. *Courtesy of the Boeing Company*

The right seat position featured the tried-and-true electromechanical instrumentation typical of production aircraft at the time. *Courtesy of the Boeing Company*

The left seat position was equipped with a very early electronic flight instrument system (EFIS), which today is standard in nearly every modern cockpit. *Courtesy of the Boeing Company*

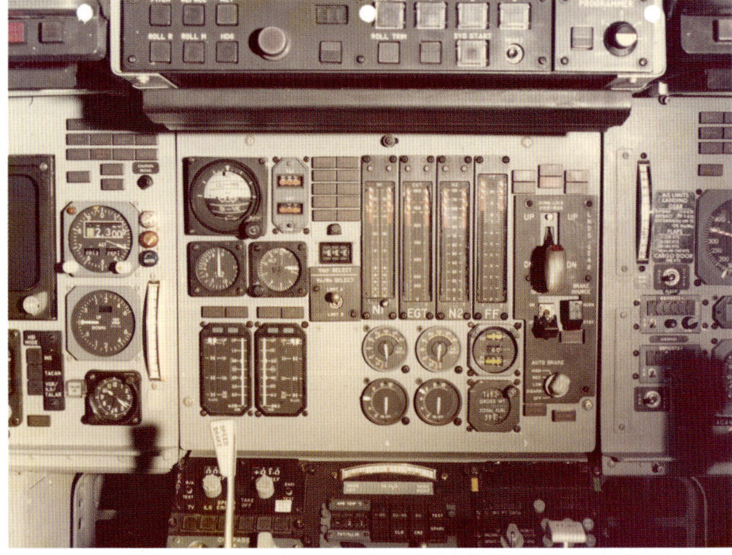

The center instrument panel was a mixture of typical Boeing instrumentation and tape-type gauges. Engine instrumentation is as follows: N1 (fan rpm) percent × 10, EGT (exhaust gas temperature degrees C, N2 (engine core rpm) percent × 10, and FF (fuel flow) in pounds per hour × 1,000. Oil pressure and quantity are also supplied on the round dials below. *Courtesy of the Boeing Company*

The aft portion of the fuselage was found to cause a substantial amount of cruise drag. The composite tail cone was revised and canted down slightly, which provided improved performance. *Dan Dornseif collection*

USAF people from the Flight Dynamics Laboratory in Dayton were quite critical of the drag estimates Boeing had made for the effect of the upswept body. They felt that Boeing was not allowing nearly enough drag for this feature. On the other hand, Boeing aerodynamicists felt that the problem was understood and that the drag estimates were right. Their belief was based on the many studies that had been made relative to Boeing's proposal for the C-5 airplane and other tests that had been performed on upswept bodies. This position was a perfect example of my ego getting in the way of my better judgment. It so happened that the USAF people were right! The fact was that Boeing had not run sufficient tests on the YC-14 configuration to really understand the aft body drag. The testing techniques used were inadequate, and the resulting data were full of anomalies that could not be sorted out. Because of the low emphasis on cruise performance at that time, Boeing elected not to pursue the problem in detail. When the airplane actually was flight tested, the drag was about 10% higher than had been predicted, much of it involving the aft body, including the influence of the protruding landing-gear pods.

A year and a half later, in January 1975, the USAF issued a requirement that the AMST airplanes must carry the very large main battle tanks, including the M60, and the British Chieftain and Centurion. The heavy longerons that carried the tail loads through the body alongside the cargo door and ramp were then modified so that there was barely adequate clearance to load these very large combat vehicles onto the airplane.

Another element that had to be considered in the body design was the heat and noise from the engine jet that flowed across the wing, over the USB flap, and down along the side of the body. With the flaps down, temperatures along the aft body just behind the wing were estimated to be as high as 300° Fahrenheit. However, these temperatures did not pose a problem to the conventional aluminum structure. The noise levels in the same region reached as high as 165 decibels on takeoff. This noise level could create a fatigue problem in the structure, and initially it was thought that considerable weight would have to be put in the structure to keep it from deteriorating. However, good detail design overcame any potential problems, and actually there was very little weight penalty because of these high noise levels. Also, the noise was fairly high on the side of the body ahead of the inlet, at about 140 decibels. This level required special soundproofing in the cockpit area, which was accomplished using conventional techniques.

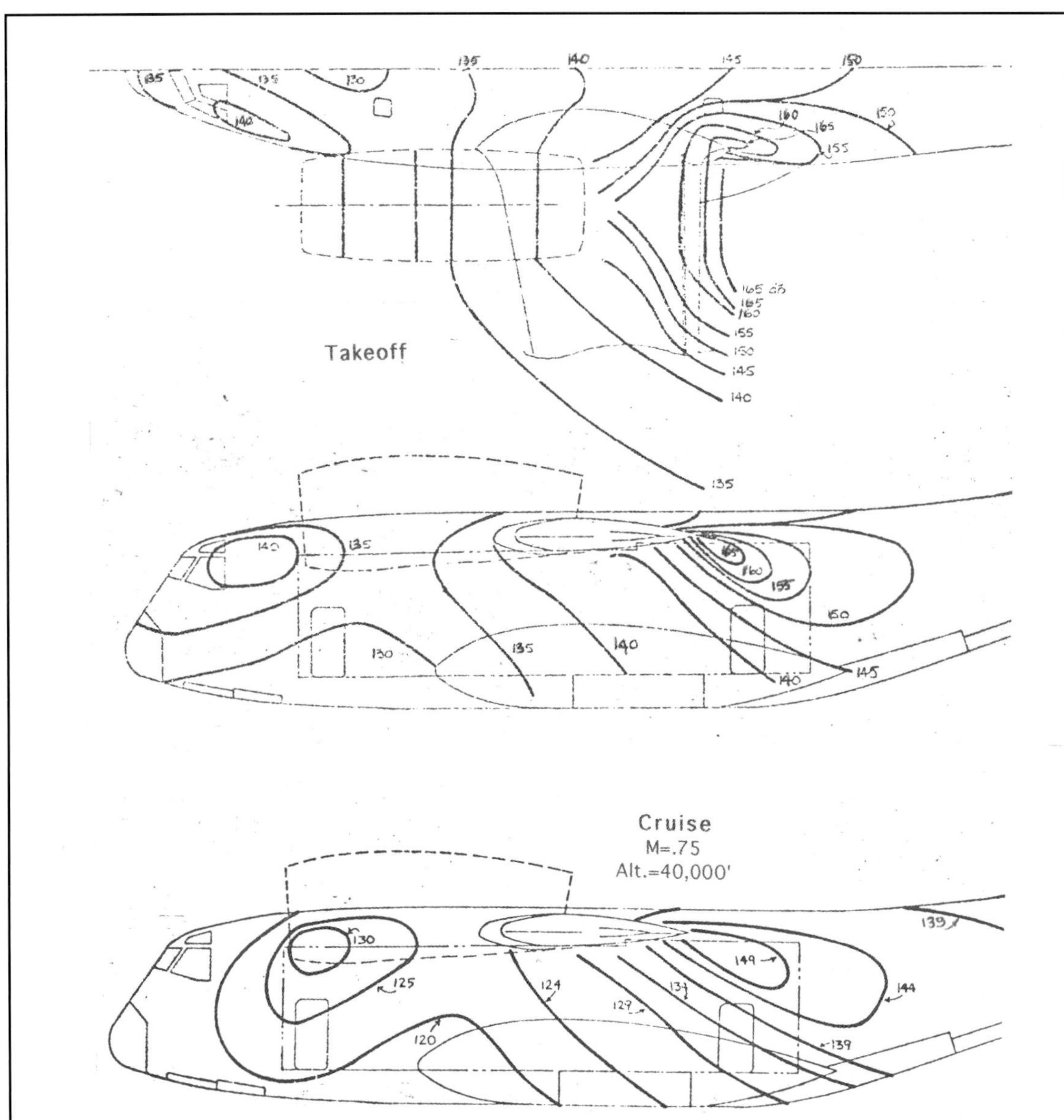

Noise levels from engine operation. Although noise affecting the body and wing was quite high on takeoff, it was far less at cruise speeds. Special attention was given to detail design of the structure to withstand these noise levels, but no appreciable weight was added. *Courtesy of the Boeing Company*

A final consideration of the body design was the suitability for dropping paratroopers. The Tactical Air Command desired that the jumpers go out the side doors so that two strings of paratroopers could be dropped at the same time. The doors were placed carefully so that the paratroopers avoided the temperature and velocity of the engine jets while the airplane was in the drop configuration. However, for these door positions, the large landing-gear pods (required for aerodynamic efficiency) interfered with the paratroopers' exit paths. A lot of design work was done to ensure that the gear pod could be folded out of the way to make a clear platform for the jumper to exit the airplane. On the prototype, the gear fairing was removed in this area just for the jump test, rather than to make and install the complicated mechanism that would be needed on the production airplane.

Jet temperatures and velocity. The troop drop door was clear of the high velocities and temperatures of the jet exhaust that was deflected downward by the USB flap. *Courtesy of the Boeing Company*

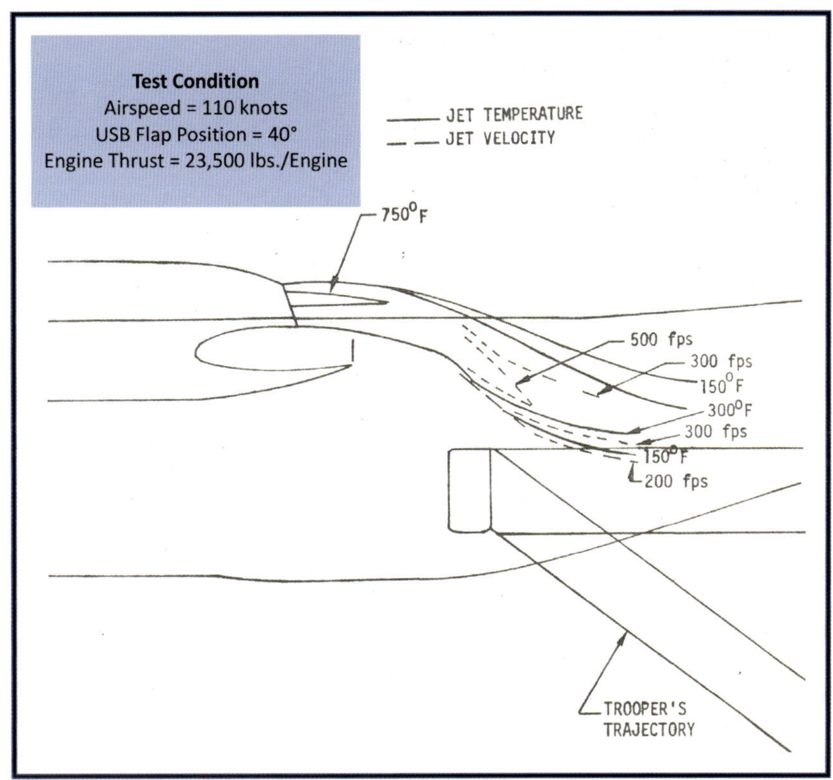

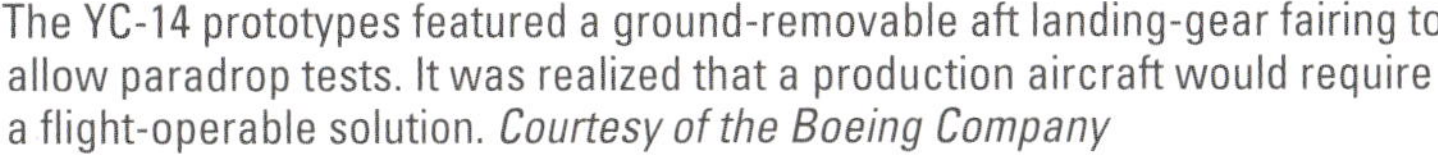

The YC-14 prototypes featured a ground-removable aft landing-gear fairing to allow paradrop tests. It was realized that a production aircraft would require a flight-operable solution. *Courtesy of the Boeing Company*

A paradrop being performed from airplane number two during flight test. Note the absence of the ground-removable fairing. Thrust vectoring was such that the jumper would not encounter the jet efflux upon departure from the aircraft.

Engine Nacelle

The details of the nacelle installation and most of its design features are discussed thoroughly in (Ref. 7). The discussion herein is limited to a few items covering the general design philosophy.

The basic shape of the engine nacelle was made cylindrical, strictly as a cost-saving measure, which was appreciable. The inlet and noise suppression features were adapted from the CF6-powered 747 installation under development at the time. The desired planform location of the nacelles was as close to the body as possible, in order to reduce engine-out yawing and rolling moments while also providing the lowest high-speed drag. The location finally was determined by the ability to drop the engine straight down out of the nacelle for maintenance without hitting the body (see illustration below). The nacelle longitudinal position was determined by placing the engine as close to the front spar as possible without having so much deformation of the exit airflow that it would bother the engine turbine. The nozzle for the engine core flow was turned upward slightly in order to put the hot core flow in the upper portion of the final mixed-flow nozzle. This turning up of the hot flow alleviated the temperature problem on the wing upper surface.

The thrust reverser, although very simple and effective, was of a nature that if it ever deployed in flight, disastrous rolling moments would be created. For this reason, there were redundant side latches to hold the thrust reverser in place, as well as a lock on the actuator itself to keep it from inadvertently deploying the reverser. The basic nacelle structure was cantilevered off the front spar of the wing, using a saddlelike shape that came up over the top of the engine to attach to the engine core at the normal engine mounting points. This saddle arrangement, although heavy, was devised so the nacelle fittings would match the attach points of existing engines. Nacelle fluid drainage was more difficult to handle than would be the case for a podded engine. Fluids coming off the bottom of the nacelle tended to flow along the bottom of the wing and into the wing's rear spar cavity, particularly when the flaps were down. For this reason, the fluids were collected into drainage lines that led to a mast extending from the bottom of the nacelle.

The engine nacelle was unique in design because the CF6-50 power plant was designed to be mounted from above, as is typical with podded engines. Note the large drain mast extending from the bottom of the nacelle. This solved a problem with engine fluid seepage collecting in the cowling and wing structure. *Courtesy of the Boeing Company*

The engine installation was absolutely unique. Boeing had had no previous experience with this kind of configuration, and yet they wanted to be absolutely sure that it worked well at all times. The whole reputation of the unique high-lift system depended on the nacelle operating with as few problems as possible. For these reasons, the program management staff relaxed their stringent requirements on weight within the nacelle. The goal was to make it work—period. For this, they were willing to let the weight go

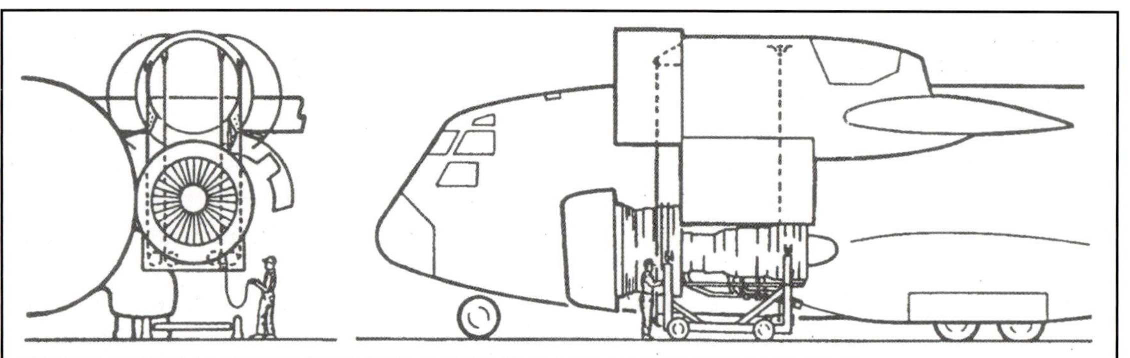
The engine installation was designed to make field removal and replacement of an engine possible with a minimum of special equipment. *Courtesy of the Boeing Company*

The thrust reverser is shown in the deployed position. The inboard variable-camber Krueger flap is also visible. These were "bent" into a more curved shape when deployed for optimum aerodynamic low-speed performance. When retracted, they were less curved and faired perfectly into the lower surface of the wing leading edge. *Courtesy of the Boeing Company*

up if required. The use of very exotic materials or any difficult construction techniques was avoided wherever possible. As a result of this philosophy, the two nacelles weighed about 3,000 pounds more than they would have weighed if more-sophisticated design and construction techniques had been used. Estimates indicated that if a more refined approach had been taken, these nacelles would have weighed approximately the same as ones suspended below the wing in a pod.

The inlet had an unusual attachment feature. In typical podded engine installations, the very high inlet loads, which are forward, are balanced out by the high nozzle loads, which are aft, leaving no net load from these items to be carried by the engine mounts. In the YC-14 installation, the nozzle loads were carried by the wing rather than by the engine, whereas the inlet loads were still carried by the fan case. To alleviate these fan case loads, a series of attachment points were located between the inlet and the nacelle structure. These attachment points actually consisted of cylinders and pistons that were pressurized by bleed flow from the engine core. With this arrangement, the higher the engine thrust and the higher the pressure within the engine core, the higher the load in the pneumatic cylinders that held the inlet to the rest of the nacelle structure. These higher cylinder loads then balanced the higher inlet loads that were created as the engine generated more thrust.

One of the design requirements for the inlet was to provide smooth airflow to the fan and compressor under the conditions of high angle of attack associated with very slow flight. Wind tunnel tests with the inlet flow duplicated ensured that there were no separations inside the inlet and that there was stable airflow into the fan under all anticipated conditions.

The goal of a properly functioning nacelle was well met by the final design. There were no problems of consequence with the nacelle throughout the entire flight test program—a real tribute to the propulsion project engineer, Luke Kimes, and his team.

Horizontal Tail

The size of the horizontal tail and the corresponding control system were determined by a number of specific requirements. These requirements included the following abilities:

- Lift the nosewheel at takeoff with a forward center of gravity (nose-heavy).
- Flare for landing with a forward center of gravity.
- Provide adequate stability during cruise flight with an aft center of gravity (tail-heavy).
- Supply adequate stability in the difficult slow-flight regime for STOL takeoff and landing with a rear center of gravity.

The requirement to lift the nosewheel at the very low speeds associated with two-engine takeoffs was a big determining factor in the horizontal tail size. Under these conditions the airspeed is low and thrust is very high. Because of the high-mounted position of the engines, a large nose-down pitching moment, caused by high engine thrust, needed to be balanced by the counterforce (nose up) created by the horizontal tail.

The proposal airplane had a horizontal tail mounted on the end of a long, extended body and a vertical tail with quite a high sweepback, providing more control leverage. However, this proved not to be enough. As the design progressed, it was found that the proposal calculations had not taken adequate account of the aerodynamic effect of operating close to the ground (ground effect) and the powerful nose-down pitching moments of the engines. More pitch authority was needed than the proposal configuration could supply. The size of the horizontal tail, of course, was tied in with the decision on the body length as well as the sweepback of the vertical tail. The NASA data that Boeing obtained during the design refinement period indicated that it was very desirable to get the horizontal tail high and somewhat more forward than was shown in the proposal, in order to avoid the very large downwash

The horizontal and vertical tail structures were designed to be aerodynamically powerful, while using a minimum count of unique components to reduce costs. *Courtesy of the Boeing Company*

coming from the powered-lift system. This fact was a feature in determining the body length and the vertical tail sweep. Also, the longer body and highly swept vertical fin of the proposal configuration had large aeroelastic effects that detracted from the airplane's stability at cruise Mach number. All of these parameters influenced the horizontal stabilizer position and the vertical stabilizer size and sweep. The final design had a fairly large tail size, made necessary for controllability during STOL operations.

The control system consisted of a double-hinged elevator that could produce very large elevator inputs and an all-moving stabilizer to provide trim. The elevator was moved automatically, slightly trailing edge down, for takeoff stabilizer settings so that more elevator travel was available to create a large increment in pitching moment at the time of nosewheel liftoff. The airfoil of the horizontal tail was symmetrical between the spars so that the same components could be used in the right- and left-hand position, providing another cost-saving feature. Since aft-mounted horizontal stabilizers produce downward lift to control pitch, the airfoil leading edge was curved in the downward-lifting direction; that is, the leading edge was canted upward to prevent stabilizer stall under conditions of very high downwash from the wing.

Vertical Tail

The vertical tail was sized mostly by the requirement to be able to control the airplane if one engine failed at low speeds on the ground. If an engine fails during takeoff and the remaining engine is operating at high thrust, the pilot must be able to control the asymmetric thrust and either bring the airplane to a stop or continue the takeoff. As discussed previously, the location of the horizontal tail helped determine the most desirable sweepback of the vertical tail, and thus this parameter was also connected with the body length decisions. Eventually, a vertical tail with relatively low sweep was chosen to reduce the elastic effects on the longitudinal stability. This shape put the horizontal tail high and relatively far forward compared to typical T tails, where it was affected less by the very strong downwash from the USB flaps. A double-hinged rudder, similar to that used on the Boeing 727, was incorporated to provide very large control forces at low speeds. The small dorsal fairing that was on the proposal aircraft configuration was eliminated during this design refinement, strictly as a way to save a slight bit of cost. In retrospect, that decision probably was a mistake, because later developments have shown that a small fairing in the intersection between the body and the vertical tail is very helpful at reducing the aerodynamic drag of that intersection. The fairing between the horizontal and vertical tail was shaped to give low aerodynamic interference at cruise Mach numbers, while being large enough to house the structure and the control and actuation mechanism in the vertical tail for the horizontal tail surfaces.

Landing Gear

The landing gear was one of the fundamental features of the airplane that made it a good STOL configuration. As mentioned previously, it was desirable to make the STOL landings without a landing flare, so that the airplane could be positioned close to the approach end of the runway at touchdown. This requirement led to a very long stroke on the landing gear and to its trailing-arm configuration. The stroke actually was about 3 feet between gear touchdown and gear compressed. The other requirement for the landing gear was the ability to support operations on a field having a California Bearing Ratio (CBR) of 6. A CBR of 6 is a surface hard enough on which to drive a car, but one that can be penetrated easily with a shovel. It was required that the airplane be able to make four hundred passes on that kind of a field without destroying the surface. The main landing gear consisted of a separate support for each pair of wheels. Each pair of wheels was attached to a trailing arm, which in turn was fastened to a vertical support member anchored rigidly to the body. An oleo strut connected each trailing arm to a movable

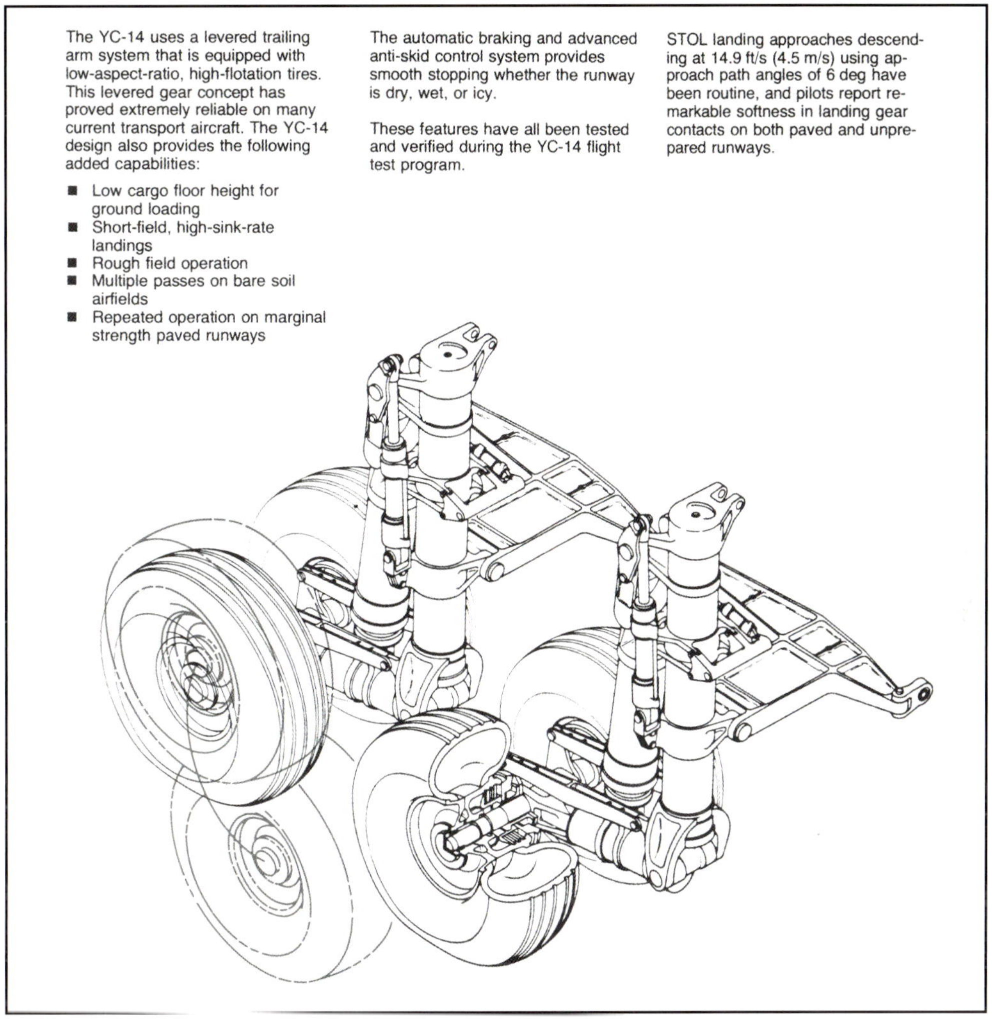

The main landing gear had a stroke of approximately 36 inches. It could withstand high-sink-rate landings and could roll over 6-inch rocks without damage. *Courtesy of the Boeing Company*

The YC-14 uses a levered trailing arm system that is equipped with low-aspect-ratio, high-flotation tires. This levered gear concept has proved extremely reliable on many current transport aircraft. The YC-14 design also provides the following added capabilities:

- Low cargo floor height for ground loading
- Short-field, high-sink-rate landings
- Rough field operation
- Multiple passes on bare soil airfields
- Repeated operation on marginal strength paved runways

The automatic braking and advanced anti-skid control system provides smooth stopping whether the runway is dry, wet, or icy.

These features have all been tested and verified during the YC-14 flight test program.

STOL landing approaches descending at 14.9 ft/s (4.5 m/s) using approach path angles of 6 deg have been routine, and pilots report remarkable softness in landing gear contacts on both paved and unprepared runways.

support member attached to the fuselage. Gear retraction was accomplished by moving this upper support for the oleo strut, which pulled the trailing arm and wheels into the wheel well directly above their normal extended position.

As the details of the landing gear developed, the pod to enclose them kept getting bigger and bigger. Considerable wind tunnel testing was completed to minimize the drag of this pod as much as possible. It was found that there was a good deal of mutual aerodynamic interaction between the gear pod shape and the aft body shape, so that relatively small changes in the gear pod could have large effects on the drag. Here again, Boeing did not do as much development work as they should have done during this design refinement period, and as a result the landing-gear pod required modification during flight testing to further reduce aerodynamic drag.

Flight Control System

Designing the systems that control the movement of the large aerodynamic surfaces of a STOL airplane is a very difficult challenge. At the low speeds associated with STOL flight, large control motions are needed at rapid rates. Under high-speed conditions, precise control of the surfaces is needed to avoid oversensitivity or control hunting, which causes continual oscillation of the airplane. For a STOL airplane, the dynamic pressures at high speed when compared to those at low speed are about twenty-one times stronger. The fact that this ratio is considerably higher than that for a supersonic transport (where the ratio typically is fifteen times stronger) gives some appreciation for the difficulty of the problem. The control power requirements in the low-speed flight regime are dominated by the need to control the airplane with an engine out. The sudden failure of an engine under powered-lift conditions requires rapid motion of the control surfaces to their extreme positions. On the other hand, in cruise flight, where the longitudinal stability is relatively low, particularly at aft center-of-gravity positions, the control of the surfaces must be very precise to avoid continual pitch oscillation. Full displacement of the aerodynamic controls under these conditions actually could destroy an airplane. The basic approach on the YC-14 was to supply large aerodynamic surfaces so that STOL flight would be controlled properly. During higher-speed flight, the number of operational aerodynamic surfaces was reduced and their travel was limited to values that would not damage the airplane.

The basic hydromechanical controls were quite conventional, with control cables going directly to valves at the control surface actuators. These cables were driven by conventional yoke and pedal controls in the cockpit. This hydromechanical system was augmented by an electronic control to give superior flying qualities in all flight regimes. At the initiation of the program, the decision was made to use a digital electronic control system. Most of the electronic controls of that period were analog. The digital system had the advantage that it could be changed late in the program, and even during flight tests, by simply changing the software, whereas an analog system would require changing electronic components. Boeing had had experience with a digital flight control system on a 737 that was modified for very low-speed flight for NASA. This digital control system had worked very well, and Boeing was confident they could do the same with the YC-14.

Although digital systems offer considerable versatility, extreme care must be taken to control their software to avoid difficulties in flight. In the proposal airplane, the augmentation system was in series with the pilot's input, so the pilot could not feel the augmentation system's action. This electronic control provided automatic stabilization in pitch and roll, including autopilot functions such as altitude and heading hold. Initially, three parallel electronic systems were envisioned, each one driving one-third of the available aerodynamic surfaces on each axis. These three systems were completely independent of one another, the so-called "brick wall" approach to isolation. The system voting was done by the aerodynamic surfaces themselves. If any electronic system had an error that drove it hard over, it could be overpowered by the other two systems that were working properly. This system was a relatively simple augmentation system, and about $300,000 was planned in the proposal to develop it with the aid of an electronics manufacturer.

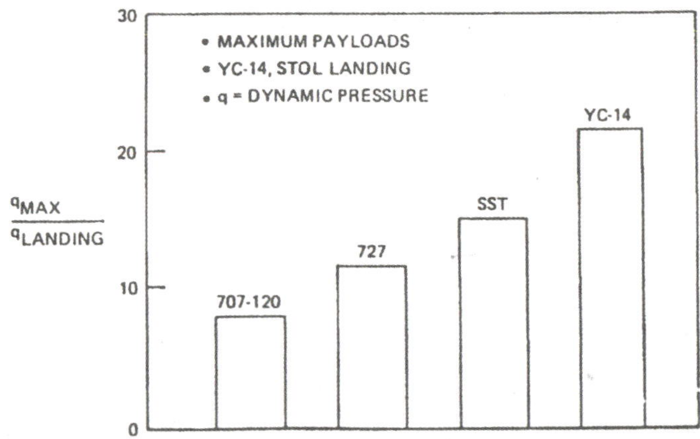

Dynamic pressure comparison. The flight control system had to operate through a range of dynamic pressure twice that of the 727 and 40% greater than that of a supersonic transport. *Courtesy of the Boeing Company*

NASA 515 was used to test experimental flight control designs and was instrumental in the development of modern electronic flight instrument systems (EFIS). This aircraft was the first Boeing 737 built and flown, the origin of a successful breed. NASA 515 resides today at the Museum of Flight in Seattle, Washington. *Public domain*

As the design refinement period progressed, it became evident that the airplane could never meet its engine-out performance during go-around without reconfiguring the flap system for lower drag. The roll dynamics of a sudden engine failure could be controlled adequately by the pilot utilizing his normal lateral control that moved the spoilers and ailerons on the wing. Once the roll was stabilized, the airplane was placed in a very high-drag configuration, with the flaps down and the spoilers up on the wing with the operable engine. To relieve this high-drag situation, the augmentation system sensed which engine had failed, and then on the opposite wing slowly retracted the spoilers while retracting the flaps at the same time to keep the rolling moment on that wing constant. Concurrently, it commanded the USB flap on the dead-engine side to extend full down to get as much lift as possible. The USB flaps behind the engines actually were in two components, a fore flap and an aft flap. During this engine-out recovery, not only was the flap on the dead-engine side driven full down, but the fore flap was rotated slightly. This motion opened up aerodynamic slots between the wing trailing edge and the fore flap and between the fore flap and the aft flap, thereby markedly increasing the flap's effectiveness.

Putting this reconfiguring task onto the electronic augmentation system meant that it now had to sense the engine failure and then exercise control over major aerodynamic surfaces of the airplane through large ranges of travel. With such large authority, the "brick wall" system utilizing aerodynamic voting no longer was applicable. Instead, the system had to incorporate three channels with electronic voting to eliminate the consequences of any single failure. This system was much more complex than was originally anticipated, because now the three channels had to compare signals so that any malfunctioning channel could be voted out. This operation required precise control of the computational timing of these three digital systems so that they would be comparing identical situations.

During this period, the Marconi-Elliot Company, an English electronics company, had been selected to design and build the augmentation system. They had made their bid on the basis of the brick wall system and had planned to utilize the computers developed for the Tornado fighter jet. To their credit, they hung in with the program while the three-channel system was developed. It was a long, tedious process requiring the development of both hardware and sophisticated software. The interchannel communication on this computing system was done with optical links. The electronic signal was converted to light, transferred to the adjacent computer along a fiber-optic path, and then converted back to an electrical signal. This process was to avoid any possible short circuit transferring from one computer to another and

Table 1 Electrical flight control system features

- Command and stability augmentation
  - Sprial, dutch roll, turn coordination
  - Pitch & roll rate command, attitude hold
  - Trim offload
- Speed and path control
  - Throttle and USB flap speed control
  - Direct lift control spoilers
- Configuration management
  - Fly-by-wire USB flap
  - Engine-out sensing and flap clean-up
- Pilot assist modes
  - Aerial delivery
  - Attitude and heading control

Courtesy of the Boeing Company

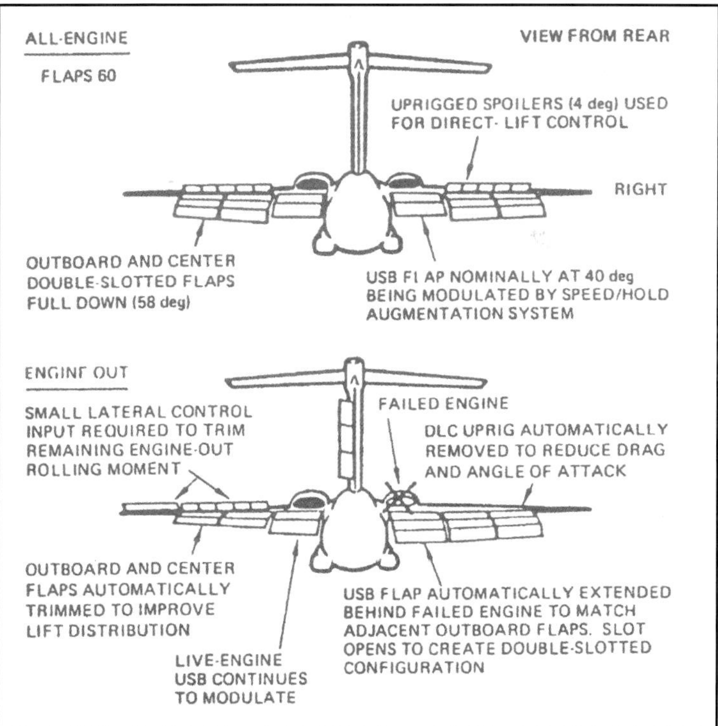

Automatic reconfiguration of the flap and spoiler system following engine failure during a STOL landing was done automatically by the flight control system. *Courtesy of the Boeing Company*

thereby rendering the whole system inactive. These optical links worked very well, and it was a very sophisticated system for its time. The cost of the system escalated to an estimated ten times what had been planned originally. Some of this cost was covered by Boeing, but much of it was covered by Marconi-Elliot as an investment in getting into this type of business.

Philosophically, this system was like the autofeather devices used to automatically reduce propeller drag after an engine failure. Similarly, stick pushers have been used to move elevators and keep airplanes out of high-pitch-attitude situations in order to avoid pitch instabilities. However, I believe this case was the first one where major control surfaces were moved automatically to solve a performance problem. Such practices are fairly common in modern fighter designs, but the YC-14 was a real pioneer in this field. The system proved to be very reliable during flight testing. Controlling a simulated engine-out was a very easy operation for the pilot, requiring nothing but instinctive reactions.

The augmentation system also provided speed control during STOL approaches. When the proposal airplane was first developed, it was thought that speed would be controlled by a separate lever on the throttle stand. Once this lever was set to a particular speed condition, the pilot would just move the control column to point the airplane where he wanted it to go. If he pushed the column forward and the airplane started to accelerate, the USB flap would go down farther, deflect the thrust more, and keep the airplane from accelerating. Conversely, if the pilot pulled the airplane nose up to a shallower glide slope, the USB flap would retract slightly so there would be enough forward thrust to handle the situation. In the final design, this extra handle was eliminated, and the desired speed was set by a dial on the Electrical Flight Control System panel in the cockpit. The speed control did the same thing as planned originally, it moved the USB flap rapidly to hold constant speed at differing approach slopes without changing engine thrust. Additionally, an integrator was included that gradually changed engine thrust to accommodate a new stabilized glide slope angle. The proper thrust permitted moving the USB flap to its central position again, where it was ready to accommodate any further changes. The final system also included the normal autopilot functions, turn coordination, and compensation for small speed instabilities at high Mach numbers.

Precise control during STOL approaches was aided by a very sophisticated electronic attitude display. This display featured a cathode-ray tube that showed values of airspeed error, bank angle, altitude, and flight path direction, in addition to the artificial horizon. It also showed flight path acceleration—that is, fore and aft along the flight path, so that a pilot could tell if

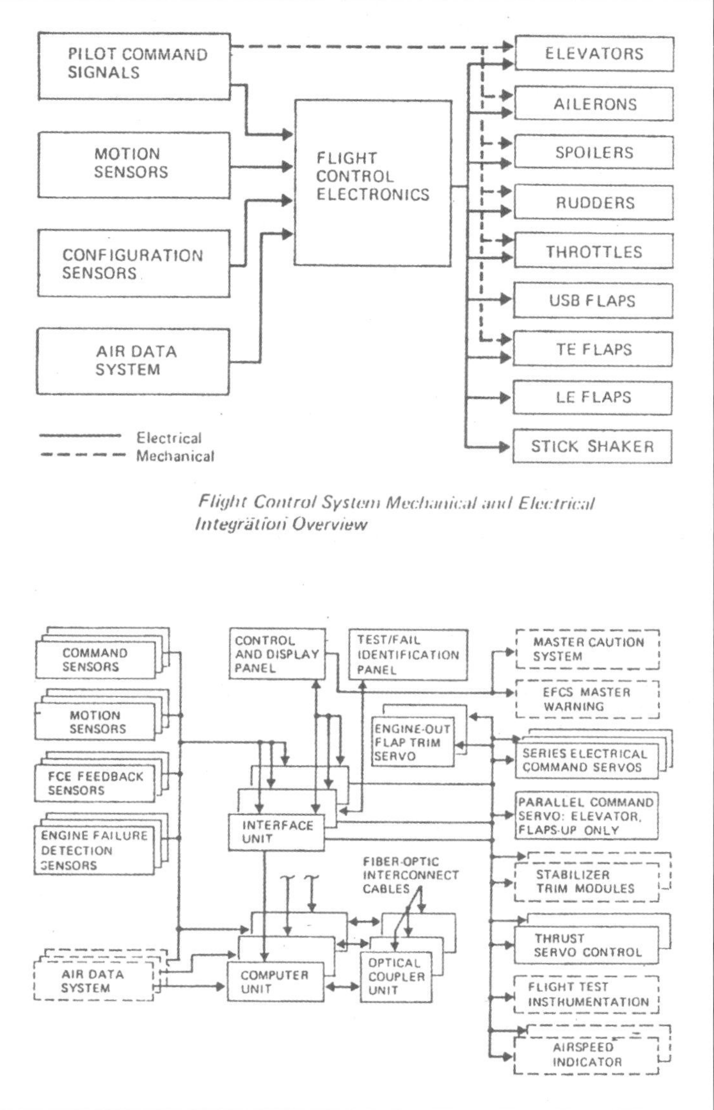

Flight Control System Mechanical and Electrical Integration Overview

The control system as built on the YC-14. The YC-14 electronic control system had three separate channels with electrical voting to handle single-system failures. Information transfer between channels was done using optical links to prevent the propagation of electrical short circuits. *Courtesy of the Boeing Company*

there was adequate thrust to maintain a particular glide slope. Superimposed on this flight data information display was a picture of the external scene created by a forward-looking TV camera. To make a precision STOL approach, the pilot could set up a landing configuration, set the augmentation speed control to hold constant speed, and then aim the flight path indicator at the TV picture of the runway. This system proved to be very capable, and the pilot could determine far out from touchdown if he was making a good approach to hit the runway right at the approach end. This cathode-ray tube display worked well and was a predecessor of the many electronic displays that are now used universally in the military aircraft and commercial transport airplanes of the world. The development of the flight control system is described in detail in Refs. 11 and 12.

A great deal of flight simulation was done to ensure that the flight control system would be adequate. The studies began with fixed-based simulators to determine the basic control laws that were needed, particularly during final approach. Eventually the entire system was duplicated on the moving-base STOL simulator at the NASA Ames Laboratory. Here, the final control law gains were refined and the failure modes were evaluated to ensure that the pilot could maintain control at all times.

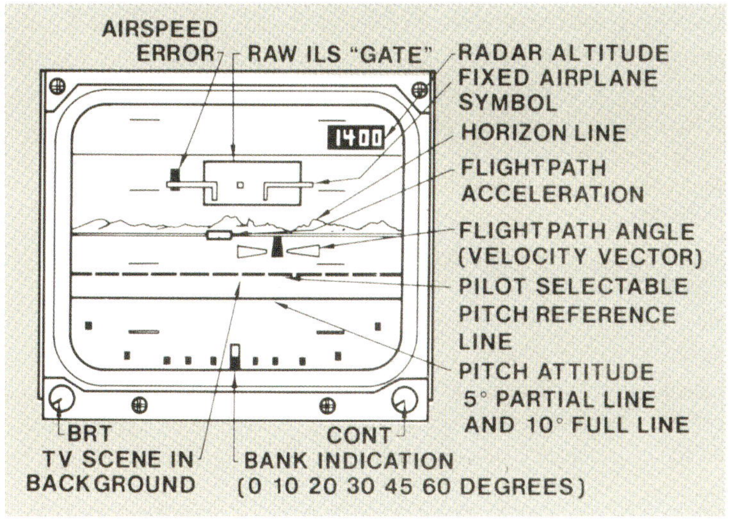

The left-seat pilot station on the YC-14 used an early EFIS to provide the pilot with flight path information combined with outside imagery from a camera mounted on the aircraft. *Courtesy of the Boeing Company*

Boundary-Layer Control System

From its inception, the YC-14 configuration had a boundary layer control (BLC) system across its entire leading edge as a way to generate higher aerodynamic lift coefficients. The BLC system also was a way to generate symmetrical lift augmentation during engine-out cases, because the boundary layer control air was cross-ducted from the operating engine. As shown in the original proposal, the BLC system utilized relatively low-pressure, low-temperature air, resulting from a two-stage ejector using engine compressor bleed air as the primary source. The ejector output air was carried across the leading edge of the wing in ducts and exhausted through slotted nozzles.

The YC-14's BLC system went through a great deal of development during the configuration refinement period, including a number of tests on the nozzles themselves. The system evolved into one using a single-stage ejector, with the primary flow coming from the fourteenth stage of the compressor and the secondary flow coming from the eighth stage (see drawing on page 58). This arrangement resulted in boundary layer control air that was fairly hot, but careful design kept it from bothering the surrounding structure. A lower-temperature system would have had lower pressure and would have required very large ducts with correspondingly high total-pressure losses. Furthermore, it is desirable for a BLC system to have high enough pressure to choke the exit nozzles so that the flow automatically distributes itself across the span. In order to reduce the heat radiating from these ducts, they were coated with a very fine layer of gold, because gold has a lower coefficient of heat radiation than bare aluminum.

Wind tunnel tests were run for the engine-out condition to see whether it was preferable to have the BLC across both the port and starboard sides of the wing, or to operate only on the side of a failed engine to compensate for the asymmetric lift caused by this flight condition. It was found that concentrating the BLC flow on the dead-engine side decreased the lift loss on that wing, but carrying it on both sides increased the effectiveness of both ailerons, making that solution preferable. The cross-ducting ran through the inside of the cabin, close to the front spar of the wing. The heat and volume of the air in the duct were such that if the duct were to be ruptured, the interior of the cabin could rise to fatal temperatures very quickly. Such an occurrence was prevented by surrounding the duct with a separate secondary duct that was vented to the outside of the airplane. If there were a leak in the cabin segment of the primary duct, the air would be contained by the secondary duct and sent overboard and not exhausted into the cabin.

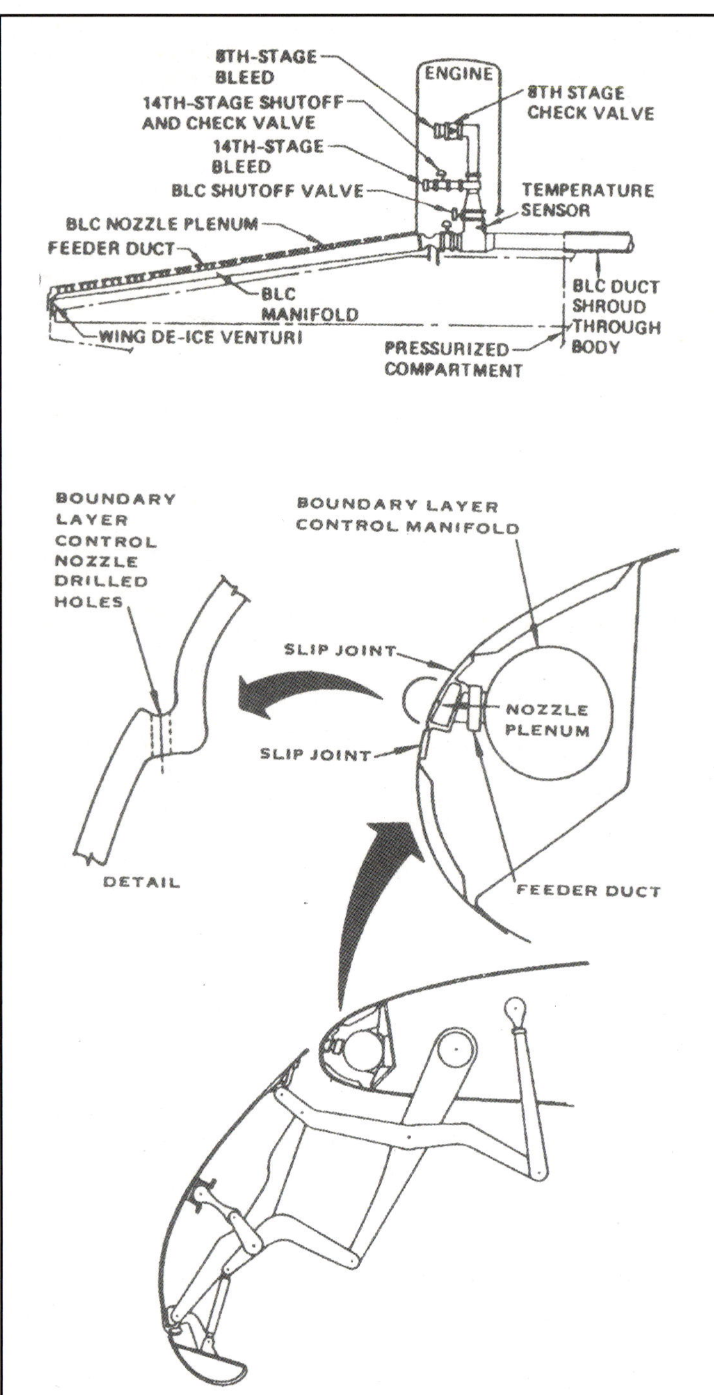

The leading-edge boundary layer control system. Variable-camber Krueger flap segments were installed at the wing leading edge. When the flaps were extended, engine bleed air was directed over the leading edge to avert aerodynamic stalls and improve lift. *Courtesy of the Boeing Company*

Full-scale testing of small segments of the slotted BLC nozzle indicated that it would be impossible to hold the proper nozzle dimensions across the entire span. Instead, a series of round holes were used, and further testing was required to refine the details and spacing of these holes so that the effectiveness was equivalent to that of a continuous slot. The aluminum skin of the wing just aft of the slots had to be protected with a thin layer of temperature-resistant epoxy coating.

Competition Comparison

Toward the end of the configuration refinement period, I presented a paper titled "Upper Surface Blowing Technology as Applied to the YC-14 Airplane" at a Society of Automotive Engineers (SAE) meeting. At the same meeting, a paper was given by Irving Held, who was in a position similar to mine at the McDonnell Douglas Company. It was my first chance to look at the performance of Boeing's competitor, the YC-15. As might be expected, the YC-15 showed posttakeoff climb performance with one engine out superior to that of the YC-14. However, the YC-15 could not make an all-engine go-around at landing-flap setting. It was forced to retract the flaps slightly to go around at all, whereas the YC-14 showed excellent go-around capability with two engines operating. In general, I felt that the YC-14 performance looked good relative to the YC-15, with the only exception being that the YC-14 control system had to be more complex in order to move the flaps asymmetrically in the event of an engine failure.

Final Configuration

By the end of October 1973, the configuration iterations had been completed, and the final configuration was essentially in place (see drawing on page 60). As compared to the proposal configuration, the body was slightly shorter, with more upsweep angle at the aft end, the landing gear was larger, the horizontal tail was larger, and the flight control system was much more sophisticated and versatile. Additionally, the exhaust nozzles and thrust reversers were slightly more complex. The design team did feel, though, that they had a configuration that would meet the performance goals they had indicated in the original 1972 proposal (see appendix 2, figure A-09).

A number of other interesting things happened during this year of configuration refinement. A group from the Boeing AMST team made a very interesting visit to the Little Rock Air Force Base for observation of C-130 operations there. They found the C-130 to be a very easy airplane to fly, and it was being well used by the Tactical Air Command. However, its cargo-handling

The large BLC cross-duct is seen in this photo just forward of the wing center section, where it passes through the YC-14's cabin. The green reservoirs (*two on the left and one on the right*) store fluid for each of the three hydraulic systems. *Dan Dornseif collection*

system was old-fashioned, and the preparation required to make a cargo or personnel airdrop was extremely complicated and rather makeshift.

In mid April 1973, the USAF finally gave the program an official designation, calling the two competitive airplanes the YC-14 and the YC-15. The "Y" designation indicated a preproduction airplane. If it had been purely experimental, it would have had an "X" designation. This "Y" designation meant the airplane was going to be evaluated as though it were an immediate predecessor to a production aircraft, indicating much more emphasis on its operational characteristics than its technology. This designation was a substantial change from what had been defined in the original proposal, and the cost implications were severe. It led to Boeing putting a complete operational cargo-handling system on the airplane to demonstrate cargo loading and offloading, cargo airdrops, personnel airdrops, and so forth. A single-point refueling system was added as well as an auxiliary power unit (APU) so the airplane would be self-sufficient in the field.

Management Changes and Corporate Reviews

In August 1973 the program manager, Maynard Pennell, was suddenly transferred away from the program. Pennell had been the chief engineer of Boeing when the 707 was designed, and was one of the company's primary aircraft designers. He had not wanted to leave the YC-14 program and retired soon after he was transferred. His position as program manager was taken over by Jim Foody. Bill Cook moved into the position of director of engineering, and I took over as chief engineer for technology.

The following October, a separate Boeing team came in to audit the YC-14 operation and program cost estimate. This team was headed by Dan Downey, a prominent engineer with a propulsion system background, and involved people mostly from the Commercial Airplane Company. They went through the program in detail, and their conclusions were that the YC-14 team was solving their technical problems well, but that they would never complete the program within the defined budget. Their estimate

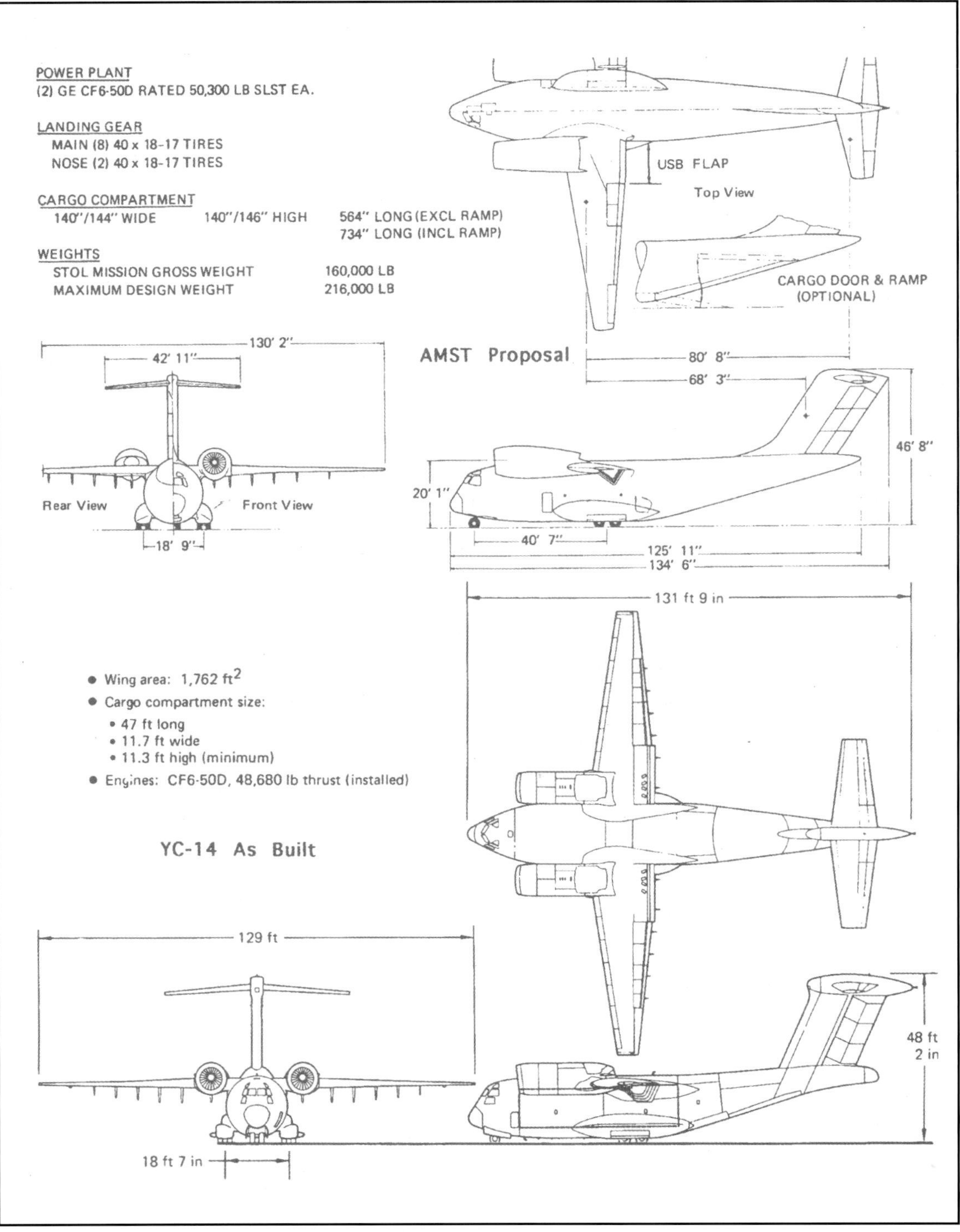

Configuration comparison. As compared to the proposed airplane, the YC-14 had a shorter body of smaller diameter with more upsweep, a larger horizontal tail, less sweep on the vertical tail, a simpler cylindrical nacelle, a larger landing-gear pod, an extended chord on the USB flap, a more complex thrust reverser, and a revised aerodynamic lateral control system. *Courtesy of the Boeing Company*

for completion was $130 million, which incidentally was exactly the same as the grassroots estimate made at the time of the proposal.

During the year, the YC-14 program had two major Corporate Management Council reviews. The Management Council consisted of the top vice presidents of all the various fields of the company, including Engineering, Finance, Operations, Materiel, and so forth. It was headed by the company president, and on top of that, the company chairman of the board. During the first review in mid-June 1973, the team was still in the throes of trying desperately to make their configuration work. Bill Cook told the Management Council that before the proposal, the team had been looking at relatively simple airplanes utilizing boundary layer control and deflected thrust for STOL operation. He felt that if Boeing had bid that airplane in the proposal, Lockheed would have won the proposal competition at a lower price. Instead, Boeing proposed a more complicated airplane, but one having much-higher potential. Now, Boeing was being forced to do the kind of research in aerodynamics and propulsion that was done by NASA on the system that the Boeing competitor, McDonnell Douglas, was using. At the end of the review, the Management Council felt that the YC-14 team had the program under control and was proceeding as best it could.

The second major review was at the end of November 1973. By then, the YC-14 team had most of its challenges pretty well in hand, but the cost was escalating. The program manager indicated that the team had only a 10% chance of making the contracted cost, probably about a 50% chance of making $105 million, and a 95% chance of making the $130 million cost the company audit team thought it would take. The Management Council's reaction was that a slight overrun was probably acceptable, but they could not stand for the kind of overruns that occurred on the 747 program. The YC-14 team was given orders to proceed, but to attempt to meet the contracted cost.

Throughout the year, the designers had a constant battle trying to keep the weight under control. All airplanes tend to grow in weight during their design period. Oftentimes the performance can be made up by increasing the gross weight and just letting the field lengths for landing and takeoff go up a little bit. Such was not the YC-14 case, of course, and the team tried desperately to keep the weight at the original proposal value. They did not have the necessary resources, however, and the weight slowly increased.

By the end of 1973, Boeing had completed five thousand hours of wind tunnel tests (both high- and low-speed evaluations) and had largely sorted out the aerodynamic problems. Only the fine-tuning of the final details remained. Additionally, by the end of the year a thrust reverser configuration had been tested that showed a 42% reverse-thrust value, which was very good. Later refinement increased that value even more. The high-speed wing configuration had been lofted numerically and was completely finalized. The fire protection to be placed on top of the wing just aft of the engine had been developed, and the basic concept had passed its initial fire test. The YC-14's challenges were gradually coming under control.

Second Proposal

During the congressional budgeting process in late 1973, inadequate funds were put in the USAF budget to continue the AMST program at the planned rate. The USAF was faced with a quandary of what to do within the budget it had. On January 11, 1974, Boeing was visited by USAF secretary John L. McLucas. At the completion of a discussion about the Boeing airplane, he asked the Boeing senior management a critical question: If the USAF did not have adequate funding, would Boeing rather see the AMST program continue over a more extended time period with two contractors, or would they rather see a competition immediately, with only one contractor proceeding? The Boeing management replied they were in favor of continuing the program with two contractors completely through the flight phase. This way, they felt the USAF would get the best possible airplane even though it might take longer. This showed the level of confidence Boeing had that the YC-14 would prove to be a superior airplane.

However, General Stewart, who was in command of the USAF facility at Wright Field, felt that there was not going to be adequate money either in fiscal year (FY) 1974 or 1975 to keep both contractors going. Therefore, he asked the AMST Prototype Office to conduct the competition and decide which contractor should continue. The RFP came to Boeing on January 22, 1974, with the proposal due on February 21. A frantic month was spent preparing the proposal. The Boeing team could see all the work they had done over the past two or more years hanging in the balance, with a chance to lose it all on the basis of one paper proposal. The team worked day and night preparing the data that showed the airplane's potential performance was well substantiated and that the testing could be completed satisfactorily.

A few days before the proposal was to be submitted, a rumor circulated that perhaps the USAF was not going to be interested in this proposal after all. Finally, Jim Foody, YC-14 program manager, called Colonel Thurman, who was in charge of the Prototype Office, asking him if the USAF had decided not to require the proposal. Foody was told, "No, indeed," the USAF was not going to want the proposal, and Boeing did not have to submit anything. Following a month of intense work on the proposal, this last-minute realization naturally caused great frustration for the entire team, but there was little time to dwell on this. Instead, the team resumed the program efforts to bring the YC-14 to reality.

The USAF contracts were rewritten at this time to extend the timing by one more year and keep the funding very low during FY 1974. The stretch-out actually was going to increase Boeing's cost because their overhead would continue, and their design effort could not proceed in the optimum fashion. In negotiating the contract, the total value was increased to about $106 million, about $10 million more than the original value. At that time, Boeing's own estimate of the cost was somewhat higher, at $114 million.

During this same time period, the characteristics of the YC-14 were programed into the moving-base simulator at the NASA Ames Research Center at Moffett Field. A fixed-based simulator had been used to study the STOL characteristics in Seattle, but the moving-base simulator with a good visual display proved to be a valuable tool. The airplane was demonstrated to be very controllable through the most-serious types of emergencies, including the loss of thrust on one engine and the failure of various hydraulic system components. The simulation proved to be a reinforcing test for the YC-14 concept.

Production Airplane

By April 1974, Jim Foody had become convinced that the prototype that Boeing was designing might not garner a large production market. Others within the company were beginning to sense a shift in the policy of the US government away from further involvement in the types of military conflicts where the YC-14 would be most useful. Instead, it appeared that the defense philosophy would be one wherein the United States would support its allies with lots of supplies and equipment. Thus, a longer-range airplane with possibly a larger body would be needed. To give proper attention to development of the production airplane, Bill Cook was moved to the position of director of engineering for production airplane development, and I was made director of engineering for the prototype.

Bill Cook briefly held that position, until July 5, 1974, when he retired unceremoniously from Boeing. He had become quite disenchanted because he felt there was a marked lack of support from the company for the development of the production version of the airplane. He felt the company was making a big mistake and, because of this, was missing an opportunity for a large production program. Thus departed the one person who probably had the most influence over the philosophy and configuration of the YC-14 airplane. He was a person with an outstanding technical reputation and often was relied on by T. Wilson, chairman of the board, for his technical judgment. He felt so strongly about this issue that he retired well before the normal retirement age. About six months later, I was made director of engineering for both the prototype and production airplanes.

Even with this transition in YC-14 program leadership, the aircraft design had reached a point where it was extensively defined. Even while some details were still in flux, as is typical with most new airplane programs, the time was drawing near to make the YC-14 a reality. Focus began to slowly shift toward the construction of the test aircraft.

CHAPTER 4

Detail Design and Construction

The YC-14 program signaled many firsts in aircraft design, the most prominent being the use of upper-surface blowing combined with boundary-layer control to allow controlled flight at extremely low speeds. Among the innovative concepts featured in the development and manufacture of the airplane were the use of work package teams to do the detailed design and the use of digital mathematics to define all elements of the configuration. Continuing aerodynamic and propulsion design modifications were made during this period. These revisions, along with several changes in management personnel, led to the ever-present program cost challenges.

A lower cutaway drawing of the YC-14. *Courtesy of the Boeing Company*

Work Package Teams

During 1974, a year of detail design was accomplished on the airplane. The design was done a little differently than was the usual procedure at Boeing, in a number of respects. The airplane was divided into approximately thirty-five work packages. Each of these was designed by a team that contained not only engineers but also representatives from Materiel and Manufacturing, including Tooling. The objective was to make the design easy both to manufacture and maintain. Having the production people involved in this detail design effort was very beneficial. They contributed a great deal toward making the design easier and less expensive to build. The manufacturing people urged the Engineering Department to make low-cost drawings, even sketches, because they had a high-caliber manufacturing team that could accept that kind of direction. As it turned out, most of the drawings were of pretty high quality—the engineers just could not force themselves to produce a low-standard paper definition of the airplane. The engineering and manufacturing people were located in the same area of the plant, which made coordination between them greatly simplified. This proximity and continuous contact gave each element of the team a better appreciation of the problems of the other elements. The work package team approach has since become the de facto standard for aircraft design at the Boeing Company.

Digital Definition and Tooling

The YC-14 was the first airplane at Boeing to have appreciable portions of its configuration defined by digital mathematics. Although wings and fuselages had been lofted mathematically on previous airplanes by using continuous equations, this was the first airplane to have the exterior defined digitally. This approach meant that detail design could be accomplished from a digital reference. It also meant that a digital system could be used to define all the tools that were needed to hold the detail parts for machining and drilling, giving assurance that the parts would fit properly. A similar digital definition was used for the major jigs and fixtures that held the detail parts for assembly. Only two master tools were built for the entire airplane. Master tools are heavy, precisely built structures that locate the interface of major assemblies. The same tool is used to build both sides of the interface, so that proper fit is ensured. One of those master tools was for the wing-to-body joint, and the other was for the nacelle-to-wing

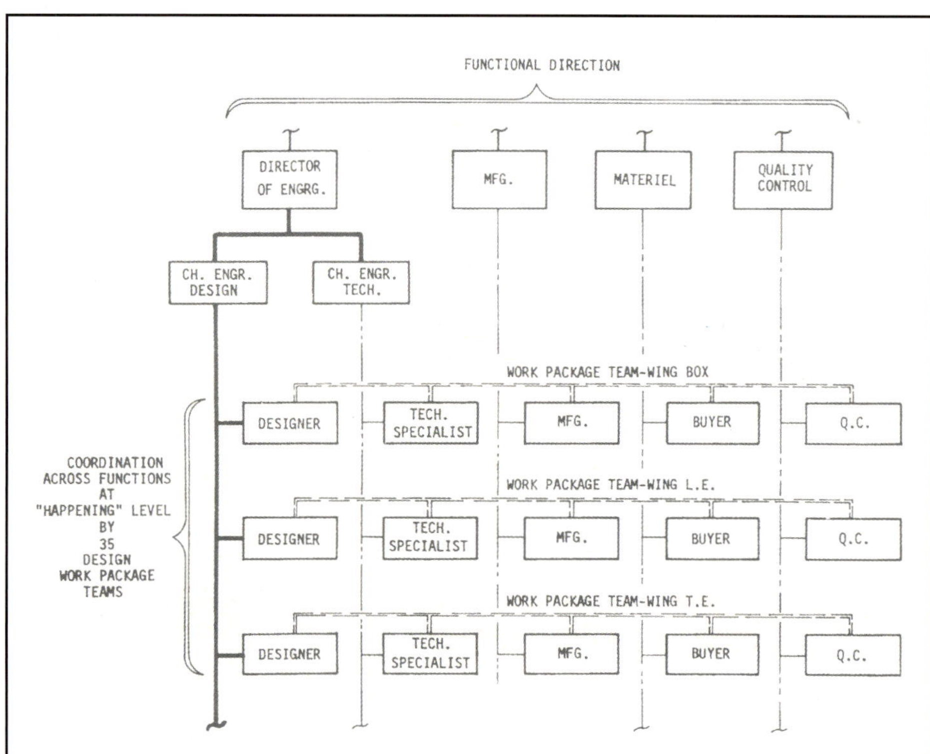

YC-14 design work-package teams. *Courtesy of the Boeing Company*

joint. Both of these areas involved the precise mating of very heavy pieces of structure, making these master tools an absolute necessity. All the rest of the tooling was set up by a digital dimensional-control system. It actually worked very well. In fact, the whole nose section was defined digitally and sent to the Boeing plant at Wichita, Kansas, for construction. Interestingly, when the first nose section came back, it was in far-better condition than those being delivered for the 707 and 727 fuselages, of which hundreds had been built. Wing tooling was defined completely numerically, and the entire wing box (including the spars, ribs, stringers, and skins) went together with only two unplanned shims required to produce the proper fit. Also, only about 60% of the planned man-hours were needed to complete the assembly.

A good deal of the production tooling for items such as wing ribs and body frames was done with wood rather than metal. In many cases, Mylar copies of the drawings were laid out on large pieces of plywood, and those became the tooling. This technique actually worked very well, and probably ten or so airplanes could have been built on it. Obviously, wood was much less expensive than the heavy steel tooling used with major production programs. There were fewer than normal tooling jigs and fixtures used to hold the pieces for major assembly, because the parts were built very accurately and their positions could be defined using the precise numerical references. However, a wooden mockup was used because the YC-14 was quite complex, with many components (tubing, wires, cables, BLC ducts, and so forth) that had to fit inside and around the aircraft's structure properly. It was felt that a mockup was the only way to ensure that everything would go together without interferences. The mockup gradually increased in quality as the year progressed, and eventually was converted to metal. Manufacturing activity in 1974 included long-lead-time items such as the machined body frames, including the wing attachment fittings.

Another view of the YC-14 engineering mockup. *Courtesy of the Boeing Company*

The assembly of the YC-14 mockup as seen in October 1974. The flat sides of the cockpit, required for optimum pilot visibility, are evident. *Courtesy of the Boeing Company*

The machined body frames were long-lead-time items for the YC-14. This photo was taken in November 1974. *Courtesy of the Boeing Company*

Cost and Weight

The design of the vertical fin was a good example of the heavy emphasis placed on cost reduction. In the original proposal, the vertical fin was a constant airfoil section to reduce cost. Another way that Boeing wanted to reduce the cost of the fin was to make it out of a bonded honeycomb material. The USAF was not in favor of honeycomb, because historically they had experienced difficulties with it in the field as a result of inadequate adhesives. Boeing engineers felt that honeycomb could be used on the prototype, would be less expensive, and would hold up through the prototype program. As one of the designers examined the shape of the airfoil between the front and rear spars of the vertical fin, he noted it was very close to a circular arc in that region. It was defined as a circular arc, which permitted the fin structure between the spars to be composed of three honeycomb panels on each side, a total of six for each fin, all identical in contour. This approach provided a large savings, by using six identical parts per airplane instead of six unique parts. If there had not been such a high emphasis on reduced cost, the design engineer probably would not have considered the possibility of using a circular-arc airfoil.

Throughout the detail design process, the aircraft weight continued to climb. The YC-14 team was always short of stress analysts to study the parts sufficiently to eliminate excess weight entirely. Boeing did reach an agreement with the USAF, however, that helped alleviate the weight issue. A great deal of weight was

CATEGORY/ITEM	WEIGHT REDUCTION (Lbs per Airplane)
A. Replace off-shelf special equipment with special design.	
1. Master Electronic Processing Unit	146
2.Control Augmentation Roll Servos	40
B. Production quality manufacturing	
1. Trimming	4
2. Use vacuum chuck to reduce gages	53
3. Replace machined blocks with forgings	4
4. Chem-milling	12
C. Material Selection	
1. BLC duct: .040 CRES to .030 Inconnel	42
2. USB skins: 15-5 CRES to 6-2-4 Ti.	60
3. Body Forgings: 7075 to 7050	120
D. Configuration changes	
1. Leading-edge Krueger Flaps: 16 to 14 segments	159
2. Leading-edge drive to single torque tube	173
E. Delete prototype features	
1. Flight Test Director's station	105
F. Production design	
1. Separate machined fittings (where beneficial)	6
2. Integral machined fittings (where beneficial)	20
3. Integral machined stiffeners	28
4. Aluminum skin-stiffener to Fiberglass honeycomb	171
Total: approximately 300 items totalling over 5700 pounds	

Typical prototype nonoptimum weight items. *Courtesy of the Boeing Company*

put in the airplane strictly because it was a prototype that Boeing wanted to build rapidly and inexpensively. Boeing termed this weight "non-optimum weight" and convinced the USAF it should be considered to be part of the demonstrated payload for the prototype airplane. The USAF agreed with a large percentage of the identified non-optimum weight. Most of this additional weight occurred in the nacelle, which, of course, was a design entirely different from any that had been previously built. Also, the propulsion system designers did not want to make any compromises that would jeopardize the nacelle functioning properly. The main goal for the nacelle design was to make absolutely sure it would work. It was felt that Boeing could argue about weight improvement on the production airplane, but they would have a difficult time explaining a condition where the nacelle did not work properly. All of the compromises were done to make it work even though it would be heavy. A group weight statement of the complete airplane and non-optimum weight items is shown below.

In August 1974, the design of the structure around the cargo door was modified to accommodate the M60 main battle tank. Carrying this tank never was a requirement for the original proposal airplane, but a slight longeron modification permitted the airplane to be compatible. Boeing felt that being able to carry the M60 would be a significant operational advantage for their airplane. Later on, carrying the tank did become a requirement.

Flutter was another item that hounded the YC-14 team throughout 1974. The large T tail and a relatively flexible aft body made flutter a serious consideration. The problem was amplified by the fact that both the rudder and elevator were double-hinged, giving each surface both high inertia and an extra degree of freedom. Flutter analyses continued throughout the year. Flutter models were built and tested (just the aft body and T tail at first, and eventually the complete airplane) to provide assurance that there would be no flutter issues.

ITEM	WEIGHT-LBS
WING	22560
HORIZONTAL TAIL	3780
VERTICAL TAIL	4174
BODY	25775
MAIN LANDING GEAR	8863
NOSE LANDING GEAR	1855
NACELLE	13542
THRUST REVERSER & DOORS	2535
TOTAL STRUCTURE	83084
ENGINE	17217
EXHAUST SYSTEM AND VENTS	443
ENGINE CONTROL	193
STARTING SYSTEM	120
FUEL SYSTEM	968
TOTAL PROPULSION	18941
FLIGHT CONTROL	6143
INSTRUMENTS	909
HYDRAULIC & PNEUMATIC	2825
ELECTRICAL	1990
AVIONICS	566
FURNISHINGS & EQUIPMENT	2074
AIR CONDITIONING & ANTI-ICING	1099
LOADING & HANDLING	1319
TOTAL FIXED EQUIPMENT	16925
UNIDENTIFIED WEIGHT*	2144
WEIGHT EMPTY**	121094
CREW	400
UNUSABLE FUEL	338
ENGINE OIL (INCLUDED TRAPPED)	114
CREW EQUIPMENT	73
MISCELLANEOUS	125
ALLOWANCE FOR AIR FORCE LOOSE EQUIPMENT	3000
TOTAL NON-EXPENDABLE USEFUL LOAD	4050
OPERATING WEIGHT	125144

* UNIDENTIFIED WEIGHT OCCURED SINCE WEIGHT CALCULATION AND TRACKING WERE STOPPED AS COST SAVING MEASURES BEFORE THE DESIGN AND CONSTRUCTION OF THE AIRPLANE WAS COMPLETE.. ITS VALUE WAS ESTABLISHED WHEN THE COMPLETED AIRPLANE WAS WEIGHED. ITS DISTRIBUTION THROUGHOUT THE AIRPLANE IS UNKNOWN.

** INCLUDES 5724 POUNDS OF IDENTIFIED NON-OPTIMUM WEIGHT.

The YC-14 group weight statement. *Courtesy of the Boeing Company*

Flutter model of the complete airplane. *Courtesy of the Boeing Company*

Continued Design Modifications

Toward the end of 1974, the propulsion and aerodynamic specialists were still making small modifications to the USB nozzle. Each time they ran another wind tunnel test, they would find the nozzle flow was not quite as expected, and they would have to make additional modifications to the nozzle shape to optimize it. Fortunately, all these changes could be accommodated late in the design period. The fly-by-wire (FBW) flight control system also became more complex throughout the year. Challenges with aircraft performance and control continued to be solved by adding capabilities to the FBW system. A turn coordinator was added to put in a small rudder motion as a turn was initiated. A rudder limiter was added to reduce the amount of rudder motion at high speeds, to prevent overstressing the vertical stabilizer. Also incorporated was a pitch attitude hold system to control the airplane during paradrops at very low altitudes. This attitude-hold system allowed the cargo to be extracted from the cargo compartment while the airplane was held steady at constant attitude. This continued complication of the FBW system soon saturated the capability of the computers that were planned for the airplane, which were satisfactory when the airplane used a brick wall three-channel system. However, when system complication increased, the requirements were soon beyond the computers' capacity, and the software had to be revised accordingly. Boeing continued to have struggles with computer memory capacity and computational timing throughout the remainder of the YC-14's development.

Throughout this period, Boeing was negotiating with NASA to obtain full-scale data on a USB high-lift system. Boeing wanted some financial help for their ground tests that had been planned, and NASA desired additional flight test data. The two organizations compromised, and each gained a bit of both. NASA contributed about $1 million to the program and received a great deal of pressure distribution data at full scale that they could not have gotten otherwise.

By the end of 1974, about 40% of the YC-14 engineering drawings had been released to Manufacturing. The YC-14 design team was about 30% of the size used to design the 727, with a peak of about 425 engineers on the entire program. By the end of the year, Boeing had completed about seven thousand hours of wind tunnel testing.

Supplier Support

Boeing had a number of major subcontractors on the program, and generally speaking, they provided excellent support. General Electric supplied the engines, and they provided top-notch support throughout the development and testing period. Marconi-Elliot, the flight control system designers, stuck with Boeing through the amplification of the requirements and finally provided an outstanding system. Many of the suppliers gave the program such things as valves, pumps, and generators at approximately 25% of their value, while others just loaned Boeing the equipment to use during the prototype program.

However, one of our suppliers that did not work out so well was North American's plant in Tulsa, Oklahoma. They became a subcontractor in a rather roundabout way. When Jim Foody was trying to get support for the airplane in Congress, he talked to Congressman Carl Albert, who was Speaker of the House of

Representatives and the congressman from a district near Tulsa. His first reaction upon hearing the story on the airplane was "How much of it is going to be built in Tulsa?" Jim Foody returned from that contact and told the YC-14 team they had to get a million-dollar effort into the Tulsa plant. In order to do that, Boeing had to convince the USAF that they could not do a specific work package as cheaply themselves as they could get it done by sending it out. Boeing put together a work package that included the cargo ramp and the cargo door, both of which were fairly straightforward structural elements. As it turned out, North American got into a great deal of difficulty, both in the engineering and the manufacturing of these two major pieces. YC-14 Engineering spent more money just coordinating North American's designers and correcting their mistakes than they would have spent completing the job in-house. Manufacturing had problems as well, but fortunately, when the parts arrived in Seattle, they fit as built, and the AMST program had achieved the support of Congressman Albert.

Boeing's equipment suppliers were very enthusiastic about the airplane and over and over again would help maintain their equipment or modify it in any way that was needed to make it work. All in all, the support that Boeing received from the industry was truly outstanding.

Corporate Review and Management Changes

By the end of the year, there was once again a discussion in Congress concerning whether or not the AMST program should be continued. Eventually, it was included in the budget, but this continual hassle within the government regarding the AMST program status was a large deterrent to getting good support throughout the Boeing Company. Boeing's upper management was very reluctant to invest a large amount of their own money in a program for which the customer did not show much enthusiasm.

This attitude of not wanting to risk the company's money on a program with an unsure future was demonstrated clearly to the AMST team at various management meetings that occurred during 1974 and 1975. On December 20, 1974, the YC-14 program management met with the president of the Aerospace Company, Ollie Boileau, and his Management Council. The council recognized that the funding was going to remain low during 1975, but toward the end of the year, when FY 1976 began, the funding would increase so that the effort could accelerate to a more reasonable schedule. Boileau was fairly positive about the program and thought the YC-14 team had done a good job in getting the airplane designed and progressing to assembly. He was very concerned about having to risk as much as $20 million during the early part of 1975, with the looming possibility that the program might suddenly be canceled.

The detailed engineering drawings were flowing out rapidly at this point, and the chief project engineer was tracking carefully to see that they were being released on a schedule acceptable to Manufacturing. Surprisingly, YC-14 Engineering was criticized for this situation. Because Engineering had no late releases, the upper management felt they really were not squeezing their manpower hard enough. Most programs at this stage were well behind in their engineering-drawing releases, and this is what the management expected of the YC-14 program. YC-14 Engineering felt that they actually were doing a better job for which they got no credit.

In January 1975, the YC-14 Program Management had a meeting with the Corporate Management Council, headed by T. Wilson, chairman of the board. The group included Mr. Allen, chairman emeritus; Mel Stamper, president of the Boeing Company; Ollie Boileau, president of the Aerospace Company; and several other corporate and Aerospace Company vice presidents. Before the formal presentations began, the Management Council was taken through the mockups in the shop areas to show them how the airplane was going. Generally, their reaction was very favorable. It looked to them as if it was coming right along, and they were glad to see some pieces of hardware. I had the opportunity to talk to T. Wilson and Mr. Allen to point out that the work package concept was working very well and showing good cooperation between Engineering and Manufacturing. Mr. Allen remarked that it used to be that Manufacturing was almost like another company, and it sure took Boeing a long time to get around to doing it right. At this meeting, it was pointed out that the company might well be at risk for about $17 million by the end of FY 1975. The total cost of the program now was estimated to be $124 million, including a $5 million allowance for possible changes between the present time and the end of flight test.

At the end of this meeting, T. Wilson reviewed his position. He felt that the YC-14 team had a competitive airplane, but that they should not underestimate their competition. He felt that the program seemed to be under good control, and that the airplane was going together well. On the other hand, he was "damn disappointed" that the team did not meet the cost estimates that had been made when the program began. He said the overruns were not necessarily a disaster, but conversely the team did not get an "A" either. He did feel Boeing should take the risk during FY 1975 and proceed with the YC-14 planned schedule, with the expectation that the funding would catch up when the money from FY 1976 arrived. He was very concerned that the team was predicting a large overrun at the end of the program. He was not

Assembly of the YC-14 prototype wing structure during June 1975. The assembly was considered 50 percent complete at this point. *Courtesy of the Boeing Company*

impressed by the fact that other people in the company weren't surprised by how much it was costing to create the airplane. What he wanted was somebody who could show him how it could be done for a lesser cost. The YC-14 team was disappointed that "T" never seemed to appreciate the fact that the people associated with the program in the beginning had estimated the cost would be on the order of $130 million. It was the corporation that decided to bid the program at only $96 million, or, in the case of the stretched-out program, $106 million. By any standard that the YC-14 program could be judged against from other data in the company, an outstanding job was being done to design and build the airplane. The YC-14 effort was the most efficient, modern, large airplane program that Boeing had ever undertaken.

Shortly after this meeting, I got another cost shock. The designers who were producing the drawings would not stand behind the estimates they had made when the cost projection had gone to the corporate headquarters. My chief project engineer kept saying that more man-hours were needed to get the drawings out; otherwise, Manufacturing would soon be in a terrible mess. My background experience was in the Technical Staff areas and not in project design. Thus, I relied heavily on my chief project engineer to give me good advice. I found, however, that he did not recognize how seriously the corporate management felt about the YC-14 cost situation, and would not bring his man-hours down to meet the budgeted allotments. I ended up going through the details of many of the individual project engineers' manpower estimates. I always felt uneasy putting a lot of pressure on them to get rid of manpower when I really didn't understand their task loading as well as I did with my Technical Staff. My Technical Staff consistently ran slightly under their allotted budget, but my project engineers ate up all the extra and then some. I had to face this issue with Dick Taylor, who was Jim Foody's boss and vice president of the Aerospace Company in charge of the program. Dick was very unhappy to have my estimated man-hours suddenly escalate 5% right after he had made a commitment to the corporation. However, he also recognized that the program couldn't let Manufacturing come unglued because of late drawing releases, and so he did not prevent me from continuing my course.

As a result of this corporate attention, the YC-14 program had another audit of their effort by a team from the Commercial Company. The audit team's conclusion was that the YC-14 program was an extremely high risk, and that this level of risk had not been indicated to the corporate management. They had no criticism of how well the YC-14 team had done their job to that point, and offered no advice on how to reduce man-hours and thereby lower the program costs. A short time later, the YC-14 program was reviewed by Edward C. Wells. Ed Wells, the designer of the B-17, was the top technical vice president of the corporation. The president and chairman of the Board of Directors at Boeing relied upon him to make final technical judgments about the company. At the end of his review, Ed wrote a memo to T. Wilson in which he agreed that the YC-14 airplane that was being designed probably was the one that should be built to win the prototype competition. It was as small as possible and additionally utilized a great deal of high-lift technology. He did feel, however, that the effort on a production airplane should concentrate more toward strategic applications, where he felt the customers' desires were shifting.

Shortly thereafter, corporate management took steps to split the activity between the prototype development and the tasks being accomplished on the production airplane. In the middle of March 1975, Roy Rotelli, a hard-nosed project manager, was brought in as deputy program manager for the prototype under Jim Foody. No deputy was appointed for the production airplane, and thus Jim Foody handled that aspect. I served the function of director of engineering for both the prototype and the production organizations. Rotelli's task was to get the cost down on the prototype. After evaluating where the YC-14 program stood and really looking at the Engineering Department, Rotelli became convinced that the team was not overmanned at all, and was quite amazed that so much had been done with the relatively small number of people who were available. He continued always, though, to force down the cost of the airplane even though it might sacrifice the quality of the prototype design. He removed from the design many of the items that had been put in to demonstrate the capability of the airplane beyond just STOL takeoff and landing operations. Because Boeing's strategy for years had been to supply the USAF with demonstrated operational performance, I often was put in a position of trying to defend our earlier decisions.

Several months later, in mid-July 1975, additional organizational changes were made. A separate Military Airplane Development Group was started within the Boeing Aerospace Company. It was headed by Bill Maxwell, an Aerospace Company vice president who, as an Air Force general assigned to the Federal Aviation Administration (FAA), had been in charge of the supersonic transport program. Under him, as head of transport airplanes, was W. T. "Bill" Hamilton. Also, a vice president in the Aerospace Company, Hamilton was a very experienced airplane aerodynamicist, probably the most qualified airplane designer in the entire Aerospace Company. He was made program manager for transport airplanes, replacing Jim Foody, who was placed as deputy program manager for the production airplane. Dick Taylor, who had been the vice president in charge of the AMST program, was shifted to Boeing's Washington, DC, office. As usual, the move was played as one to strengthen the organization, but it seemed evident to me that both Dick Taylor and Jim Foody were being punished for the cost overruns on the YC-14 program. In fact, Dick Taylor told me years later that, at the time, he did not feel he was being treated harshly. His bosses had convinced him that his particular talents really were needed in the Washington office. Jim Foody, on the other hand, was very unhappy about this turn of events. He even considered leaving the company but elected to stay and see what he could do to help. Soon thereafter, he was removed from the production program entirely and assigned to the 747 Division. He was given very little to do there and felt that his future with Boeing appeared quite bleak. Eventually, he quit Boeing and became a vice president at Fairchild. I had always felt he had been an extremely effective program manager, particularly in dealing with the politics of the Department of the Air Force, the Department of Defense, and Congress. He was never surprised by congressional action and, instead, anticipated it. If a congressman gave a speech on the floor relative to the AMST program, the chances were that Jim had helped the staff write it. He always felt that Boeing could have influenced the program a lot more than it did, and could have kept the program moving toward a satisfactory conclusion. I thought that Jim also felt he could overspend a few million dollars every year and get the prototype finished, and the production airplane launched. After that happened, the program would be so successful, nobody would ever remember the overruns. In view of all the organizational changes, I feel that T. Wilson never saw it that way.

Meanwhile, the estimated total cost of the completed program continued to rise. By the end of May 1975, it was estimated to be $140 million, and $147 million by the end of July, an escalation of about $20 million over a six-month period. Engineering wasn't the only group accruing costs; in fact Manufacturing was creating them much faster. By this time, the wing had been pulled from the major wing jig two weeks ahead of schedule at about 60% of its anticipated cost. The body was going together well with no major problems, and the landing gear was ready for installation.

Although the manufacturing effort in the Seattle area was going very well, the situation elsewhere was not. The engine nacelle was being built at Boeing's plant in Wichita, and the Manufacturing people there were experiencing great difficulty. By now the estimated cost of the nacelle was about $13 million, compared to $7 million budgeted for the job. Also, because of the increased complications of the electrical control system, its cost was rising

The wing structure was lowered onto the first YC-14 fuselage on July 10, 1975. *Courtesy of the Boeing Company*

too. At the end of July, the situation was again taken to T. Wilson and the Corporate Management Council. The best estimate of the cost to complete the YC-14 program now was $147.4 million, with the variation ranging from $140 million to as high as $160 million. In addition, the total USAF obligation of $106 million would run out in August 1975, and from then on, the entire program cost would rest with Boeing. All of this bad news had to be faced in light of the fact that although the prototype airplane program was firm within Congress and the USAF, there was no strong indication a definite market existed for the production airplane. T. Wilson had not been prepared beforehand for the size of the current cost estimates, and his immediate reaction was "That's a big lump!" He went on to say he was not very happy with the situation. Boeing at that time made about $80 million in profit per year, and here the YC-14 program had blown away $40 million of it in one sweep. Losses of that amount had nearly brought programs to a complete halt at other companies. In spite of that, though, his real concern was with the company's cost credibility. Boeing was not creating a good image of cost control on the prototype airplane, which would make it even more difficult to sell the idea that the production airplane would have low cost. Everyone on the program interpreted T's reaction as one of being extremely peeved, and well he might have been in light of the other problems he faced in the company at the same time. It took corporate management a week or two to decide whether to authorize the program to continue or not. During that period, Bill Hamilton had another three-hour session with T. Wilson and Ollie Boileau in which he reviewed the program in general, pointing out that the competition was very tough. Boeing had taken over a year to optimize their configuration because the complexities of USB and the electronic flight control system were not really understood when the program began. On the other hand, the comparison of the YC-14 accomplishments to that of any other airplane made it look very good. At the end, the program was directed to proceed according to its existing cost estimates, but every effort should be made to keep the cost managed properly. The program managers had to go back to the Management Council a week or so later and demonstrate in detail why they thought their current cost estimate was viable.

In late August 1975, McDonnell Douglas flew their airplane (the YC-15) for the first time, right on schedule. From all indications, their flight went well, and they completed three flights over the next three days. This news indicated to the YC-14 team again that their competition was going to be extremely tough.

The nose and main landing gears seen during construction of the first prototype in August 1975. *Courtesy of the Boeing Company*

The McDonnell Douglas YC-15

The YC-15 demonstrating its short-field takeoff capability. *Courtesy of the Boeing Company*

The YC-15 was McDonnell Douglas's entry in the AMST competition and was the direct competitor to the Boeing YC-14. Both airplanes were essentially designed to replace the Lockheed C-130 Hercules and operate at higher cruise speeds to expedite airlift response and increase the number of daily sorties per aircraft. Considering the groundbreaking USB design of the YC-14, McDonnell Douglas took a somewhat more conventional approach to the design of its competition entrant. Like the YC-14, the YC-15 used a supercritical wing, which minimized cruise drag and made the similar compromise of having a limited amount of wing sweep. While this eased production costs, it also greatly enhanced the handling and lift characteristics during STOL operations. Part way through their test program, they shifted to a wing about 20 percent larger than their original design. To save costs, the YC-15 used components from existing aircraft, most notably the nose section derived from the wide-body DC-10 airliner, giving the airplane a "familiar" appearance.

Given some similarities, the YC-15 was very different from the YC-14. Instead of employing twin high-bypass engines mounted above the wing surface, the YC-15 employed a four-engine, underslung arrangement—a configuration similar to the C-141 and C-5 transports already in operation. One disadvantage to this on a smaller aircraft such as the YC-15 was that the only engines available in this thrust class at the time were noisy and thirsty low-bypass turbofans. The YC-15 was fitted with conventional leading-edge slats. It was also equipped with a double-slotted trailing-edge flap system that was designed to be deployed into the jet exhaust of the engines, deflecting this downward in order to enhance low-airspeed lift for STOL operations.

In the end, the YC-15 was never ordered into serial production. The YC-15 did, however, form a very rough basis for the much-larger C-17 airlifter. The shift in rationale within the DoD, changing the desired requirements for large airlifters, led to the demise of the AMST program. The revised requirements took large airlifters farther from the front lines and tailored their operations to longer, more-improved runways. While the more conventional YC-15 design failed to meet many of the goals set forth by the AMST program (in which the Boeing YC-14 excelled), it eventually formed the basis for the successful McDonnell Douglas (later Boeing) C-17 airlifter, in service today.

YC-15 Characteristics

ENGINES: 4 P&W JT8D-17 TURBOFANS RATED AT 16,000 LB THRUST (7,260 KG)

	SQ FT	SQ M
WING AREA:	1,740 OR 2,107	161.7 OR 195.8
	FEET	**METERS**
WING SPAN	110.3 OR 132.6	33.6 OR 40.4
OVERALL LENGTH	124.2	37.8
OVERALL HEIGHT	43.3	13.2
FUSELAGE DIAMETER	18.0	5.5
CARGO COMPARTMENT		
LENGTH	47.0	14.33
WIDTH	11.7	3.57
HEIGHT	11.3	3.44
LOADABLE RAMP		
LENGTH	12.7	3.76
WIDTH	11.7	3.57

Courtesy of the Boeing Company

By late October, the YC-14 Engineering team completed its first final design status review, where a segment of the detailed design was examined by applicable specialists from throughout the Boeing Company to check for design errors. The first study was on the fuel system, and it was followed by similar reviews of all the major assemblies.

By year's end, the situation at Marconi-Elliot, the manufacturer of the FBW control system, continued to deteriorate. With help from Boeing people sent to England, they gained control of the software issues, but the hardware was well behind schedule. Although Marconi-Elliot continued to say they were going to be able to deliver their units on time, the Flight Test organization started doing preliminary planning on what flying could be accomplished without an electronic control system on board.

Detailed planning of the flight test program began in October 1975. This timing was much later than some of the USAF people associated with the program felt was required, but engineering work had to be done in series, and a full staff complement to accomplish the flight test planning was simply unavailable. An experienced flight test manager, Ken Hurley, was brought on board to manage the flight test program for the next year and a half. Hurley was a highly organized person and an ideal choice to lead the flight test activities, particularly the challenges associated with the nine-month assignment of the flight test team to Edwards Air Force Base in California. Before coming to Boeing, he had a very successful Air Force career, including a tour as an SR-71 Blackbird reconnaissance systems operator.

Full-Scale Upper-Surface-Blown Flap Test

As part of the engine, nacelle, and USB flap development program, Boeing always had planned to run a ground test of a complete, full-scale configuration before installing it on the airplane.

An actual production nacelle was used for this test. A segment of the wing behind it was duplicated along with the USB flap. This assembly was attached to a duplicated segment of the fuselage so that noise and pressure levels on that area could be measured. The whole apparatus would test whether or not the flow would turn properly in full scale, as had been anticipated from the model tests. This installation was made at a Boeing test facility located north of Seattle on the Tulalip Indian Reservation, where there was lots of land, so the test rig could be separated from any areas that would be bothered by the noise. By the end of the year, about two weeks of test running had been completed, and most of the

Test of the USB installation, December 1975.
Courtesy of the Boeing Company

news was very good. The performance of the nozzle was good, the nozzle-effective-exit area was proper, and noise levels were lower than estimated. The airflow over the top of the flap looked very good, and the flap did not vibrate more than one would expect. The noise levels at idle thrust were found to be very low. It was possible for people to stand under the wing and talk to each other, because the inlet noise was well forward and the exhaust noise was shielded by the wing. There was one failure of a small attachment bracket holding the flap, but it had been known from analysis that this bracket was weak. There was no trouble beefing it up to where it was adequate. There was much relief that a very good verification of the airplane's powered-lift capability finally had been demonstrated at full scale and in an environment very closely simulating the final airplane. During these tests, sound levels and pressure distributions were measured over the USB flap and the adjacent fuselage for NASA under the special research contract referred to earlier.

There was one troublesome failure during this test, however. During a routine borescope of the engine after a number of tests had been run, damage was found on a number of compressor blades. The further the inspectors looked into the engine, the more damage was evident. General Electric felt that the engine was damaged to the point where it had to be removed and repaired. To their credit, they spent essentially no time trying to place blame but instead put their efforts into getting the engine repaired. It was removed immediately and sent to Southern California for repair during the Christmas holidays. By the time work began in early 1976, the engine was ready to go again. The damage was found to have been caused by a small SAE 10-32 bolt that somehow had been dropped into the engine. The cause of the damage was determined by looking at the marks the bolt had made on individual compressor blades. Fortunately, the bolt did not go through the hot section and into the turbine, so that the damage was limited to the compressor itself.

Early in January 1976, an engine was reinstalled in the Tulalip test rig. An investigation had pretty well determined that the SAE 10-32 bolt causing the damage had entered the engine through the variable bypass valve doors just downstream of the booster. The quality control procedures used to inspect the engine were reviewed completely to make sure that no more foreign objects were left in the engine. General Electric even went to the point of x-raying the engine from the inside by putting an isotope in the hollow shaft and x-ray film around the outer part of the core so that they could see any loose items. In one final inspection, looking around the front of the compressor, they found a little washer. This occurrence was a real shock. It meant that there were two engines in a row with something in them waiting to ruin them with initial startup. The washer was retrieved, and, ironically enough, it appeared to be about the size used on a 10-32 bolt. These two instances brought on procedures that required all openings in the engine be sealed over before any work was done on the surrounding cowling.

The test runs on this engine installation were made with the USB flaps fully down at 70°. The airflow turning was evaluated there using the test rig balance and found to agree very closely with the static tests done on scale models earlier in the program. By mid-February 1976, the thrust reverser had been operated on the Tulalip test rig. Its operation looked very good and indicated that the desired reverser performance would be met without any problem.

Design and Assembly Status

By the end of 1975, the assembly of the airplane was coming along well. The basic systems were being installed, including the hydraulic, electrical, and control cable systems. All the systems located along the rear spar of the wing were nearly finished. The lateral control spoilers were in place, the boundary-layer control system at the leading edge was completely installed, and the leading-edge Krueger flaps were being attached. Both the horizontal and vertical stabilizers were out of the assembly jigs, and the large fiberglass

Technicians work on the unique thrust reverser assembly during final assembly. *Courtesy of the Boeing Company*

fairing was being fitted to the top of the fin. The landing-gear fairings were being fitted to the fuselage, and the cargo door and ramp were being installed. The airplane went together very well, and most items were ahead of schedule by this time, although there was a little delay in getting the flaps installed on the airplane. Functional tests of the systems were underway, and all planning was aimed for flight in mid-August 1976.

By the end of January 1976, the horizontal and vertical stabilizers had been installed on the airplane, and the fuselage of the number two airplane already was assembled. The analysis of the airplane continued as the assembly proceeded, and periodically someone would find something that was not quite proper. For instance, just before the horizontal tail was lifted into place, a substantial error was found in computing the stiffness of the elevator power actuator support structure. The stiffness was tested by loading the elevator and was found to be softer than the value that had been used in the flutter analysis. A reanalysis came to the conclusion that the airplane speed might have to be limited from a flutter standpoint. A similar situation was found in the vertical tail structure. Through an error in communication, the wrong value of loading due to rudder deflection was used in the fin analysis, and the fin, therefore, was not strong enough to take full rudder deflections at high speed. This error brought on the need to reduce pressure in the rudder actuator as speed increased. Thus, another requirement was imposed on the flight control system. On the other hand, the most recent aerodynamic data, when put into the simulator, indicated the airplane had appreciably better control characteristics than estimated early in the program. Stall recovery appeared to be quite straightforward. The basic aerodynamic data in the STOL flight regime remained very irregular as a function of angle of attack, even for the final configuration. Therefore, the control engineers recognized that the airplane's flying qualities probably would not be ideal without the help of the FBW flight control system.

In February 1976, the first set of Marconi-Elliot electronic flight-control system equipment came into the plant and was immediately put into Boeing's laboratory and set into operation. These lab tests indicated that all three channels of the system would work together properly and that the interfaces with the other aircraft equipment, such as the digital air data computer, were satisfactory. By early March the Marconi-Elliot equipment was running as a three-channel system, being fed signals from the airplane equipment, and actually flying a simulation of the airplane. The electronic control system finally was beginning to fit into place.

Airplane number one as she stood on February 3, 1976. *Courtesy of the Boeing Company*

Airplane number one seen in the late stages of final assembly.
Courtesy of the Boeing Company

By mid-March 1976, the USB flaps were on the airplane, as were the other trailing-edge flaps, and test personnel were able to operate the USB flap with a hydraulic system. Because the USB flap was going to control glide path during STOL flight, it had to move relatively rapidly. It moved smoothly under the hydraulic control over large angles, yet it would oscillate, if required, at rates as high as twenty-five cycles per second. It was a very impressive sight to see this large flap move back and forth at that frequency.

Diminishing levels of manpower continued to be a problem, and Engineering management kept reducing the work statement so that the tasks could get done with fewer people. It was decided to write very simple reports describing the aircraft systems. Also, it was decided to stop keeping track of the non-optimum weight put into the airplane. This decision meant Boeing would be unable to convince the USAF that a production airplane wouldn't have additional weight and thereby get credit for it as payload on the prototype. Probably another 1,500 pounds of weight was put into the airplane, for which Boeing never received credit because of this decision.

Another Corporate Review

In early March 1976, the program received another review by the Corporate Management Council. Again, the team was headed by T. Wilson and included Ed Wells; George Schairer, corporate vice president of research and development; Ollie Boileau; and six other company vice presidents. The YC-14 team was able to report to this review committee that as a result of the Tulalip engine test, the risk relative to USB performance was largely eliminated. Also, the risk on the schedule for the electronic control system was less than previously indicated. The Engineering and Test organizations were right up against their budget plans, but the assembly of the airplane had gone better than anticipated, so Manufacturing was operating at less than their budgeted rate. The whole atmosphere at the meeting was much more friendly than the gathering that had occurred earlier, when the Management Council first was exposed to the fact that the program probably was going to cost approximately $145 million. At the end of the review, T. Wilson congratulated the group on the progress that had been made. He was looking forward to the flight testing and felt Boeing was going to learn a great deal from the airplane. He went on to say that the program now had gotten its manpower under control, and it should begin to think about what could be done to increase the value of the prototype airplane. He even questioned the decision to stop the tracking of non-optimum weight, but Rotelli convinced him that no further work should be done in that area. Because the estimated cost had stopped escalating, Wilson even said that cost credibility and schedule were important, but performance was the most important thing, and the YC-14 team should concentrate on getting optimum performance.

The Management Council still was concerned about the overall competitive situation and whether or not the production airplane would ever become a reality. The estimated cost of the three hundredth production C-14 now was nearly $13 million, as compared to the $5 million that was estimated at the beginning of the program. They were concerned that the USAF's thinking on transport needs was shifting to a more strategic mode, and they were extremely concerned that Lockheed would continue to push the C-130 modernization and get the characteristics the USAF wanted. A comment was made that if Lockheed were to put a large body on the C-130 so it could take the oversized vehicles, they could effectively kill the whole AMST program.

Functional and Vibration Tests

By the end of March 1976, the airplane was essentially completed by Manufacturing and was turned over to the Engineering Department for functional tests. Also, the first flightworthy computing units were arriving from Marconi-Elliot, which was a big milestone, essentially eliminating the final major risk in the program schedule.

By the end of April, the ground vibration testing of the airplane had been completed. This testing was done in a new way for Boeing. The airplane was mounted on very soft supports, and an element such as an aileron was shaken mechanically through a wide range of frequencies. The resulting motion of the airplane was measured in many places across the wing, fuselage, and tail. The motions were analyzed by means of a Fourier analysis to study the airframe oscillations. This procedure was a very rapid way of doing the ground vibration testing and indicated that the structure had the stiffness characteristics that were anticipated, and thus the flutter analysis done earlier probably was adequate.

Little things kept cropping up, of course, during the final construction of the airplane. For example, it was found that the nose gear doors were too close to the ground. Although there was enough clearance as the airplane rested statically, heavy braking at low speeds might rock the airplane onto the nose gear to the point where the landing-gear doors could be damaged. Just damaging the landing-gear doors themselves would not have mattered much, but there was fear that the doors might tear off and go down the body and damage the undersurface of the fuselage. Therefore, the landing-gear doors were modified to provide adequate ground clearance. To save money, YC-14 Engineering had never run a landing-gear shimmy analysis. Landing-gear shimmy is similar to an undamped shopping-cart wheel cycling back and forth. At the last minute, a very crude analysis was run so that there would be some idea of what to do in case a shimmy actually occurred during the taxi tests.

The aft corner of the nose landing-gear door was removed to prevent ground contact during maximum performance landings. *Courtesy of the Boeing Company*

During this period, the program began to get visits from the USAF's Executive Independent Review team. This team was made up of experienced Air Force people who examined the design in light of their background and gave comments as to any changes they thought were necessary. They, of course, asked a great number of questions, all of which had to be answered in spite of the very busy schedule. They submitted a fair number of comments, and a few of them did result in minor revisions to the airplane.

Just before moving the airplane out of the factory, an inspection called an "On-Airplane Safety Inspection" was performed. This inspection is standard on every new Boeing airplane. The experts on the various aspects of airplane design and construction from throughout the company were brought in on a Saturday, and they reviewed the airplane all day long. They looked at the systems and structure and wrote any comments they had concerning items they thought should be changed. Any unsatisfactory comments were resolved systematically, so that no fault could slip through unconsidered. This inspection was the final stamp of approval by the company Engineering Department that the airplane was ready for flight test.

CHAPTER 5

Ground and Flight Testing

One of the highlights of any airplane program is the aircraft rollout. It is a milestone that represents the completion of the assembly in the factory and is the first public display of the finished airplane. After ground and taxi tests affirm that all systems are operating properly, the program's most dramatic and defining event takes place as the airplane makes its first flight.

The first YC-14 finally sees daylight during this "unofficial" rollout for ground testing. Traffic is stopped while the aircraft is tugged across East Marginal Way at Boeing Field. *Courtesy of the Boeing Company*

Rollout

Airplane One was rolled out of the factory on the night of May 25, 1976, and onto the ramp for outside testing. To test the engines at high power with the flaps deflected, where they would create high vertical forces, a special massive concrete ballast had been poured underneath the ramp so that the airplane could be fastened down and would not get away.

The official rollout ceremony for the airplane occurred on June 11, 1976. It was quite a celebration, with a great number of people present from the USAF, the airlines, the press, and the subcontractors. Because of the uncertain weather, which was often a problem for outdoor celebrations in Seattle, the main activities were held inside a very large flight test hangar at the north end of Boeing Field. As the speakers were talking, the airplane was rolled up outside the closed doors of the hangar. At the proper time, the hangar doors were raised to present the airplane. It was fortunate that the program was done that way, because there were sporadic rain showers all day. After the ceremony, there was a large luncheon for the people on the program and the visitors, but it was a rather short activity. By two o'clock in the afternoon the airplane was back in its working position and fueling tests had begun.

Courtesy of the Boeing Company

The official YC-14 rollout ceremony occurred on June 11, 1976.
Courtesy of the Boeing Company

Ground Tests

By the end of June, engine runs had begun, and the engines were soon tested at 100% takeoff thrust with essentially no problems. The noise levels in and out of the airplane were about as anticipated. Inside the airplane in locations where the jets scrubbed the outer fuselage skin, it was necessary for the engineers to wear helmets, because the noise level was about 126 decibels. Outside the airplane the noise levels with the engines at idle were quite low, and it was easy for people to converse anywhere around the airplane. At high power, large vortices formed that would flow into the inlet. With no wind, these vortices would originate on the side of the body just ahead of the engine nacelle. They were made visible by water vapor because of the unusually low temperatures and wet weather existing at the time of these tests. With a tailwind, the vortex would start on the ground as much as 20 feet ahead of the airplane and then lead into the inlet. Although these vortices obviously were very strong, there was no problem with them picking up foreign objects and damaging the engine. As a matter of fact, at the conclusion of these high-powered ground tests, the engines were examined by General Electric, who reported that they were in the best condition ever seen for engines run under similar conditions. This observation indicated the value of having the engines high up on the top of the wing and away from the ground. The BLC system was operated during these tests and found to work satisfactorily. Any rainwater that had settled into the upward-facing BLC nozzles was blown out readily when the system was pressurized.

In early July, another ground vibration test was run with the electronic flight control system operating to ensure that there was no coupling between the airframe vibrations and the flight control system. This type of coupling had been a problem on a number of USAF airplanes. It was found that there were no such issues with the YC-14, and the airplane was cleared for flight as far as flutter was concerned. Final ground tests included checking for electromagnetic interference, to make sure the electrical power systems of the airplane did not interfere with the electronic control system and electronic data systems. Also, the emergency power unit was tested. This unit was a hydrazine-powered turbine driving a hydraulic pump to maintain flight control in case of a concurrent failure of both engines.

There was sort of a donnybrook very late in ground testing when the USAF objected to the type of seats that were in the airplane for the test crew. These seats were not for the flight crew but were for the test crew managing the instrumentation. At Boeing, most of the data obtained in flight tests are recorded by instrumentation on board the airplane and are monitored by the flight test engineers in flight. The USAF insisted the seats were not adequate, and it turned out they were right. No analysis ever had been done on those seats. Fortunately, the test team was able to obtain proper seats from another Boeing Air Force program and install them in the airplane. I thought the whole situation was highly embarrassing for Boeing.

Another organizational change occurred in late July. Roy Rotelli, who had been managing the prototype program, was moved up with Bill Hamilton, who managed both the YC-14 and C-14 programs, and I was made program manager for the YC-14. Since the job remaining on the YC-14 primarily was one of engineering evaluation, I retained the position of director of engineering. I felt my biggest task was to get the airplane through evaluation on budget. It would require a great deal of discipline to avoid spending money to fix things that were not optimal, but largely inconsequential. Always present was a temptation to improve performance, or at least bring it up to the standard that had been set for the aircraft. In reality, most such things could not be done because of the lack of funding.

Initial Flight Tests

Initial flight testing of a new airplane concept is an exciting period demanding careful attention to hundreds of details. The YC-14 test plan was developed to take advantage of the different features incorporated into each of the two test airplanes.

Flight test begins. *Courtesy of the Boeing Company*

Test Plan Concept

Planning for the flight test of the YC-14 started to some extent at the beginning of development. During the year preceding the first flight, planning activity intensified, resulting in detailed plans for instrumentation, taxi conditions, flight conditions, support requirements, and emergency procedures. The flight test program was organized under a joint test force (JTF) with a director and three deputy directors. The director and one deputy director were from the Air Force Flight Test Center (AFFTC) at Edwards Air Force Base, California. The second deputy director was from the Air Force Operational Test and Evaluation Center (AFTEC), based at Kirtland Air Force Base, New Mexico. The third was Boeing Company test manager Ken Hurley, who also headed up the Boeing test team. For a short time, there also was a NASA participant director.

The test program was conducted at two locations. Three months were spent in Seattle, where initial safety testing and basic flight envelope expansion were accomplished. Both airplanes and personnel then were moved to Edwards Air Force Base, where the remainder of the testing was performed. Boeing developed a separate flight test instrumentation plan for each of the two test airplanes. During the planning phase, individual test conditions were assigned either to the number one or number two airplanes according to the configuration and operational timing. Initial safety envelope expansion and handling qualities testing were scheduled on airplane one. The number two airplane had several operational installations not present on the number one airplane, such as a cargo-handling system. Thus, the tests of actual operation were scheduled on the number two airplane. Instrumentation that was required for tests on the number one airplane was not installed on the number two airplane, and vice versa. The instrumentation concept was patterned after the standard Boeing approach of telemetering data to the ground stations only for critical limited-crew flights such as flutter evaluations. On flights where test crews could operate onboard instrumentation, the data were recorded on board and processed on the ground. The USAF never favored this approach, preferring to telemeter all the data. However, it worked very well under the circumstances of prototype development.

The initial plan called for 260 flight hours on both airplanes to accomplish the highest-priority tests, with roughly a hundred more hours reserved for reflight and unexpected development testing, for approximately 365 total hours. It was felt by many that this number of hours was an ambitious effort to accomplish in just one year, but actually 601 hours were flown. There were approximately 650 channels of instrumentation in the initial flight test plan, but as the program developed, the instrumentation package grew to somewhere near 1,100 data channels.

Taxi Tests

The airplane rolled under its own power for the first time on the afternoon of July 30, 1976. The initial taxi tests were to check the brakes and for a possible shimmy in both the main gears and the nose gear. The first day, the airplane reached 80 knots on a taxi test, and the brakes and steering all worked well. There was little of the wallowing on the gear that I was afraid might occur because of the relatively narrow tread and soft oleos on the airplane. The nose gear indicated no sign of shimmy, but the main gear indicated an oscillatory load at about 80 knots, equivalent to about 5% of the design load of the landing-gear beam. Over the next day or so, the taxi speed was advanced to 120 knots, and the oscillatory loads never did increase. It eventually was decided that the loads probably were caused by an out-of-balance wheel, because there was no problem whatsoever with the main gear for the rest of the program. However, there were some problems with nose gear shimmy experienced later in the program.

Taxi tests being conducted on the first YC-14 in August 1976. The Cessna 150L taking off in the foreground lends to the large size of the YC-14. *Courtesy of the Boeing Company*

The final day of taxiing was devoted to checking the control characteristics of the airplane. The lateral control under single-engine operation was done both at low speeds and at speeds associated with V1 at takeoff. (Author's note: V1 is a speed occurring during the takeoff roll that is defined as "critical engine failure" speed. If an engine fails before this speed is reached, the takeoff is aborted, and the airplane is stopped. If the engine fails above this speed, the takeoff is continued on the remaining engine[s]. Therefore, V1 is the lowest speed where aerodynamic control must be sufficient to handle zero thrust on one engine and full thrust on the other[s].) Finally, a nosewheel liftoff was performed at around 72 knots. The demonstrated control power was about as predicted, and the crew was quite happy with how the airplane operated on the ground. There was one final inspection of the engines by General Electric personnel. They reported, as before, that the engines were in the best condition they had ever seen after the kind of operation performed during this ground testing. The engines looked absolutely new.

During these taxi tests, it was necessary to spend a lot of time letting the brakes cool with the engines at idle. During this cool-down time, experiments were performed to see how ground personnel could operate around the airplane with the engines idling. The airplane was found to be very innocuous relative to such activity. The front access door was easily available, with no problems. The airplane cargo ramp could be lowered, and personnel could climb in and out very easily without any interference from the engines, because the exhaust flow was high above them. It was found also that the area around the ramp was quiet and that it was easy for people to stand on the ramp and talk to one another with the engines idling.

First Flights

The airplane was ready for flight on August 6, 1976, but the operation was plagued by inclement weather. Low clouds persisted, and the flight finally was canceled around three o'clock in the afternoon. The next two days were a weekend, and it rained continuously both days. Actually, it was very unusual weather, even for Seattle, to have this much rain in August. The morning of Monday, August 9, was still cloudy but there were indications it might improve. Ken Hurley and I flew in his own airplane to hunt for good weather and found that the clouds were breaking up to the west, and good weather soon would be in the Seattle area. Boeing weather requirements for a first flight included a 3,000-to-5,000-foot ceiling at Boeing field, and a visual flight route to 16,000 feet, where the testing could be done. The first flight occurred around three o'clock in the afternoon on August 9, 1976. As the airplane taxied onto the runway, I found my heart really pounding. I had stationed myself at the approximate predicted takeoff point. The chase airplane (a Canadair F-86E MK.6) took off first, turned downwind, and the pilot started the YC-14 brake release countdown as he began his turn onto the base leg of his pattern. The YC-14 took off right in front of me, and there have been few thrills in my professional career that can match the feeling I had as I watched the plane lift into the air for the first time.

A group photo of YC-14 program team members in front of airplane number one in September 1976. *Courtesy of the Boeing Company*

The first flight of the YC-14 on August 9, 1976 with the Canadair F-86E chase plane in tow. *Courtesy of Bob Carver*

Another perspective of airplane number one during its first flight from Boeing Field. *Courtesy of the Boeing Company*

YC-14 first flight cover, flown aboard the aircraft on its maiden flight. *Dan Dornseif collection*

The first flight went very well. The airplane handled well, and the electronic flight-control system worked well. The airplane was brought back onto the ground with a nice smooth landing and taxied back in to receive the congratulations of T. Wilson and others who had gathered for the first flight. The crew on the first flight was Boeing project pilot Raymond McPherson and Air Force pilot Maj. David Bittenbinder.

The next flights were to clear the escape system, and this was done by dropping a dummy from the escape chute over the Whidbey Island Naval Air Station, located about 57 miles north of Seattle. The flight rate during August and September necessarily was fairly low. There were inspections after each flight and, of course, problems were discovered, but no real show stoppers. The test crew gradually cleared the airplane for flight in instrument meteorological conditions, operated the cargo door and ramp while in flight, and tested the STOL mode at altitude. The pilots quickly developed a great deal of confidence in the airplane, because it handled well and responded to their control inputs precisely. By the end of September 1976, the airplane had flown to speeds as low as 79 knots on both engines and 90 knots on one engine. The airplane was extremely docile under these conditions, and the pilots felt they could easily conduct a single-engine landing, if necessary.

After the first flight on August 9, 1976. *Front row, left to right*: T. A. Wilson, Boeing chairman of the board; Jim Foody, former YC-14 program manager; Omar Bygland, YC-14 chief project engineer; Maynard Pennell, vice president of Boeing Aerospace Company; John Wimpress, YC-14 program manager and director of engineering; Ray McPherson, YC-14 project pilot. *Courtesy of the Boeing Company*

Airplane number one is seen in flight, with the Puget Sound in the distance. This allows a good view of the USB flaps in their fully retracted position. Note the modification that placed the USB trailing edge farther aft than the adjacent outboard flaps. *Courtesy of the Boeing Company*

This photo shows a closer view of the USB flaps, extended variable-camber Krueger flaps, and exhaust nozzles. It is noteworthy that with the trailing-edge flaps retracted, the vortex generators installed behind the engine nozzles are retracted. *Courtesy of the Boeing Company*

Airplane number one during testing at Edwards AFB. The left rudder deflection indicates that the aircraft is being tested with the right engine not producing thrust. Note the full extension of the USB flap and its exposed slots augmenting lift on the failed-engine side. The fly-by-wire flight control system would sense an engine failure and automatically change the flight control configuration, independent of pilot input. *Courtesy of the Boeing Company*

Airplane number one seen during tests at Boeing Field. Note the fully extended outboard flaps and retracted USB flaps. *Courtesy of the Boeing Company*

The McDonnell Douglas YC-15 seen in flight. Note the large trailing-edge flaps and leading-edge slat arrangement. *Courtesy of Mike Freer via Wikimedia Commons*

There were two minor structural problems during this early development testing. One problem was associated with the cove seals on the vertical fin. These seals closed the gap between the vertical fin and the rudder to reduce drag. They were made of fiberglass and actually rubbed on the rudder at high rudder deflections. They were found to be too flexible and would break off in flight. After trying a number of different solutions, it was decided to make the cove seals much shorter, allowing them to gap slightly, in spite of the drag. The other problem was excessive deflections of the flexible leading-edge Krueger flaps at high speed. These flaps tuck into the wing lower surface near the leading edge. They were not sealed and vented properly, so that air loads got in behind them and caused them to bulge out. It was necessary to measure the pressures inside the wing and establish how these flaps should be sealed and vented so that there would be negative pressures inside to suck them closed. Eventually the problem was solved satisfactorily. Everyone was very pleased with the early operation of the USB flaps. The flaps moved as directed, were very steady even at high thrust, and gave the flight crews complete assurance that the STOL mode was going to be satisfactory.

In early September, I visited the Farnborough Air Show as part of an exhibit emphasizing the YC-14. While there, I observed the YC-15 demonstration flights. They were truly spectacular. The airplane was lightly loaded, perhaps 20,000 pounds under its normal STOL weight. It consistently took off in less than 1,000 feet and landed with what appeared to be less than a 600-foot ground roll. Its maneuverability around the field was outstanding, showing rapid roll rates and the ability to pull high-g turns. Seeing this airplane perform in this manner gave me a distinct feeling as to the tough competition that Boeing faced and our need to make the YC-14 truly superior.

The Close Call

In early November, the test crew had what I consider to be the closest call, from a safety standpoint, on the entire flight test program. High-speed flutter checks were being made in the cruise configuration. During these tests, the airplane was put in a specific condition of speed and altitude. Then, the control surfaces were pulsed to see if they tended to induce any kind of structural oscillation on the airplane. Because of the potential hazardous nature of these flights, they were done with only the two pilots on board. All the data were telemetered to the ground, where they were monitored by a flutter specialist to see if any reduction in damping was beginning to occur. The flutter checks on this flight had been conducted for quite some time at high altitude, so that the airplane was thoroughly cold-soaked. The airplane was brought down fairly quickly to 12,000 feet, and the flutter checks began there, gradually accelerating to higher and higher speeds. The testing had been carried to a little over 360 knots when the leading-edge flaps began to show gapping again. The airplane was starting to slow down, when suddenly the chase plane pilot stated that hydraulic fluid was streaming from one of the flap support brackets. The YC-14 pilot reported that the hydraulic pressure in one of the three systems dropped rapidly, as did the quantity, and the airplane immediately was diverted to land. It took about another fifteen minutes to touchdown, and there was no further incident other than the pilots elected to make a flaps-up landing, rather than lower the flaps.

It was found that the hydraulic failure was a rupture of a plug in one of the actuators caused by extremely high pressure in the hydraulic system. All the trailing-edge flaps on the YC-14 were controlled by hydraulic actuators. To hold the flaps up in the cruise configuration, the system locked the local hydraulic fluid at constant volume so that the flaps would hold in place even though the hydraulic pressure was turned off. This hydraulic lock was maintained by a check valve that allowed fluid to enter the local system but not escape until a control valve was opened by the pilot moving the flap controls. While the airplane was cold-soaking at high altitude, the hydraulic fluid condensed, and the system moved more and more fluid through the open check valve. When the airplane came down to low altitude and started to warm up, the hydraulic fluid naturally expanded. It could not get through the check valve in the other direction and eventually reached extremely high pressures and ruptured the actuator plug. The reason for this failure was that the pressure relief valves intended to compensate for just this kind of hydraulic thermal expansion had never been installed in the system. Further investigation showed that all three of the hydraulic systems had been built the same way. The YC-14 Design Requirements Document stated very plainly that pressure relief valves should be included in the hydraulic system anywhere there was a hydraulic lock. However, the relief valves were not installed. Because of the relatively small YC-14 team, the usual process of engineering checks and balances was reduced in scope as compared to those on most Boeing products. The YC-14 hydraulic system was relatively conventional and was designed by competent engineers, so that the resulting hydraulic-system configuration did not get the careful review and analysis afforded to the more distinctive areas of the airplane, such as the control system or electronics. Thus, the mistake was not discovered. It is surprising that such an omission could escape detection in a company as sophisticated as Boeing, being missed both in the Detail Design Review and in the On-Airplane Safety Inspection. The event is a perfect example of how a relatively small error can have very severe consequences in an aircraft development. All three of the hydraulic systems had the same disease, so to speak. Boeing was fortunate that only one of them had ruptured and that the airplane had been flying in a location where it quickly could be brought back to land.

This whole incident shook me up considerably. Never before had I been involved in a situation where an error, made within my area of responsibility, had had such a dangerous potential. Certainly, one of the most difficult events in my professional career was to go to the flight crew the following day and tell them they had been in danger of losing all three hydraulic systems, and it was the fault of my Engineering Department. The Air Force pilot, Dave Bittenbinder, could have made life extremely difficult for me over this incident, if he had so elected. I'll never forget his response to my explanation of the problem. He said, "Wimpress, I don't mind your scaring the hell out of me after I'm back on the ground." Incidentally, years later Ken Hurley told me Ray McPherson said this was the only time during the program when he felt apprehensive.

This episode taught me a short but severe lesson: never divert from long-established procedures without giving the process careful thought. If changes are made, follow the subsequent actions thoroughly to be sure no compromises are made to airplane safety. When assigned to the Boeing 757 Commercial Airplane Program, the next airplane on which I had a major engineering responsibility, I made sure that every element written into the Design Requirements and Objectives (DR&O) documents was met. I did so by insisting that each sentence of those documents be signed off for compliance by a responsible engineering manager.

During the flutter tests, Boeing obtained the first indication that the cruise drag was high on the airplane. The pilots reported they had to use about 10% higher revolutions per minute (rpm) on the engines than their handbook indicated. Although surprised at this report at first, I was not too concerned, knowing how difficult it is to get really good, stable conditions for measuring drag. However, it was a forewarning of problems to come.

Another Management Change

In early November the AMST program had yet another organizational change. Bill Hamilton, the vice president in charge of the AMST program at Boeing, became vice president of engineering for the Aerospace Company. Frank Verginia replaced Hamilton as head of the AMST program. Thus, the most airplane-oriented vice president in the Aerospace Company was taken off the only ongoing airplane program within the organization. Frank Verginia was another completely unknown personality to the USAF—an entirely new face. He knew absolutely nothing about the airplane, so the team had another big educational task. These constant changes in the upper management of the program made me feel that the Boeing Aerospace Company really did not consider the AMST program to be a high priority.

Airplane number one seen during unimproved field testing at Edwards AFB. *Courtesy of the Boeing Company*

Flight Tests at Edwards Air Force Base

The two YC-14s and the flight test program were moved to Edwards Air Force Base in early November 1976. The route of flight to Edwards was determined and alternate landing sites were scouted. A thorough briefing was assembled, showing how to handle an emergency on the ground, and this briefing was taken to every potential emergency landing site along the flight route. The two airplanes went down to Edwards Air Force Base essentially together, and engineering data were collected on both airplanes and the trip was accomplished without any problems.

Test Philosophy

Upon arrival of the planes at Edwards, the immediate effort was to conduct STOLs and to prepare for specific operational tests such as airdrops, ground handling, and interfacing with the military vehicles. Throughout the flying program there were very few spare parts. There were essentially only two sets of hardware for anything that was truly prototype in nature, and only one spare engine for the two airplanes.

Airplane number two was painted in the standard USAF camouflage used during the 1970s. Here it is seen touching down, prior to thrust reverser deployment. *Courtesy of the Boeing Company*

Airplane number two was flown to Yuma, Arizona, to assess the loading operation of various Army equipment. *Courtesy of the Boeing Company*

Test planning had to be predicated on flying only one airplane at a time. Because the configuration of each airplane dictated which tests could be accomplished with that airplane, the detailed scheduling problem was difficult at best. Normally, the test team tried to schedule one airplane to fly as much as possible when it was in flight status, while the other was being prepared for its next sequence. The number one airplane was the primary STOL development aircraft, and the number two airplane was primarily the systems and operational test aircraft. For example, airplane one did not have a cargo system or operational thrust reversers, while airplane two had both. Conversely, number one had considerably more instrumentation installed. Testing was often assigned on the basis of where the necessary instrumentation resided. Duplication of instrumentation was avoided as much as possible. The electronic flight control system (EFCS) was a prime development item and was constantly being updated. Airplane number one was kept in the latest configuration so that the STOL work was not compromised. The EFCS on number two was merely kept in a sufficient configuration to support other tests until the end of the program, when both aircrafts' EFCSs were kept fully updated.

In mid-December 1976, the number two airplane was returned to Seattle over the Christmas holidays to be painted in camouflage colors. Before that time, both airplanes had been just bare metal with a clear protective coating.

By January 1977, it was determined that the test team was falling behind in their scheduled testing rate, and the testing increased to a six-day workweek. Since the shift of the program from that of a technology demonstrator to that of an operational prototype, a number of tests had been added to the program, including evaluation of the high-speed cruise drag. As the program was conceived, the YC-14 was to emphasize the demonstration of a STOL airplane. As the program developed, the YC-14 continually was evaluated in terms of its being a production airplane. Because of the competitive environment and the desire to show the airplane in the best light possible, a lot of money was spent demonstrating the operational aspects of the airplane. For example, airplane number two was flown to the Army Proving Ground in Yuma, Arizona. A number of Army outsized vehicles, such as trucks, vans, tanks, and a self-propelled howitzer, were loaded to confirm that these vehicles could be carried.

By late January, as the testing fell further behind schedule, a seven-day workweek was instigated. Testing was done six days a week, and maintenance was done on the seventh. Good management practices dictate that overtime cannot be sustained efficiently at above approximately 10%. Normal is usually 4% to 6%, but our team was at about 25% at this point. However, mitigating circumstances were that team spirit was very high and people were away from home, so they wanted to work. The test team sustained this schedule for several months without a discernible loss in efficiency. The YC-14 maintenance team included some twenty-five very highly qualified Air Force people who were learning about the airplane as they helped. They were an integral part of the team and supported it with enthusiasm and skill. The aerospace ground equipment (AGE) supplied to the program by the USAF would not meet that same standard, however. Equipment such as starting carts was in deplorable condition and almost unusable. Finally, a special team was brought in from Boeing to update and maintain the equipment, so that by early February 1977, AGE was greatly improved.

STOL and Soft-Field Tests

During February and early March 1977, most of the test activity involved accumulating data on STOL operations and fine tuning the EFCS. Keeping the EFCS updated to the latest configuration always was a problem. The program had only one spare EFCS channel. If there was a failure in any channel that required a spare, there was always the question of whether or not the spare was in the proper configuration to match the other two channels in the airplane. Finally, during one of the major airplane layups, all the boxes of all the channels were brought up to a common standard, which made spare interchanging appreciably easier.

By March 1977, the STOL configuration had been evaluated very completely, and STOLs had become routine. By the end of March, all of the soft-field work had been done. As mentioned earlier, the soft field was defined as a CBR of 6. This condition has been likened to the consistency of a well-prepared golf course sand trap. A "runway" was prepared just west of the main Edwards runway. The desert was graded, tilled, leveled, and measured for CBR. Multiple landings were made, taxi tests were performed, and the capability of the YC-14 to operate on soft fields was demonstrated. The airplane negotiated ruts as deep as 30 inches with no significant trouble. It also ran over all the standard bumps that were available at Edwards AFB without problems of any kind.

From the early days of the flight test program, the pilots had complained that the nose wheel steering was inadequate in some conditions. The problem was confirmed during taxi tests on dry pavement at Edwards, and a modification to the nose gear steering system was developed.

Using existing parts, a third steering actuator was installed along with Teflon bearings. The addition of these changes raised some questions about nose gear shimmy, but it was felt that the extra steering power was a requirement.

Touchdown on the dirt runway at Edwards AFB. The first photo shows the USB flaps partially down, the nosewheels still in the air, and the reversers yet to be deployed. The second image shows the reversers in use. The dust cloud remained behind the airplane because the discharge flow was upward and did not touch the ground. *Courtesy of the Boeing Company*

This group photo was taken at Edwards Air Force Base during the YC-14 testing. In the background, airplane numbers one and two, the only two YC-14s built, stand at the ready. *Courtesy of the Boeing Company*

Periodically, I visited the flight test operation at Edwards Air Force Base. Once was to celebrate a milestone event, and another was to participate in a test where I had a special interest. *Author's collection*

Airplane number two demonstrating a STOL landing at the 1977 Paris Air Show. Note the extended USB flaps and vortex generators behind the exhaust nozzle. *Courtesy of AIAA*

By early April 1977, the program had exceeded all its projected goals in terms of flight hours, test conditions accomplished, and data accumulated.

European Demonstration

Boeing had a strong desire to demonstrate the airplane to the Army in Europe, where they felt it had considerable application. The possibility of coupling this demonstration with a showing of the airplane at the Paris Air Show provided a unique opportunity. The USAF would approve such a demonstration only if the flying was part of the Initial Operational Test and Evaluation (IOT&E) normally used to demonstrate an aircraft in an operational environment. The planning for this trip began in late January and included an extensive series of demonstration flights. Fields visited included Wright-Patterson Air Force Base, United States; Mildenhall, England; Rhein-Main, Germany; Frankfurt, Germany; Heidelberg, Germany; Paris, France; Keflavik, Iceland; Goose Bay, Labrador; Andrews Air Force Base, United States; Pope Air Force Base, United States; Little Rock Air Force Base, United States; Loring Air Force Base, United States; and the Azores Islands. To make such a wide-ranging trip with a prototype airplane with one set of spares seemed a monumental task, and it was.

The airplane was leased to Boeing by the USAF for parts of this trip, which gave Boeing operational control of these portions. One of the reasons for this arrangement was that there would be passengers flown on the airplane for demonstration purposes, and the USAF was not in a position to handle that requirement. Approximately thirty airline-type seats were installed in the cargo compartment for crew and observers. Also installed was a closed-circuit TV camera system showing the view out the front of the airplane, which was displayed to the observers during ground and flight operations. These seats were full in virtually dozens of STOL demonstration flights.

In late April 1977, preparation began on the number two airplane for the IOT&E trip. Many changes had been made to this airplane during the preceding few weeks, and it was necessary to be sure that everything was correct. Ken Hurley's team conducted a point-to-point check of all changes made, to be sure the configuration was proper. To accomplish this check, the airplane was scheduled for lay-up between April 25 and May 7.

The newest modification to the nose gear steering was not available during the lay-up schedule. Everyone desired to have this modification installed even though there was still the specter of a shimmy problem. The modification required making irreversible changes to the existing

Airplane number two seen on display at Mildenhall, England. *Courtesy of the Boeing Company*

nose gear parts, adding further risk. The landing-gear parts showed up one week prior to departure. Number two was put into lay-up again for the gear. It was flown less than forty-eight hours before departure and encountered severe nose gear shimmy.

The only other nose gear available was on the number one airplane, and nobody was sure the gears were interchangeable. Major structural parts of the prototypes often were not, each being custom built. Still, the decision was made to interchange them. At two o'clock in the morning on the day before departure, Ken Hurley got a call from the shop chief saying the gear was installed, but each time it was retracted there was a loud cracking sound that could not be located. A complete magnifying-glass inspection of all structures and components associated with the gear was conducted. The concern was that the heavy shimmy encountered the day before might have damaged something in the hidden structure. The inspection revealed nothing, and so the decision was made to proceed with the trip. Inspection after every few days of flying was directed. Apparently, the gear just had to settle itself into its new fittings, because the problem went away. This incident was not important in itself, but serves to illustrate how operating with prototypes differs from operating with production airplanes, where more spares usually are available and parts interchangeability is ensured.

The entire demonstration trip was phenomenally successful. The YC-14 was accompanied for most of the trip by a C-141 to carry spare parts. On the over-water legs, the YC-14 was operated by a limited crew, with the rest of the team on the C-141. Over land areas, the YC-14 carried its own people. The entire support team used on the trip consisted of eighteen Boeing employees and five Air Force personnel, along with a cadre of backup people standing by at home in case of difficulties. The cadre never was needed. The airplane did not miss a single demonstration. It was flown by over twenty different pilots with skill levels from minimum to superior. The comments always were favorable, with landing performance singled out as most impressive. Landings and full stops were made routinely in less than 900 feet, some as short as 600 feet. Dozens and dozens of STOL landings were made under all kinds of conditions, including narrow, short runways. In spite of all the STOL landings made by crews inexperienced in the airplane, not a single tire was blown on the entire trip.

The long-stroke landing gear worked exceptionally well. I watched dozens of STOL landings and never once saw the main gear wheels come off the ground once they had touched down. The airplane would hit relatively hard on a STOL landing. The gear would compress and then rebound, but the wheel itself would never come up off the ground. After the airplane touched down, braking could begin immediately and remain on continuously.

The Paris Air Show

The YC-14 was considered the first exhibit airplane for the Paris Air Show that year, and it performed every day. The McDonnell Douglas YC-15 was also there and flew many demonstrations. Naturally, the Boeing people thought the YC-14 performance was superior. The YC-15 never aimed for the end of the field while making a STOL landing, as did the YC-14. Instead, they aimed for a point well down toward the center of the field. Thus, the landing performance of the airplanes never could be compared directly. The YC-14 made a number of flights with the seats in the cargo compartment filled with observers and with various visitors doing the actual flying

A Russian team was at Paris that year with one of their airplanes. During one day of the static display, a half-dozen Russian visitors toured both the YC-14 and YC-15, which were parked next to one another on the ramp. They went over our airplane very thoroughly, and after having seen both airplanes, the head of the Russian delegation pointed to the YC-14 and said, "That one will win." Their faith in the YC-14 configuration was reflected several years later when the Antonov Design Bureau produced the An-72, which closely resembled the YC-14.

It was at Paris that I felt that the top Boeing management finally began to appreciate what this airplane could do. Although they had been told how well the airplane was performing during its flight testing at Edwards, it was not until they actually saw it that they fully recognized its dramatic performance. After this top management group, headed by T. Wilson, had the occasion to be more closely associated with the airplane, fly in it, and talk to the crew members and the enthusiastic visitors, the support for the airplane and the AMST program increased markedly at the corporate level.

The YC-14 put on a spirited performance during the 1977 Paris Air Show at Le Bourget Airport. The McDonnell Douglas YC-15 is seen parked in the background. *Courtesy of the Boeing Company*

The YC-15 is seen at the Paris Air Show with the then-experimental CFM56 engine installed in the number 1 (left outboard) position, with the standard JT8D engines in positions 2, 3, and 4. *Courtesy of the Boeing Company*

Demonstrations in Germany

During midweek of the Paris Air Show, the YC-14 was taken to Germany to demonstrate it to the Army and to the German Air Force. At Rhein-Main, a major German air cargo distribution center, the airplane taxied into the cargo-handling area, lowered the ramp, and backed up under its own power to the loading dock. This same maneuver required an extended period of complicated ground handling for the C-5 or the C-141 to position up to the loading dock, whereas the YC-14 did it on its own in a matter of a few minutes. The airplane went on to Heidelberg, Germany, under conditions typical of western Europe—a light drizzle and about a 3,000-foot ceiling. The runway there was relatively short, very narrow, and covered with puddles of water. This base was used mostly by small, twin-engine turboprop airplanes, with an occasional C-130. The airplane maneuvered easily under the ceiling, landed right at the end of the runway, and stopped about halfway down in a mass of spray from the puddles. It then went into reverse thrust, backed up to the end of the runway, took off again, circled around, and landed once more. This was a very "dramatic STOL" demonstration of the YC-14's ability to operate from a small, out-of-the-way field.

Significant accomplishments:

- 13,542 miles of ferry flights
- 177 STOL landings
- 54 guest pilots
- 251 guest observers
- airplane flown 27 of 30 days

Everyone was extremely pleased with how the airplane performed on the European trip. The relative ease with which it was maintained and its ability to hold a tight schedule, involving many separate flights, was an outstanding demonstration for a prototype airplane, which had been in flight test for less than a year.

The airplane returned to Edwards AFB on June 23, 1977. A few tests remained, including minimum control speed with engine out and the loading of the M60 main battle tank. This tank was not flown on the YC-14, but it was loaded under its own power on the ground. During this time, a number of different US Air Force pilots were checked out on the airplane, and NASA pilots were given a chance to fly it as well. The image on page 98 shows the second prototype prior to taxi during one of these final flights at Edwards. The flight test program ended on August 8, 1977, exactly one year after it began, and the test team returned to Seattle.

Airplane number two demonstrating at Heidelberg, Germany, in June 1977. The YC-14 takes off on a rain-soaked day midway through the Combat Deployment Test of the Initial Operational Test and Evaluation (IOT&E). Observers at each point on the tour were favorably impressed with the new dimension being offered to tactical airlift: a highly maneuverable, wide-bodied, obviously powerful, and rugged airplane. *Courtesy of the Boeing Company*

The number two airplane during a late test flight at Edwards AFB. This photo shows the excellent visibility for the pilots. *Courtesy of the Boeing Company*

Test Results

The technical results of the flight test program are described in Boeing document D748-10130-1, "YC-14 Advanced Medium STOL Transport Final Flight Test Report." The summary of this report is as follows:

Test Results (Boeing Document D748-10130-1)

The YC-14 successfully performed the AMST mission. It impressively verified the application of advanced technology to large STOL transport design. Significant advances were made in propulsive lift, flight controls, and landing gear. Results of flight testing showed the YC-14 performance was better than those goals expressed quantitatively (see chart on page 99). The results of the YC-14 flight testing are summarized in the following paragraphs.

Takeoff and Landing Performance Meets Program Goals

The YC-14 could operate into and out of a 1,840-foot semiprepared runway (sea level, 103°F) with a 27,000-pound payload at the midpoint of a 400-nautical-mile combat radius mission. This is better than the 2,000-foot field length goal. Two-engine takeoffs were performed within 1,100 feet, and landing rolls were 600 to 800 feet, using maximum brakes and reverse power.

High Maneuverability Emphasizes Greater Survivability

Higher climb performance was achieved by the YC-14 than any other transport in its class. The aircraft reached 1,650 feet above ground level (AGL) within 1 mile from brake release and an average 3,210-feet-per-minute rate of climb (Edwards Air Force Base, 2,300-foot elevation, 100°F). The Initial Operational Test and Evaluation (IOT&E) target was 1,500 feet AGL. The YC-14 reached 2,070 feet AGL in the first 360° turn on a spiraling "combat" departure, averaging 45° bank and a 1,900-foot turn radius (102°F at Edwards AFB). The aircraft can reach 35,000 feet in less than ten minutes. Pilots maintain a 3,000-feet-per-minute descent on approach before smoothly transitioning to the normal 1,000-feet-per-minute descent rate for a STOL landing.

High maneuverability was demonstrated in the landing configuration. This is due to the excellent handling qualities, high roll control power, and safe speed margins on final approach. Landings were continued under adverse conditions, such as simulated engine failure or heavy crosswinds, with Level 1 pilot ratings. Direct crosswinds were 36 knots, with gusts to 39 measured at the ground station, equivalent to 48 knots at the 50-foot tower height. The electronic flight control system (EFCS) provided Level 1 pilot rating with safe performance margins by controlling angle of attack and airspeed while stabilizing aircraft attitude. Touchdown dispersion was minimized. Flight tests showed that during high levels of turbulence, further improvements in the EFCS control over airspeed are desired and have been identified.

Tests have verified a 3.0 g load-factor capability at the combat radius midpoint. A 2.5 g capability for the 53,000-pound overload payload exceeded the 2.25 g goal.

Large Cargo Compartment Capacity Offers Increased Capability

The M60 main battle tank (109,200 pounds) was loaded on the YC-14. It was driven aboard by an operational Army crew member. The tallest vehicle loaded was an 11-ft-high, 5-ton RT crane; the longest vehicle was a 46.1-foot-long, 5,000-gallon fuel truck. These ground-loading tests on the flight-ready aircraft verified that the cargo compartment capacity can handle over 90% of the Army oversized equipment.

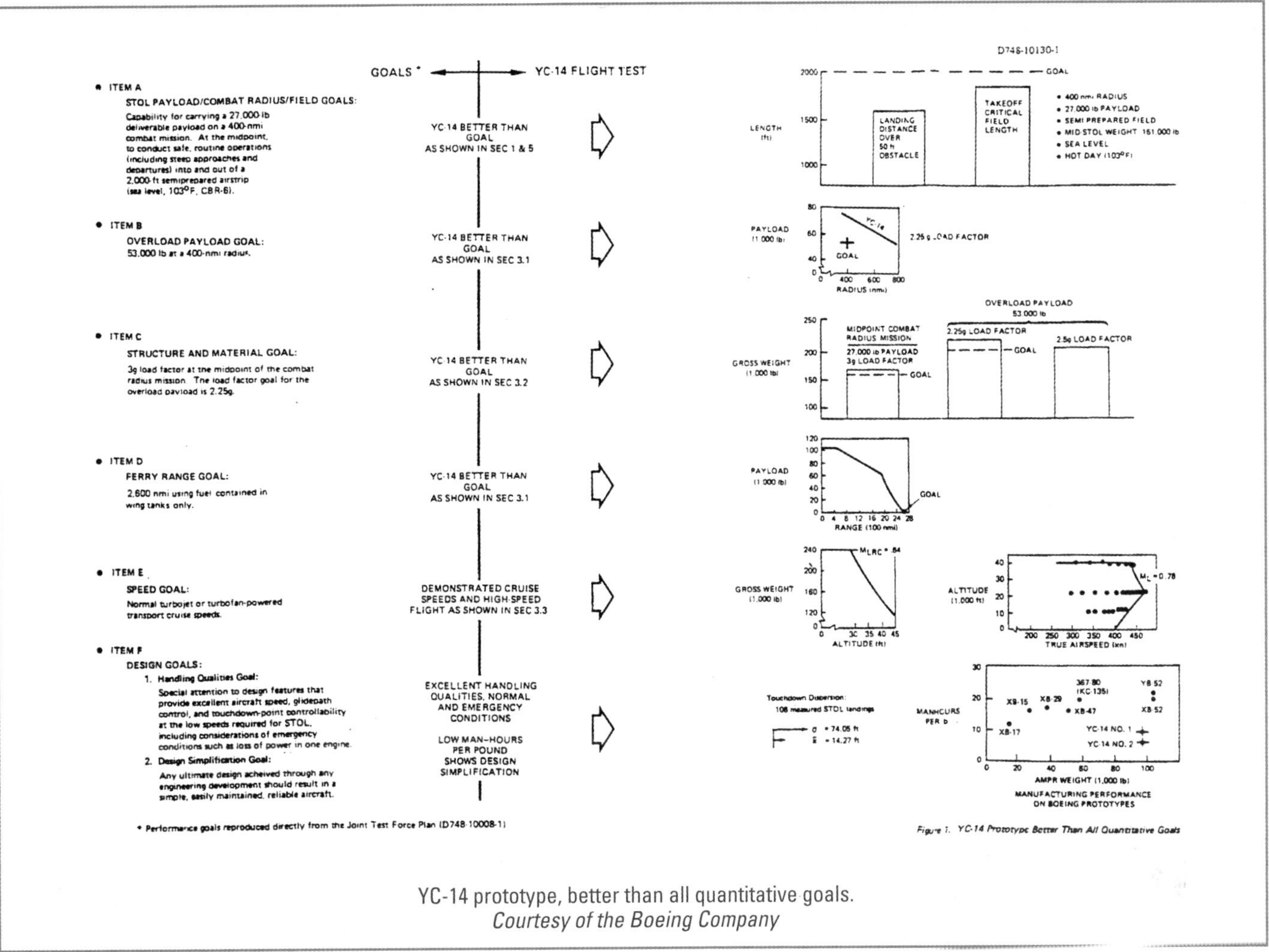

YC-14 prototype, better than all quantitative goals.
Courtesy of the Boeing Company

Airdrop Capability Enhances Combat Support

All airdrops were successfully performed. The heaviest load airdropped was a 20,000-pound platform, and the heaviest Low Altitude Parachute Extraction System (LAPES) drop was a 10,000-pound pallet. Aircraft flying qualities were excellent, with virtually no control inputs required by the pilot, an achievement attributable to the EFCS. Two troop jumps from the troop door were accomplished.

Low External Noise Lessens Combat Perimeter Detection

The YC-14 is quiet. Footprints of iso-intensity contours during takeoffs and landings are less than half the area of other transports in its class.

Rugged Aircraft Design Increases Ground-Maneuvering Performance

The capability of the long-stroke lever-action landing gear to perform at high sink rates and operate on rough fields was verified by flight test. The YC-14 landed at sink rates up to 15.4 feet per second and performed multiple passes on a semi-prepared runway. The aircraft demonstrated 180° turns within a total width of 69 feet. Good maneuverability and controllability were exhibited during backing maneuvers. Nose gear shimmy occurred during ten of the 1,368 landings. A program was initiated to develop improved stability to eliminate shimmy for the C-14 landing gear.

The YC-14 demonstrated the ability to drop large and heavy equipment during airdrop operations. *Courtesy of the Boeing Company*

Overwing Engine Avoids Ingestion

Sand and dust ingestion was avoided by the overwing engine installation, even during maximum thrust reverser operation. Visibility remained unimpaired during semi-prepared field operations. Walk-around areas were virtually unlimited with the thrust reversers deployed. Loadmasters and maintenance personnel have a quiet and safe environment in which to operate. Therefore, there was no need to shut down the engines, and, consequently, turnaround time was reduced.

Range and Payload Show High Capability

The YC-14 had a 736-nautical-mile radius capability with an overload payload of 53,000 pounds, compared with a 400-nautical-mile goal. A 2,630-nautical-mile ferry range with only internal-wing fuel was determined from flight testing. This compares with the 2,600-nautical-mile program goal.

Low Maintenance Cost Achieved by High Reliability

Aircraft reliability and maintainability were not emphasized during the prototype development program. Near the completion of the prototype program phase, the aircraft made a month-long IOT&E deployment, a representative operational maintenance environment. On that tour, the aircraft averaged only one squawk for every two flights, indicating the potential for good future reliability.

The high-performance margins of this aircraft allow reduced-thrust operation, which will extend engine life and reduce maintenance.

Unresolved Problems

Although the test program was an extremely successful demonstration of the STOL capability of an airplane involving new technology in aerodynamics, propulsion, mechanics, and flight control, there were a number of problems that never were resolved completely.

Boeing never was able to determine why the rudder cove seals destroyed themselves so quickly. They did know that similar problems had occurred on the Boeing 727, where they were fixed by simply stiffening up the seals to make them strong enough. In the case of the YC-14, much of the testing was done with these cove seals removed.

The biggest technical discrepancy of the flight test program was that of drag in the cruise configuration. Careful testing showed that the drag during cruise flight was about 10%–11% higher than had been predicted. This fairly severe error showed that the concern of the USAF aerodynamicists from Wright Field, several years earlier, certainly was well placed. By changing the fairing of the wheel well pods and by adding some small ventral fins on the back of the body, the drag was reduced about 4%, still leaving approximately a 7% discrepancy. The USAF, in their official report on the flight test, blamed the remaining 7% on the performance of the wing itself. I never felt that to be the case, because Boeing's analysis of the wing pressures and performance indicated that the wing was acting essentially as had been predicted. On the other hand, Boeing never ran the usual number of high-speed wind tunnel tests to carefully define the high-speed performance. At that time, the emphasis was on STOL and not cruise performance. I believe that most of the rest of the drag discrepancy involved the aerodynamics of the aft body and the improper measurement of engine flow effects on the wind tunnel model. Boeing just never had evaluated them properly (please see appendix 2, figure A-10, for the drag polar comparisons).

In contrast, the approach speed prediction under STOL conditions, utilizing powered lift, the USB flap, and all the new aerodynamic and control technology of the airplane, was correct within roughly 1 knot. This achievement, done mostly by aerodynamicists Tim Wang, Tom Zierten, and their team, was truly outstanding when one considers the completely novel configuration that Boeing had developed.

The third major item that never was sorted out completely during the flight test program was a small lateral tremble in the airplane that occurred during cruise flight. This vibration was essentially a body-bending mode that could be felt more strongly in the cockpit and also toward the aft end of the cargo compartment. In the center of the airplane, near the wing, it was less pronounced. It was very persistent and was felt at all airspeeds and altitudes. It seemed to be somewhat dependent on engine thrust but was there, to a slight extent, even at idle power. Boeing never was able to determine what caused this vibration, but it was noticeable enough that it certainly would have had to be eliminated to make a satisfactory production airplane.

CHAPTER 6

YC-14 Program Conclusion

Epilogue

It is interesting to reflect on the effects of the YC-14 program. It had a significant influence on subsequent production airplane proposals, as well as on the lives and careers of the people involved in the prototype development.

Production Proposal

By the time the YC-14 flight test program was completed, preparations were well underway for making a proposal for a production program. John "Jack" Steiner, famous for his design of the Boeing 727 and by then a corporate vice president, was brought in as C-14 program manager. Frank Verginia became his assistant program manager. Jim Copenhaver assumed the role of director of engineering. He had been a project engineer on the Boeing 737 and most recently had been director of engineering for the Boeing Commercial Company. I was made chief engineer of technology for the proposal airplane.

The proposal went through the usual frantic preparation. The mission requirement was essentially that of the prototype airplane, but slightly amplified to allow for more worldwide operation. The payloads remained essentially the same, and the airplane Boeing proposed was strictly a refinement of the prototype configuration. However, the production program never was to be, because it failed to get through the congressional budgetary gates. In the end, when questioned by the appropriate congressional committees, the USAF would not defend the AMST mission. The AMST program was in competition for funding with the Rockwell B-1 bomber, which at that time was a primary USAF objective. The Army defended the projected mission of the AMST airplane, saying that it would be very valuable to them in western Europe. The USAF, on the other hand, after spending several years defining the required operational capability (ROC) and another five years developing two different types of prototype airplanes, would not stand up and defend the mission as one they really needed. And with that, the AMST program died.

The Strategic Airplane

In 1981, the USAF projected the need for another transport having far less STOL capability but more strategic airlift potential than had the AMST airplanes. The airplane required to meet the new performance goals would be so large that Boeing could not compete with a twin configuration, because engines of that thrust class were not yet available. Therefore, the airplane submitted into that competition was a three-engine airplane. Two of the engines were mounted above the wing like on the YC-14, and a third was put in the tail, much like on a Boeing 727.

McDonnell Douglas submitted an airplane that was similar to their YC-15 configuration, with four engines under the wing, exhausting into an externally blown flap, with some capability as a STOL airplane. At the time of this competition, Boeing was heavily engaged in producing its line of commercial airplanes, primarily the 757 and 767 jetliners. McDonnell Douglas, on the other hand, had not yet recovered from the problems with the DC-10 and was struggling to keep the MD-80 program viable. In 1985, McDonnell Douglas was awarded the contract to develop the airlift airplane, which is now flying, ironically, as the Boeing (née McDonnell Douglas) C-17.

This is a model of the proposed Strategic Transport Trijet, with its 727-type tail design. *Dan Dornseif collection*

The Boeing C-17 airlifter. *Courtesy of the Boeing Company*

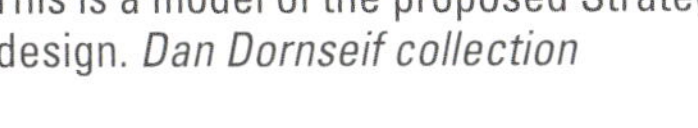

Disposal of the Prototypes

The two YC-14 airplanes were brought to Seattle to be in place to support the anticipated production program. It was felt that they would be a valuable addition to this production program because they could be used to flight test ideas and improve the design. When the AMST program was canceled, the USAF directed that the airplanes be placed in storage at Davis-Monthan Air Force Base and kept there for possible future use. The Museum of Flight in Seattle tried hard to have one of the airplanes left in Seattle for permanent exhibit, and Washington's congressional delegation indicated that such would be possible. However, the USAF insisted that both of the airplanes be moved to Arizona. It was a sobering day when I stood on the ramp and waved goodbye as Ray McPherson, the test pilot of the original first flight, took off and flew the last of the airplanes to leave on its final flight. After the airplanes were in Arizona, they were immediately stripped of all of their equipment, because much of it had been lent to Boeing by the suppliers. The number one airplane, years later, was moved to the Pima Air Museum in Tucson, Arizona, where it was put on display next to one of the YC-15s (see photos on page 104). The number two airplane still is in storage at Davis-Monthan and still displays the large "1" on the side of its nose that was placed there for the Paris Air Show.

Other STOL Development Programs

There were three serious STOL development programs occurring around the world that were influenced by the AMST program. All three programs had the opportunity to examine the extensive published data and view the flight demonstrations of both AMST prototype airplanes. Each one, without exception, chose the YC-14's upper-surface-blowing (USB) concept as their powered high-lift system.

John Wimpress stands in front of the first YC-14 built. After its last flight, the CF6-50 engines, borrowed from General Electric, were removed from the airplane. This aircraft currently resides at the Pima Air Museum in Tucson, Arizona. *Author's collection*

The first YC-14 is seen at Pima in company with its competitor, the YC-15. The YC-14 resides there to this day; however, the YC-15 is no longer on the premises. *Author's collection*

The second YC-14 prototype remains today at Davis-Monthan AFB in Arizona. *Courtesy of the Boeing Company*

NASA 715 was the test bed for the QSRA program. *Public domain (NASA)*

NASA's QSRA

NASA, after evaluating all of the various STOL concepts, chose USB for their Quiet Short-Haul Research Aircraft (QSRA). This airplane, which was developed from a de Havilland Buffalo, was modified by a Boeing team to have four turbofan engines over and ahead of the wing. During the late 1970s and early '80s, NASA 715 was tested extensively at extremely low speeds, including operations from a naval aircraft carrier without the use of arresting gear during landing or catapult during takeoff. However, the concept did not prove attractive enough either to the airlines or the military to result in a production program. Please see appendix 2, figure A-11, for technical details in the QSRA aircraft.

Japan's Asuka

The Japanese National Aerospace Laboratory, after spending several years developing a four-engine version of the YC-14 concept, abandoned further development in 1991 in spite of very successful and impressive demonstrations by their prototype airplane.

The Soviets' An-72/An-74

Boeing and McDonnell Douglas were not the only companies interested in producing a STOL-capable airlifter. Behind the Iron Curtain, Oleg Antonov was conducting his own experiments with similar objectives. In 1972, a new design study known as "Aircraft 200" commenced and by June 1973 had achieved the official designation of An-72. The gestation period for the new aircraft was lengthy, with its first flight occurring on August 31, 1977, trailing the YC-14 by more than a year.

Looking at the An-72, one immediately notices a strong resemblance with the YC-14. It's a smaller airplane, though, having a wingspan of about two-thirds that of the Boeing machine, and having engines with about one-third the power. However, the details of the nacelle and USB flap, which are so critical to making the powered-lift system work (such as the side door on the nozzle), are so identical to the YC-14 in concept that the resemblance cannot be coincidental. Antonov easily had access to the details of the Boeing design. Starting with the patent filing of January 1973, which showed the basic shape of the airplane, and continuing with technical papers given at SAE and AIAA meetings from 1973 to '75 that showed all these features in great detail, there was a steady flow of information during the period of the An-72 development. The entire power plant installation resembles the YC-14, right down to the engine drain mast used to drain fuel, oil, and hydraulic fluid seepages clear of the airframe, preventing fire hazards. In addition, the An-72 thrust reverser design was nearly identical to that on the YC-14. Antonov's team must have conducted their own tests to get the data needed to support their detail design, but certainly their starting point was the YC-14. To their great credit, they proceeded to put their design into production, building a total (including the commercialized version, An-74) of 195 airplanes.

The Japanese Asuka research aircraft was a highly modified Kawasaki C-1 military airlifter. *Courtesy of the Boeing Company*

Copying aircraft design features is not unusual. For instance, the YC-14 team got the idea of drooping the fuselage tail cones to reduce aft-body drag from seeing it done on predecessor airplanes, and presumably the An-72 history is the same.

Other areas showed marked differences between the two designs. Because of the lower wing loading of the An-72, a simpler high-lift system was used, employing leading-edge slats instead of the complex variable camber Krueger flaps used on the Boeing airplane. In order to enhance pitch control at low speeds, slats also were installed on the horizontal stabilizer, whereas the YC-14 employed a conventional stabilizer design.

The Antonov An-72 and the An-74 are an important part of the YC-14 story. While the YC-14 was a victim of changing military and political climates, the Russian aircraft has had a long and successful career. Many of these airplanes are still in operation today because of the rare and valuable performance enabled by the basic design. This evidence points to the idea that the YC-14 would have been successful in its own right had different political cards been dealt.

This view of a climbing An-72 shows distinct similarities to the YC-14. This aircraft is being operated by the Sudanese government. *Courtesy of Mehmet Mustafa Çelik via Wikimedia Commons (https://creativecommons.org/licenses/by-sa/4.0/, unmodified)*

Antonov An-72 CCCP-19795 is seen on display at the 1981 Paris Air Show. *Courtesy of Acroterion via Wikimedia Commons (https://creativecommons.org/licenses/by-sa/4.0/, unmodified)*

Management, Personalities, and Politics

It is interesting to review the management of the YC-14 program, both the personalities and the politics involved. This viewpoint, of course, is strictly my own, and others may feel much differently than I.

Management Anomalies

When the program began, the AMST team was made up of highly imaginative people who had excellent backgrounds in STOL flight and in airplane conceptual and detail design. They developed very rapidly a unique configuration promising unprecedented STOL performance.

They were given the task of building and demonstrating this airplane at a cost that none of them really felt was possible. As the emphasis of the program shifted from that of a STOL technology demonstrator to one of demonstrating an entire operational system, of which STOL was just a part, the cost problem became much more difficult. Expensive items never anticipated in the original proposal were required to make a reasonable operational demonstrator.

As the costs began to climb, Boeing corporate management repeatedly changed the program management in an effort to get the climbing costs under control. Each new program management team was not familiar with the airplane, and none succeeded in really changing the cost trends of the airplane development. They did, however, escape the blame that was placed on those initial pioneers who conceived the whole thing in the beginning.

On the USAF side as well, there was constantly changing program management. The System Program Office (SPO) at Wright Field in Dayton had at least four different leaders during the development and flight-test period. Each of these leaders came into the program essentially uninformed about STOL flight and its implications. All of them had to be educated in STOL technology and prototype aircraft construction.

The program seemed forced, as a matter of political expediency, to move a large item of construction into the North American plant at Tulsa. This was an expensive and time-consuming diversion to a program that could not afford it, but it appeared that it was the only way Boeing could ensure support by a very powerful element of Congress.

By the time construction of the airplane began, cost control was the dominant factor in the lives of the YC-14 team members. For most of the team's managers, controlling every detailed element of cost was receiving far more attention than the technical and practical development of the airplane. The program was reviewed over and over again by management councils both of the Aerospace Company and the Boeing Corporation. Most of these reviews were not particularly critical of the technical development. They were extremely critical of the cost performance and constantly directed the program management to hold the cost down. In their defense, however, the corporate management did end up paying the bill that was needed at least to demonstrate the airplane to some extent.

The full impact of the airplane's capability never was realized by top corporate management until they saw the airplane fly in Paris. There was a complete metamorphosis of their viewpoint when that happened. From then on, their support of the program became far stronger.

This continual shifting of Boeing and USAF program management, coupled with the vacillating support of Boeing's corporate management, undoubtedly interfered with the YC-14 concept demonstrating its ultimate potential. Again, though, Boeing's corporate position must be considered in light of the very difficult financial situation it was facing at the time.

Fortunately, most of the YC-14 engineering and manufacturing team members were insulated administratively from these management perturbations. Thus, their work was not affected appreciably. In fact, most of the people who worked on the YC-14 generally look back on it as one of their favorite Boeing experiences. For example, the engineering team on the propulsion system, which was a unique development, still met periodically in 1991 just to chat and reminisce. The entire team was small enough so that people could see the whole operation, and decisions were made at a far-lower level than is usual for a complex airplane design. The design approach used on the airplane of combining the designers, manufacturing, and tooling people into work-package teams was carried over into other Boeing airplane designs and became the foundation of the development program for the 777 airplane at Boeing. The leadership role of the YC-14 program in establishing this design approach was very satisfying to all of the participants.

The program was a very severe ground for managers, however, both within Boeing and within the USAF. I have already discussed Maynard Pennell, Bill Cook, and Jim Foody leaving the program—all people who helped lay the foundation for the YC-14. All of them left the company permanently either at the time they left the YC-14 program or very shortly thereafter. Dick Taylor, who had been sent to head the Boeing office in Washington, DC, returned several years later to continue an illustrious career in aircraft development. He became very well known for his work on certifying commercial twin-engine airplanes for long over-water flights, thereby opening the long-range air routes of the world to this configuration. Bob Person, who was the configuration engineer during the formative period of the airplane, went on to do a number of interesting design tasks at Boeing before he retired. On the other hand, Omar Bygland, who was the chief project engineer in charge of getting the drawings out and who put into practice for the first time the work-package team concept for efficient detail design, never again got to apply that technique in a comparable position on another Boeing airplane.

The head of manufacturing, Bud Hurst, retired shortly after the program was completed after a period of very poor health. His first assistant, Bill Shineman, continued a very satisfying career, becoming a vice president and division manager of two different Boeing Commercial Company divisions.

I was the only Boeing person to be with the YC-14 program from its very initial conception through to the end of flight testing. Shortly after the C-14 production proposal was submitted, I was asked to leave the program by the Steiner-Verginia management team, to the

I received the AIAA Aircraft Design Award on August 22, 1978, from Al Cleveland. The citation said: "Aircraft Design Award. For the conception, definition or development of an original concept leading to a significant advancement in aircraft design or design technology to John K. Wimpress in recognition of the prescience, knowledge and dedication he applied to the design and development of the YC-14 airplane. By perseverance and leadership, he succeeded in converting technical concepts into a novel and practical airplane." *Courtesy of AIAA*

extreme consternation of my associates and employees. Boeing engineers had a phrase that was used often to describe this type of transfer of power: "You can identify the pioneers by the arrows in their backs." I returned to the Commercial Company, where I was chief engineer for technology on the 757 and ended my career in 1986 as director of product development for the Renton Division of the Boeing Commercial Company. In 1978, I received the "Aircraft Design Award" from the AIAA for my role on the YC-14.

The situation in the USAF had some surprising similarities. At least one of the SPO directors left the USAF shortly after his tour on the program. The head of the JTF at Edwards Air Force Base, Colonel Floyd Stroup, resigned from the USAF very shortly after this program was completed. David Bittenbinder, one of the brightest and most promising young Air Force officers I had ever come in contact with, resigned from the USAF shortly after the production program was canceled. Colonel Kent Davidson, who was the deputy director for AFTEC during AMST tests at Edwards Air Force Base, was one of the USAF officers who did go on to have a very successful career in the Air Force, retiring as a major general.

Conclusion

In summary, I believe it can be said that the YC-14 was an extremely successful prototype airplane. It combined the leading edge of technology in several different areas to make an airplane having unique capability. It met or exceeded every single one of its STOL design goals and did a lot of other things as well. In terms of the efficiency of its design and construction, it exceeded every standard that existed up to that time within the Boeing Company, in spite of the fact that it overran its cost far beyond its contracted price. For its role as a technology demonstrator, it certainly would have to be deemed a complete success.

However, its mission as defined by the USAF ROC was far too limited and too compromised toward STOL capability to make it an aircraft of high overall utility. As the requirements pendulum swung away from STOL and toward longer range and more payload, the specific YC-14 configuration became less attractive. (There are those within the USAF community, though, who believe that the current airlift airplanes are so large and so strongly oriented toward the strategic mission that they never will be used as tactical airplanes, and that there still is a strong need for a truly tactical transport like the YC-14.) Similarly, from a commercial standpoint, there is a very limited requirement for STOL airplanes in the total transportation environment. Although the situation may change someday, currently, space and runways are not expensive enough to warrant compromising the capability of a commercial airplane to any extent to achieve very short field lengths.

The basic YC-14 configuration is highly compromised for STOL, and it is doubtful that large quantities of airplanes based on this design concept ever will be seen in the transportation system of the world. However, in my opinion, if there ever is a requirement for a large STOL airplane, it will be based on the YC-14 design.

Reflections of Y-14 Program Team Members

In this section of the book are shown the post-program observations of several direct participants who held responsible positions. These individuals responded graciously to my invitation to describe the program from their viewpoint. Their statements are given here directly as written, without changes or editorial comment.

Flying the YC-14

Ray L. McPherson, Boeing YC-14 Project Pilot

A description of the airplane's operation from a pilot's viewpoint is given by Boeing project pilot Ray McPherson. Ray McPherson was assigned to the YC-14 program in its very early stages and made countless contributions both to design philosophy and details as the configuration developed. He followed the program through to the end, being the pilot not only on the first flight, but also on the final ferry mission to storage. In 1981, Ray received the American Institute of Aeronautics and Astronautics (AIAA) Octave Chanute Award for his work on the YC-14. This award is given to "pilots or test personnel that advance the art, science, and technology of aeronautics."

Being assigned to the YC-14 program as the project pilot turned out to be the most interesting experience of my forty years of flying. I was assigned to the program about two years before the initial flight, so that it was possible for me to become involved in some of its design features, particularly in the cockpit area. Many hours were also spent in an engineering flight simulator developing the electronic flight control system (EFCS) to optimize pilot handling qualities. The results of the flight test program, and the opinions of approximately twenty pilots who were fortunate enough to fly the YC-14, verified the simulator time was well spent. Changes were made to the EFCS during the flight test program, but the basic concept of the control wheel steering attitude hold system was well defined prior to the first flight and completely acceptable to all of the pilots involved.

It provided the pilot with excellent handling qualities throughout the flight envelope. He had the impression the airplane was being flown by an autopilot at all times. He could make well-coordinated pitch-and-roll attitude changes using normal pilot techniques, but when he released the controls, the EFCS maintained the new attitude and provided platform stability normally associated with an autopilot.

Airplane number one (*foreground*) and airplane number two in formation flight. Ship one wears a bare metal finish even today at the Pima Air Museum. Airplane two was painted early on in the standard USAF camouflage, looking the part of a military airlifter. *Courtesy of the Boeing Company*

Lateral control breakout forces were approximately 2 pounds, and about 12 pounds were needed to obtain full aileron control. Pitch forces were also light, and consideration had been given to using a control stick rather than the conventional wheel and column. This would have given the pilots a better view of the forward instrument panel, but there was concern expressed by some pilots in using a control stick in their left hand. Simulator studies proved this was not a valid concern, but it was never tried in the airplane.

The climb and cruise portion of the flight envelope, from a pilot's standpoint, was fairly conventional. The climb performance of the YC-14 was its most impressive feature in this area. At a STOL weight of 160,000 pounds at takeoff, the airplane could reach a cruise altitude of 40,000 feet in about twelve minutes—considerably better than conventional jet transports. It could compete with some subsonic jet fighters of its day.

The rest of this discussion will concentrate on the STOL characteristics of the YC-14. They are what made the airplane so interesting to fly. Its unique system of powered lift, derived from a concept called upper surface blowing (USB), was very apparent because of the big turbofan engines located on the top of the wing, and the large USB trailing-edge flaps located on each side of the fuselage. The location of the engines also had other advantages, such as less tendency for foreign object damage (FOD), reduced infrared signature and noise because of wing shielding, a safer and quieter environment for ground personnel around the airplane when engines were running, and an excellent position for locating thrust reversers, which will be discussed later.

Under standard sea level conditions, the General Electric CF6-50 engines were rated at 48,000 pounds of thrust each. At a STOL gross weight of 160,000 pounds, they provided a thrust-to-weight (T/W) ratio of 0.6, which was about twice that available in jet transports of that time period. Because of the twin-engine configuration having a requirement for engine-out operation from a 2,000-foot field, STOL takeoffs with both engines operating resulted in takeoff rolls of approximately 1200 feet. Throttling back an engine at the critical engine speed of 70 knots resulted in takeoffs of less than 2,000 feet. It should be noted here that the USB system was not used for takeoff.

Several tests were conducted making STOL takeoffs with one engine shut down at brake release. Because full throttle on the good engine could not be used until about 70 knots, takeoff rolls required about 2,300 feet, exceeding the 2,000-foot STOL field length. This type of takeoff was not a design objective, but it did demonstrate the takeoff performance available in the STOL configuration.

Boeing test pilot Ray McPherson (*left*) with USAF pilot Major David Bittenbinder in the cockpit of the YC-14. *Courtesy of the Boeing Company*

One unique feature to improve engine-out takeoff and initial climb performance on the YC-14 consisted of automatically retracting the outboard trailing-edge flap on the good engine side and extending the USB flap on the dead-engine side when the loss of thrust was sensed. It required no action by the pilot to obtain the split-flap configuration, and the resulting reduction in drag and increase in lift was significant. Most designers of flap systems on an airplane take every precaution to prevent flaps from splitting during extension or retraction. The system on the YC-14 performed perfectly throughout the flight test program and measurably enhanced engine-out takeoff and climb-out performance without increasing pilot workload or reducing system reliability.

The only thing that pilots needed a little time to get used to on a STOL takeoff was the fast acceleration of the airplane and the short ground roll. Good coordination between the pilot and copilot in setting takeoff thrust and monitoring engine operation helped.

Maneuvering with flaps down at approximately 150 KIAS right after takeoff was excellent up to approximately 45° bank angles. Good climb capability during this maneuvering allowed the pilot to stay in close to the field until he could climb clear of any hazards before heading out on course.

From a pilot's standpoint, the STOL approach and landing characteristics of the YC-14 were its most interesting features. In order to take full advantage of the powered-lift system and reduce approach and landing speeds for STOL operation, the airplane was flown on the backside of the thrust-required-versus-airspeed curve. This would normally require a pilot to change his flight path control techniques on a conventional airplane. For instance, pulling back on the longitudinal control, with no change in thrust, would increase the sink rate and result in a steeper flight path angle. On the front side, the same technique would result in a shallower flight path angle. To eliminate the requirement to change from conventional piloting techniques during approach and landing, the YC-14 EFCS was designed to allow the pilot to use normal flight path control, and the airplane responded as if it were on the front side of the thrust-required curve. In fact, the YC-14 was easier to fly on a STOL approach compared to a conventional airplane, even though it was on the backside, because airspeed was automatically maintained for the pilot. This was done by the pilot dialing in the desired speed for the approach and landing, usually 85 KIAS. This speed was displayed on a digital readout in the cockpit. The EFCS then electrically modulated the USB flaps, which were fly-by-wire controlled, to maintain that speed. Using a normal 6° flight path angle on the approach, the USB flap was extended approximately 40°, but in turbulence or during excessive maneuvering, it could modulate plus or minus 10°–15° around that angle. As the USB flap angle increased, the airplane drag and lift vector changed to decrease airspeed. Reducing the USB flap angle caused an increase in airspeed. The throttles were electronically modulated to maintain the desired angle of attack so as to obtain or maintain the proper lift and maneuver margin. Because airspeed and angle of attack were maintained automatically on a STOL approach, the pilot workload was reduced considerably. I usually kept a hand on the throttles just to monitor their movement but never found it necessary to overcontrol the EFCS.

Good forward and down visibility is a major design requirement for any STOL airplane. The YC-14 met this requirement with large front and side windows. The fuselage attitude during approach was also a design consideration. It was nose high enough to keep the nosewheel from contacting the ground first on a no-flare landing, but low enough to allow over-the-nose visibility so that the pilots could easily see the approach end of the runway during the approach. It was also low enough to reduce the de-rotation time to a minimum after main gear touchdown, so that maximum wheel brakes could be applied, drag spoilers extended, and thrust reversers operated immediately after touchdown.

The STOL approach was made using a 6° flight path below the horizon rather than the approximately 3° used on conventional airplanes. Because of the low STOL approach speed of 85 KIAS, the descent rate was only about 800 feet per minute, depending on wind conditions. The slow speed and steeper angle on approach also gave the pilot time to better judge his touchdown point on landing, usually 200 to 500 feet past the approach end of the runway. The touchdown was normally made with no flare required by the pilot. Ground effect under calm or headwind conditions would usually reduce the sink rate prior to touchdown by approximately 25%, and sink rates of less than 600 feet per minute at touchdown were acceptable. A tailwind on the approach and landing had a tendency to eliminate the ground effect and increase the descent rate, so early recognition of this type of condition was an indication to the pilot that some flare prior to touchdown would be required.

A form of direct lift was also designed into the STOL approach configuration of the YC-14. The EFCS automatically extended the wing spoilers symmetrically 2° above the wing surface. If the pilot made a small nose-up input on the control column during approach, the spoilers automatically dropped down, giving a small lift increment equivalent to approximately 0.1 g. An input in the opposite direction extended the spoilers to 4° above the wing surface, resulting in a loss of lift. Because these small changes in lift could be made rather quickly, with no change in body attitude, the pilot could make small but quick changes to his flight path angle, giving him very precise control.

This precise control, combined with good visibility, slow approach speeds, and no flare landings, allowed all pilots, even those with low experience levels, to accurately and consistently make good short-field landings. Pilots have always taken a lot of pride in making good landings, and the YC-14 proved to be a good ego builder in this area. STOL landing distances of 700 to 800 feet were routine, even on dirt strips. The shortest distance measured on a concrete runway was about 350 feet, but I believe there was at least a 10-knot headwind blowing that day. Crosswind landings did not present any problems, even though at the slow approach speeds used, the crab angles were in excess of 20°. [Author's note: "Crabbing" refers to turning the aircraft into the wind to correct for crosswinds for a desired ground track, while "de-crabbing" means that this correction is eliminated at the last moment before touchdown to align the aircraft with the runway.] Depending on the direction of the wind, the pilots would find themselves looking through the side windows during approach.

Because of the attitude hold capability of the EFCS, a wings-level crab technique proved to be the easiest way to make a crosswind approach. At the proper altitude, usually about 50 feet above the runway, the pilot applied full rudder in the proper direction and de-crabbed prior to touchdown. Rudder control power at a speed of 85 KIAS provided a good yaw rate, and there was no rolling tendency during de-crab because the attitude hold capability of the EFCS held the wings level. Some crosswind landings, up to approximately 40 knots, were made without de-crabbing and were satisfactory but uncomfortable, but de-crabbing proved to be the best technique.

The thrust reversers on the YC-14 were located on the top of the engines and were actuated on the ground by the throttle levers being pulled back past an idle detent. This was a natural pilot motion, and quick opening of the reversers was possible without the pilot having to take his hand off the throttles. For the reversers to be effective on a STOL landing, the quick response to a pilot command was necessary because of the short landing roll and time to stop. The pilot also did not want the engines to decelerate after touchdown. Being on top of the engines and deflecting the engine thrust forward and up, the reversers applied additional load on the main gear for more effective brake operation. They also did not cause any loss in forward visibility because of blowing dust, so common on propeller-driven airplanes. The reversers also were very effective in ground maneuvering without any jet wash hazards to ground personnel or equipment.

The pilot's instrument panel included a TV tube in place of the conventional attitude indicator. Symbology was presented on the screen to include pitch and roll attitude, but additional data such as flight path angle, flight path acceleration and deceleration, indicated airspeed, and raw data Instrument Landing System [ILS] deviation were also included.

The picture from a forward-looking, low-light-level TV camera mounted in the nose of the YC-14 could also be superimposed on the TV screen. The pitch attitude marks were scaled to coincide with the outside world so that the pilot had an integrated flight display, including the outside world "real" horizon. It was an attempt to provide a head-down display [for] the pilot that would demonstrate approaches and landings under instrument conditions, without the use of ground aids such as an ILS. It would allow a pilot to make a precise approach and landing without looking outside the airplane. For instance, the pilot could approach a field in level flight at some convenient altitude, such as 1,000 feet. The TV camera picture on his display showed him when his intended landing spot was 6° below the horizon on his display scale. At this time, he would lower the flight path symbol to coincide with the touchdown point. It was then an easy matter to follow the flight path symbol to the touchdown point in a head-down condition without having to look outside. Although not much time and money was spent on developing this concept during the program, it did demonstrate the potential for such a system for use in remote fields with no active landing aids such as an ILS. It was rather easy to visualize forward-looking radar being used under low-visibility conditions to help a pilot complete his mission.

Not many pilots have had an opportunity to use a flight path display in their everyday flying. They learned instrument flying using a pitch attitude display and adapted to it quite well. The use of a flight path display makes flying, especially instrument flying, much easier. For instance, during flight, pitch attitude is constantly changing with speed and configuration changes, but the flight path can be a constant. This is especially true when holding level flight while decelerating to a landing configuration. Flight path can be held on the horizon to maintain level flight, while pitch attitude varies considerably. Making accelerating and decelerating turns [during] level flight on the YC-14 could be done very easily by just keeping the flight path symbology on the horizon on the pilot's display. Pitch attitude changes could be ignored.

In summary, I considered the YC-14 to be a milestone in the development of STOL military transport technology. Most of the features which pilots felt were necessary for successful STOL operation were included in its design and were proven to be successful during its six hundred hours of flying. Having the privilege of flying it and being associated with the Boeing Company and Air Force personnel responsible for its being were the most interesting experiences of my flying career.

Maj. David Bittenbinder, Air Force Project Pilot

Dave Bittenbinder was a young captain when he first came to the YC-14 program, and he became a major during that assignment. He rapidly became an expert on the airplane's flight-control system and made many contributions toward its development. Faced with the prospect of a desk job at the end of the YC-14 program, he left the active Air Force and became a test pilot on the Lockheed L-1011. At the completion of that program, he became a quality control manager and, as of 1994, was a program manager in Lockheed's famous "Skunk Works." Bob Spitzer, the young controls engineer Dave refers to, is, as of 1994, vice president for engineering in Boeing's Commercial Airplane Company.

My selection to be the Air Force YC-14 project pilot was completely unexpected. I graduated from the Test Pilot School (TPS) in June 1973 and was informed in August that I had been selected for one of the prime positions at Edwards Air Force Base. I can assume that my recent experience in C-130 operations was the driving factor in this selection. It could not have been politics, since I was in the squadron only two months, and "political, I ain't."

My first trip to the Boeing flight-control simulator laboratory occurred about September 1973. On that occasion, after crashing and burning about a million times, I announced that I figured the control system as then configured was extremely poor and would never hack it. I am still impressed that Boeing took my comments well and developed a final configuration, which I think was years ahead of its time during the flight testing of 1976 and 1977. Strangely enough, I even became fast friends with some of the flight-control guys like Bob Spitzer and others whose names I do not recall. Speaking of Bob, I often felt in awe because he knew more about everything than I did about anything—a great guy! I remember one episode when I was having dinner with him and his family, and he received a call from his church group to give aid to a troubled teenager. Bob asked me along, and en route he explained that we were to rescue this young man from one of the seediest areas in the city. We walked in, probably the only ones in the placed unarmed, and Bob convinced the young fellow to come home with us. Bob also introduced me to hang gliding during a Saturday trip to Whidbey Island. These examples give an insight to my actual relationship with the contractor, in contrast to the adversarial relationship that the Air Force, during Test Pilot School, had led me to expect.

I guess the Air Force did a good job of instilling this adversary attitude, because I really was suspicious of everything I was presented. I was convinced everyone was a salesman and could not be trusted. Over time, Ray McPherson completely destroyed this mindset. He always was open, honest, and professional. I learned so much not only about flight testing but about life from Ray that I am proud that he was not only a mentor but remains a friend.

As far as Boeing management was concerned, I thought it was excellent. All technical challenges were worked and solved. I am sure many internal scraps occurred, but they were very professionally contained and never impacted relationships with us Edwards folks. I suspect the SPO guys might have a different story, but the Air Force charters were that Dayton would handle the money and we would do the flight test job.

On the other hand, I had some beefs about the Air Force management. One was that we were not getting the Army to sign up to the program. I considered this to be suicide, because without Army support in DoD and Congress, the program just wasn't going to survive. We also downplayed real performance achievements during the program. My opinion was that when we demonstrated results far above the goals, we should spread the word. My arguments fell on deaf ears, or worse, and caused my eventual censure. I still think the approach taken was a disservice to the country as well as to the competitors. I really think you would have invested less if you had known that the program go-ahead was not aggressively supported by the Air Force and Army.

Another management anomaly that bugged me was the requirement that contractor pilots be graduates of the Air Force Test Pilots School. It seemed that every time I turned around, I had to write a waiver request for Ray. Here was a guy who wrote the book, had dozens of test programs under his belt, but never had gone to TPS (he could have taught it). Here was I, young, inexperienced, virtually no test experience, but fully qualified by virtue of a military school.

One more kudo to the Boeing management team is that in 1974, after the funding was resolved, they forecast a date in 1976 for the first flight and held it. Not only was the flight on time, but the airplane was virtually free of open items. I did not realize how impressive this all was at the time, but I sure do now. I wonder if any project has achieved that kind of success since. Boeing sure has not been vocal about the YC-14 prototype performance on programs I have worked since (ATF and A/FX), but I think they demonstrated a capability that would be worthy of note in the current world of defense acquisition.

As to the aircraft itself, what can I say? It was a sweetheart. It flew like a dream and performed better than required. The excess thrust of the two-engine design gave it fighter-like characteristics with both engines operating and met the performance requirements with one engine out. The flight-control system greatly reduced pilot workload in all flight regimes. With one engine failed, the system handled the roll and yaw, and enough margin was left to handle either a go-around or a continued STOL landing. There also were further capabilities we never got around to exploring.

Among those were the air delivery capabilities. I remember after one late-night flight-control development simulator session, Spitzer and I went off to have a quiet beer. We got to discussing airdrops, and I suggested that with powered lift we should be able to control deck angle without complex flap setting and airspeed machinations. Bob went to work, and I evaluated the flight-control airdrop mode in the simulator a couple of weeks later. It was a real improvement over what I had been used to in conventional airplanes. In flight test, especially in turbulence, we found it could use a bit more improvement, but I think the basic idea would have been a real contributor to accuracy and efficiency during combat aerial deliveries.

One area which I found to need further development was cockpit controls and displays. At the time (1974), we were at the leading edge of this technology and needed flight test to come to final resolution of what was good or bad. We were definitely on the right track and only needed more "big wind tunnel" definition to solve the equation. One excellent example of this is the forward-looking sensors. The growth potential of the low-light TV has been combat-proven by systems such as infrared on the F-117 and the "Lantern"-equipped F-16.

One real challenge was landing from a very steep glide slope. Because I did much of the landing performance work, I became very comfortable with the "ground rush" the pilot experiences with a nominal 6° glide path. As we got into the later parts of the program, we had many familiarization flights for "guest" pilots of various backgrounds, and I found them all to be rather uncomfortable with the sensation of approaching the ground so rapidly. In actual fact, due to the low approach speed, the sink rate was normal for a jet transport, and ground effect sink attenuation resulted in really smooth landings without pilot input.

Alexander Kent Davidson, Air Force Evaluator's Viewpoint

General (then Major and, later, Colonel) Kent Davidson was one of the few USAF officers to follow the AMST program from beginning to end. He was in the Pentagon when the ROC was being prepared, and represented AFTEC at Kirtland Air Force Base during the proposal evaluation as well as during the design, construction, and flight test phases of the program.

As I reflect back on my own experience on the AMST prototype program, I have a great many fond memories. For me it was a particularly unique opportunity to participate in the entire life cycle of a new aircraft. Beginning in about 1969 while at the Pentagon, I had the chance to work with Hank Van Gieson and others at Headquarters Tactical Air Command (TAC), developing the original operational requirements for a jet-powered C-130 replacement. Finally, in 1972 (with the help of David Packard and, in my opinion, a bit of luck) the AMST prototype program became a reality. I had the good fortune to be selected by TAC to head up their participation in the flight test effort. Later, when the Military Airlift Command (MAC) became the parent command, I was doubly fortunate to be able to stay with the job I had begun many years earlier. Flying both of the prototypes was a dream come true for me, and the performance and handling qualities of the prototypes certainly met and exceeded my expectations. I do not think any pilot who flew the YC-14 could avoid the indelible impression that this was a transport aircraft unlike any other transport aircraft. The very high thrust-to-weight ratio combined with a powerful control system made it possible to do things with this aircraft you could only dream about in other large aircraft. I found the aircraft to be a true delight to fly.

The "fly-by-light" digital flight-control system was well thought out. Control forces were relatively light, and the electronic augmentation system did its job well without being overly intrusive. The propulsion system was outstanding. The very large high-bypass General Electric turbofans provided what must have been the greatest margin of reserve thrust ever installed in an aircraft of this type. Although they were subjected to a considerably more stressful environment in the test program than they were designed for, these engines proved to be highly reliable and responsive as well as quiet and fuel efficient. With ample quantities of thrust and control power readily available and well harnessed, the maneuvering capability of the aircraft was essentially constrained only by the pilot's imagination (and, of course, the prototype structural placards).

The flight demonstrations by the YC-14 at Paris and many military bases produced an audience response I have never seen equaled before or since. After every flight, literally scores of people, often pilots themselves, would seek out the crew and express their amazement at the performance of the aircraft. I also had the opportunity to serve as safety pilot for many guest pilots, and it was a special pleasure to observe how well many of these pilots flew the YC-14 on their first attempt.

Flying the aircraft with confidence and precision was definitely the norm rather than the exception. The YC-14 was such a good flying airplane that it was sometimes hard to believe it was, in fact, a handbuilt prototype using a relatively large number of off-the-shelf components from other aircraft. Certainly, the prototypes had some fault, but these faults were for the most part simply minor annoyances associated with the early stage of development of the aircraft. Overall, and particularly in terms of the basic concept, this aircraft was a splendid piece of work. I think it is a great tribute to the foresight and skill of Jack Wimpress and his talented engineering team and Ray McPherson and the Boeing flight test organization, as well as the tremendous support of GE and the many other key vendors, that this most unusual and unique airplane came out of the blocks on schedule, breezed through its airworthiness and other preliminary checks, and then executed an extremely demanding flight test program virtually without a hitch.

This level of success has rarely if ever been seen in the development of a totally new aircraft and, to my knowledge, had never been previously approached on a design as unconventional as the YC-14. In point of fact, the past history of the DoD in flight testing STOL and V/STOL aircraft had been very checkered. Until the AMST, nearly all such programs had been characterized by the loss of one or more of the flight test vehicles and by aircrew fatalities. That the YC-14 completed its very challenging test program, including many tests normally conducted only with full-scale production articles, made a highly successful deployment to Europe and the Paris Air Show, made visits and demonstrations at numerous overseas and Continental US (CONUS) military bases, and did it all on a very compressed schedule without significant mishaps of any kind involving either of the two prototype airframes is the clearest possible confirmation of a quality design and a sound program.

Many people, especially those of us who worked directly on the YC-14 and 15, were very disheartened and disappointed, to say the least, when the source selection for the production program was abruptly terminated. There were a number of reasons why this happened—the entire story might be worthy of a book in its own right someday. All that notwithstanding, I find it fascinating (and more than a little ironic) that although the US was unable to proceed to production with either of its new medium-jet STOL transports, the former USSR and now the CIS produced in quantity a somewhat smaller but remarkably close copy of the YC-14, the Antonov An-72/74. By all reports, this has been a very successful design and has proven to be a flexible and dependable workhorse transport. It certainly brings to mind the old adage that imitation is the sincerest form of flattery! Jack Wimpress, perhaps more than any other individual connected with the program, should revel in that flattery. I know Jack put a great deal of himself into what was an absolutely magnificent flying machine. Jack Wimpress can be justly proud of an accomplishment few engineers will ever experience and fewer still could ever hope to match.

One of the simple truths that came out of this program for me was the confirmation of a notion I held before the program began. That notion was simply that there are many benefits, not all of them obvious, to be gained from a "higher than normal" thrust-to-weight ratio on a military transport aircraft. I would apply this philosophy independently of the number of engines the aircraft has, and would accept a moderate decrement (within reason) in cruise specifics to obtain the advantages of the extra reserve thrust. My experience flying the YC-14 showed me firsthand in many, many ways that this is the way to go with a military transport. Given the continuing and very impressive progress being achieved in engine development, I think this is a very doable concept. I think another way to frame this idea is to look at it in terms of a parallel with another well-known program.

The F-16 has been called the most successful military aircraft program of the century. Many feel that the fundamentals of the design concept were what made this such a great aircraft and paved the way for its unprecedented success in the field (and in the marketplace). The lightweight-fighter concept was built around the combination of a very high (higher than normal) thrust-to-weight ratio and a low (lower than normal for a fighter) wing loading. This combination did good things for the F-16, and I would argue that an extension and refinement of the same basic concept could do equally good things for a military transport aircraft. Unfortunately, we did not quite achieve this with the C-17, and I think we are already regretting it—but maybe next time.

James Hutton, A Working-Level View

Jim Hutton was a working-level engineer in the weights technology staff during the YC-14 development. He consulted several of his compatriots from that period in preparation for making the following observations. Jim now is a technical manager, having broad responsibility in the development of Boeing's commercial airplanes.

What was it like to be a working-level contributor supporting the YC-14 development? To a person, the response is a warm smile, nodding head, and the phrase "The best experience I ever had." Why? Reasons given are amazingly consistent and include a strong sense of personal contribution, the demonstrated trust of management, and the teaming approaches embedded in the program. Also, we were highly motivated. We recently had helped to develop the 747 and were developing the National Supersonic Transport until it was terminated. Aerospace development opportunities were few in the early to mid-1970s. The YC-14 was an "oasis" for a skilled development workforce surrounded by a "desert" of a few opportunities.

All of the reasons given included one central message: "The bosses let me and the people I worked with do our jobs to the fullest extent we ever experienced." While management left no doubt who was in charge, there was a clear commitment to trust and acceptance of the opinions of the working-level contributors. No messengers were shot, no matter how bad the news, and we surely had bad news days. We felt appreciated for exposing problems. This attitude produced an unusual personal desire to identify remedies as a participant in the development, as opposed to adding to the problems management had to overcome. While most managers desire this approach, the YC-14 management did it.

Technically, the YC-14 was challenging:

1. As a product, the Lockheed C-130 was our benchmark, and it is an excellent, cost-effective solution in the marketplace. Carrying the XM1 (now the M1A1) battle tank is an example of one "next step" necessary to compete with the C-130.
2. Considering airspeeds varying from STOL to M = 0.72 cruise, the YC-14 dynamic pressure (q) range was larger than airplanes most of us had supported. Application of USB on this scale was unprecedented. Maintaining stability, control, and good handling characteristics with USB over that q range was a particular challenge.
3. To produce a C-14 at $5 million per unit, design definition and production techniques needed to be carefully comprised.
4. Development funding was limited; therefore, our judgment, supported by a few tests, was a key to airplane development.
5. As the program matured, the airplane changed from a USB demonstrator to a product demonstrator. Added systems (cargo doors and handling systems) and capabilities (real airdrops) were defined into the airplane with what seemed like no relief in schedule and little increase in resources.

Prototyping provided a significant relief in planning and documentation for production, product support in the field, and military specifications compliance. However, design and production approaches were based on commercial airplane practices. Safety was never compromised by design intent. System redundancies, design of components, and construction of structures reflected these standards. Specific YC-14 issues were addressed (e.g., structural concepts for reacting excessive acoustic loadings on the fuselage due to USB flow impingement). Prototype tooling was one of a kind and highly innovative.

We felt the lack of testing to verify our judgment was a risk. Examples of risk abatement follow.

1. For critical structures, prototype factors, usually 25%, were added to calculated applied loads.
2. For many joints, once a fastener was selected, the joint was sized to the fastener capability instead of the applied load.
3. For very high risks, tests were conducted (e.g., fuselage acoustic loadings).
4. We were consulted prior to decisions on risk abatement.

An environment for teaming was strictly enforced. In retrospect, this was a Design/Build Team (DBT) or Integrated Product Team (IPT) approach before we knew those names. Meetings were delayed or rescheduled because a finance, operations, or engineering representative was not present—not for just big, high-level issues, but typically for any issue. Program issues continually were shared with us by the bosses, in person and directly. Engineering design groups were located in the factory. We were all involved together.

On the way to a meeting, we jokingly said to Jack Wimpress that this airplane was our "Dash 80" (the 707 prototype, where many earlier Boeing engineers had cut their teeth), and he had better not muck it up by not consulting us. Jack called our bluff. The YC-14 itself demonstrated the results.

CHAPTER 6

Appendixes

Appendix 1
A Technical Look at the YC-14

There are two principal parameters that are available to the designer of a jet-powered airplane to change the airplane's performance (in terms of range, field lengths for takeoff and landing, and cruise altitude) once the overall configuration has been chosen and the payload has been defined in terms of weight and cargo compartment size. These two parameters are the thrust loading (i.e., sea-level static thrust divided by weight [T/W]), and the wing loading (i.e., weight divided by the wing area [W/S]). These two parameters are shown as the axes of the STOL Airplane Design Chart on page 119. The configuration being represented on the plot is a twin-engine airplane having a wing with essentially no sweepback and a good aerodynamic high-lift system. Each spot on the T/W-W/S field represents an airplane of this general configuration having the same gross weight but with its own unique engine and wing size.

The ovals are lines of constant range, with the center point showing the maximum range available for this general configuration and gross weight. Although this particular figure was developed using some highly simplified equations for the effects of wing and engine size on weight and drag, it is quite typical of results that might come from a more sophisticated approach. The values have been normalized to make 1.0 the performance of a representative good STOL airplane. For optimum range, the wing loading is about 110 pounds per square foot, which is characteristic of many good subsonic transports. The range becomes reduced as the wing loading is increased above the optimum, because the lift-to-drag ratio gets smaller as the wing is reduced in size, resulting in a poorer ratio of wing area to total wetted area of the wing, body, and tail. At lower wing loadings, the wing is getting too large and heavy, so that the range is reduced. At lower thrust loadings, the airplane does not have enough thrust to reach its best cruise altitude, and its range is penalized. With higher thrust loadings, the engines become so heavy that range is also adversely affected.

There are several boundaries that put restrictions on the use of the high wing loading that is optimum from the standpoint of range capability. One boundary shown is that of the engine-out cruise altitude, here set at a practical value of 15,000 feet. This parameter can be particularly restrictive on two-engine airplanes. The boundaries of the field lengths for takeoff and landing, chosen here as 2,000 feet, particularly important in this study as well, are shown. Any airplane meeting the requirements of these boundaries must lie above or to the left (or both) of all of them on this T/W-W/S field. For an airplane using only an aerodynamic high-lift system, the landing distance depends only on the wing loading (the small effect of thrust reversing changing with T/W is ignored here). The takeoff field length is a function of both W/S and T/W, because at high thrust levels the airplane can accelerate quickly to the high takeoff speeds needed by higher wing loadings. When a powered-lift system is used, both takeoff and landing distances are functions of both T/W and W/S, and the boundaries are moved to higher wing loading because of the greater lift coefficients that can be created. One of the great values of this type of chart is that it enables the designer not only to pick an optimum configuration, but, more importantly, also to see easily where moving off optimum

Figure A-01: STOL Airplane Design Chart. *Courtesy of the Boeing Company*

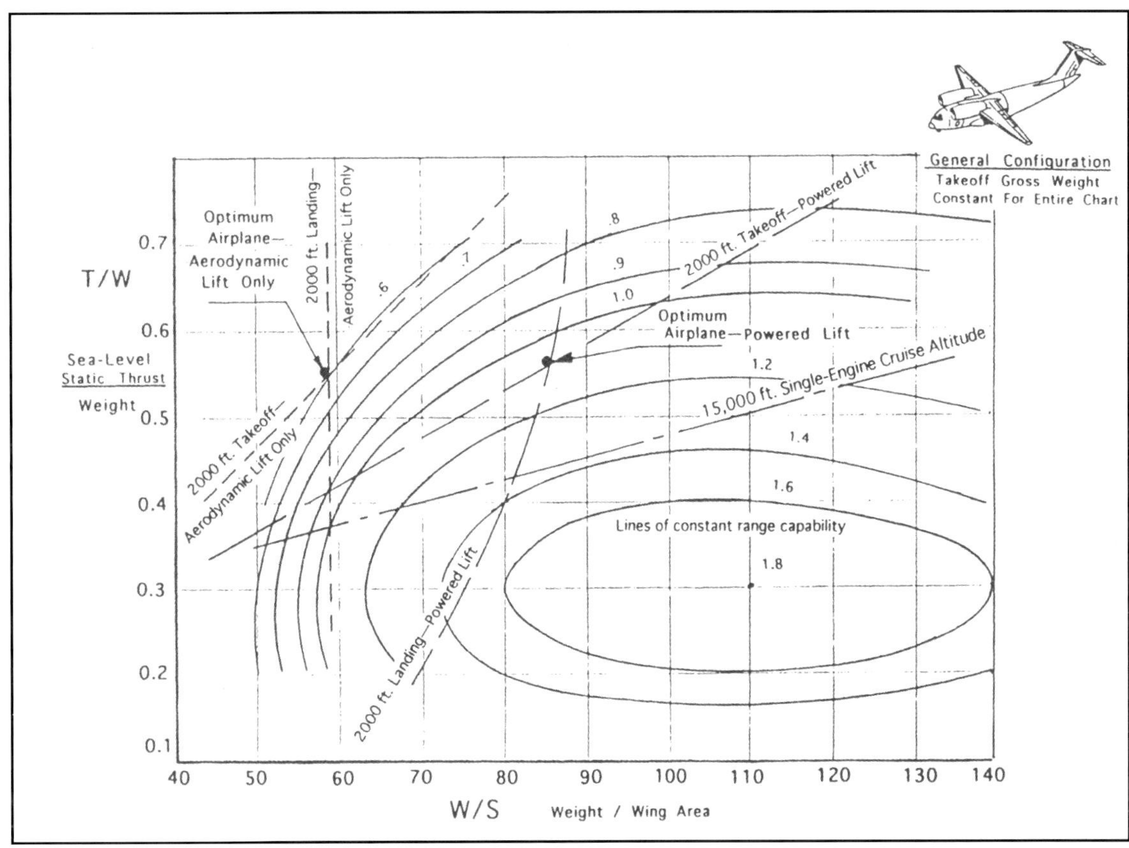

may markedly increase one aspect of performance, with very little penalty in the others. This visibility of possible tradeoffs is not nearly as evident if a mathematical optimization analysis is done on a digital computer, leading to a specific "optimum" configuration.

It can be seen from this plot that an airplane meeting 2,000-foot field lengths for both takeoff and landing and having only an aerodynamic high-lift system has a wing loading of about 60 pounds per square foot. Its range is only about 60% as great as that of an airplane using a powered-lift system, which has a wing loading of about 85 pounds per square foot. This loss in range is due to the weight of the larger wing. In addition, the lower wing loading would result in an intolerably rough ride at high speed in turbulent conditions. The engine size for the two types of airplanes is about the same. Although not shown in figure A-01, calculations have indicated that if the field length requirement is relaxed to 3,000 feet, the corresponding boundaries move to the point that the powered-lift airplane becomes limited by the engine-out altitude. This airplane would have about 25% more range and a smaller engine than its 2,000-foot counterpart. It is apparent, then, that if truly short field lengths are desired, the thrust must be deflected in some way to aid or augment the usual aerodynamic high-lift capability. It is apparent that the exact definition of how short a field is desired can have a large influence on the airplane's overall performance.

The kind of plot shown in figure A-01 was used to select the proper wing loadings for the various thrust deflection methods that were considered in the TAI studies. At the same time, rather detailed drawings were made of the inboard profiles of the aircraft, in particular how the engine installations were arranged to augment the aerodynamic lift. These studies went on for about a year, into the middle of 1971. None of the configurations looked particularly attractive to Boeing. None of them gave the really good results that they felt were needed.

Appendix 2
Technical Charts

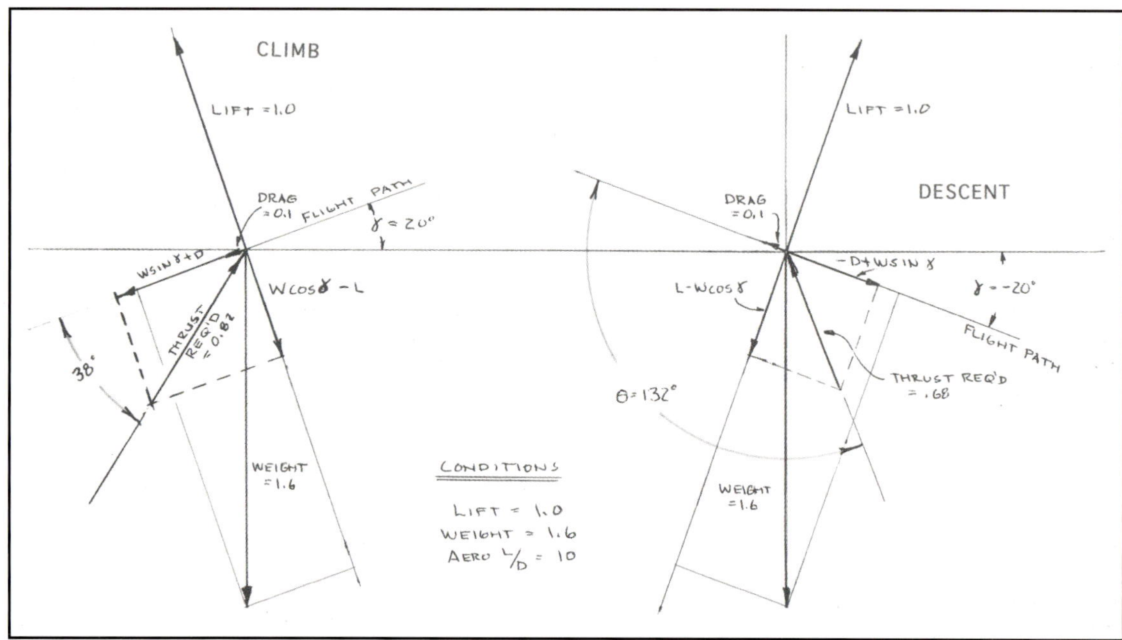

Figure A-02: The basic vectors of flight using deflected thrust. The diagram shows that descent requires 83% as much thrust as does climb, and the thrust must be deflected 94° further. The large climb and descent angle of 20° has been used here in order to make the diagram more readable. For a more realistic value of 6°, descent required 95% as much thrust as does climb, and the thrust must be deflected 25° further to 96° from the flight path.

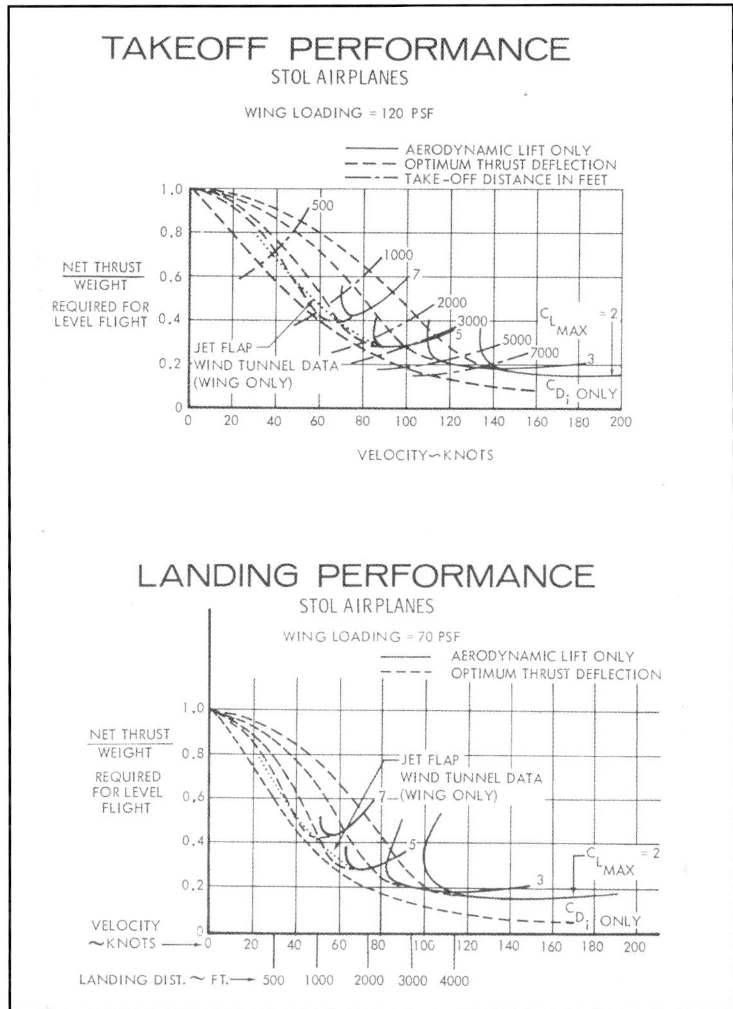

Figure A-03: Shown here is the thrust required to maintain level flight by using lift systems having various values of CL max. The two values of wing loading are those that might be associated with takeoff and landing. To fly at a speed needed to use a field length of 2,000 feet, thrust deflection is required even if a CL max is 3.0—a very high value for a mechanical high-lift system. The "CDi only" line represents a wing achieving unlimited CL max while creating only induced drag (no aerodynamic separation) and using optimum thrust deflection as velocity is reduced. The jet flap performance is close to this minimum thrust-required line since, by its nature, the jet flap produces high aerodynamic lift and near-optimum thrust deflection at the same time.

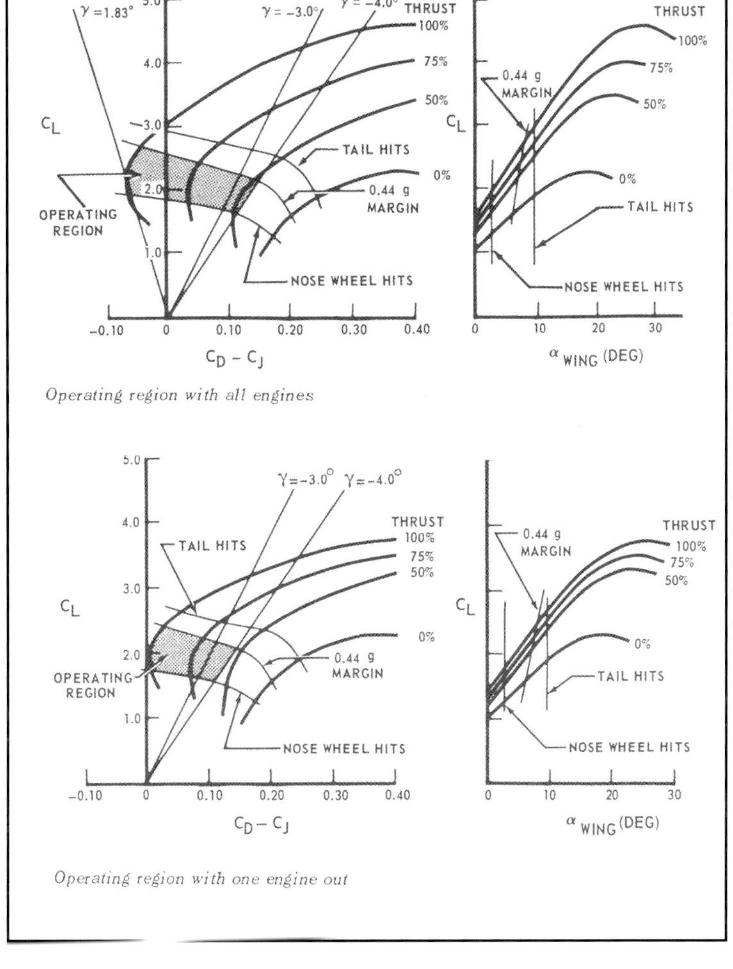

Figure A-04: The externally blown flap on the Boeing submittal to the C-5A Competition. The dark solid lines represent the net thrust-minus-drag polars of the airplane in the landing configuration. Superimposed are the attitude limitations, the requirement to descend 1 degree below the normal 3-degree glide slope, and the requirement for adequate maneuver margin (0.44 g—the same value achieved by normal FAA certification standards). The airplane can climb using all engines but just barely can fly level with one engine inoperative (without changing flap angle). Real-life restrictions thus have reduced a CL max of 4.3 to a usable CL of 2.1, still about 15% better than a mechanical flap of similar geometry.

Figure A-05: Static thrust deflection. The superior efficiency of upper surface blowing (USB) as compared to that of the externally blown flap (EBF) contributed greatly to the YC-14 performance. The differences may seem small until it is realized that for each 1% improvement in efficiency at takeoff, the payload could be increased 900 pounds. *Reprinted with permission form AIAA Preprint AIAA-75-1015 © 1975*

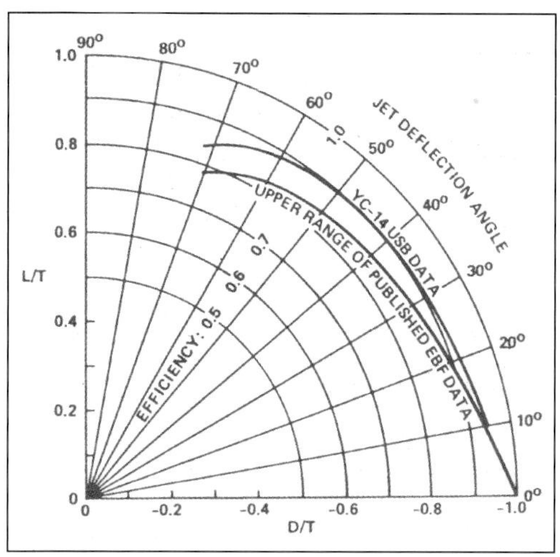

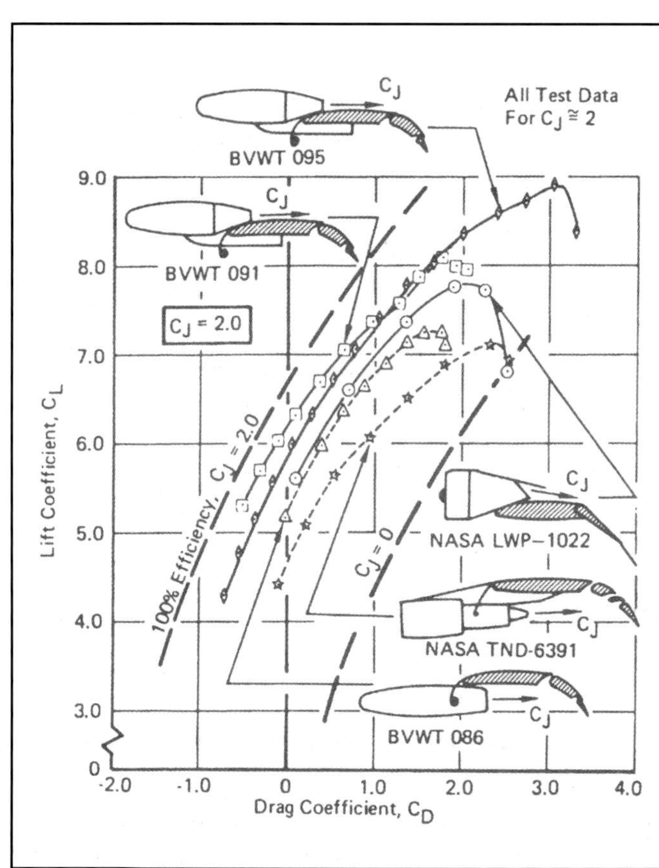

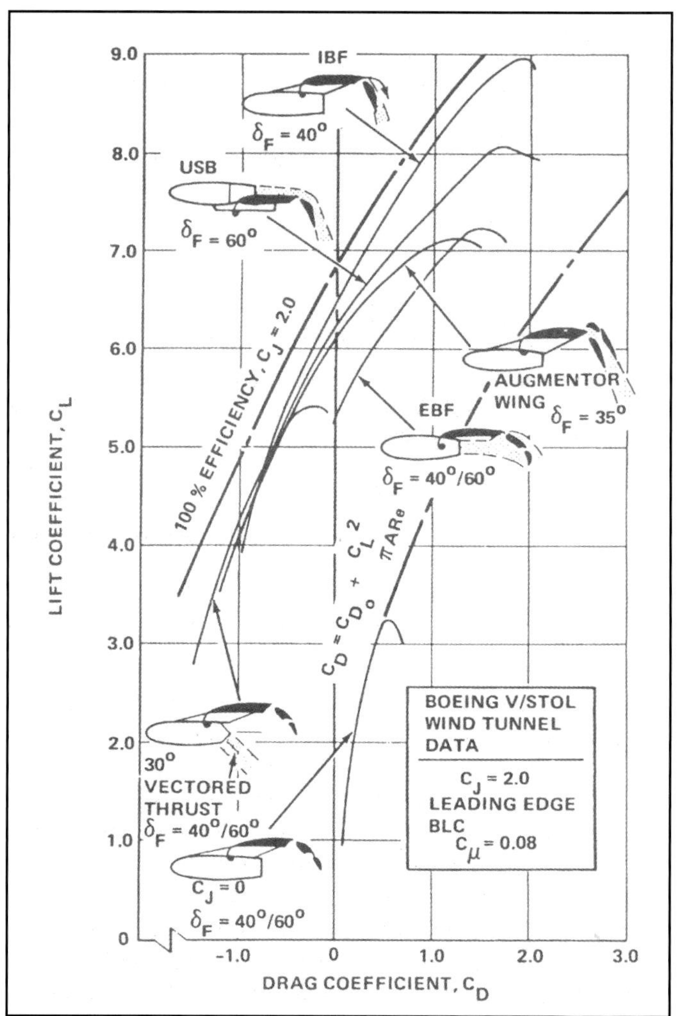

Figures A-06 and A-07: Powered-lift polar comparison. Both Boeing and NASA data agreed that the USB approach produced the best result. Although the augmentor wing and the internally blown flap (IBF) showed good performance, it was impracticable to duct through the wing the large quantities of air required. *Courtesy of the Boeing Company*

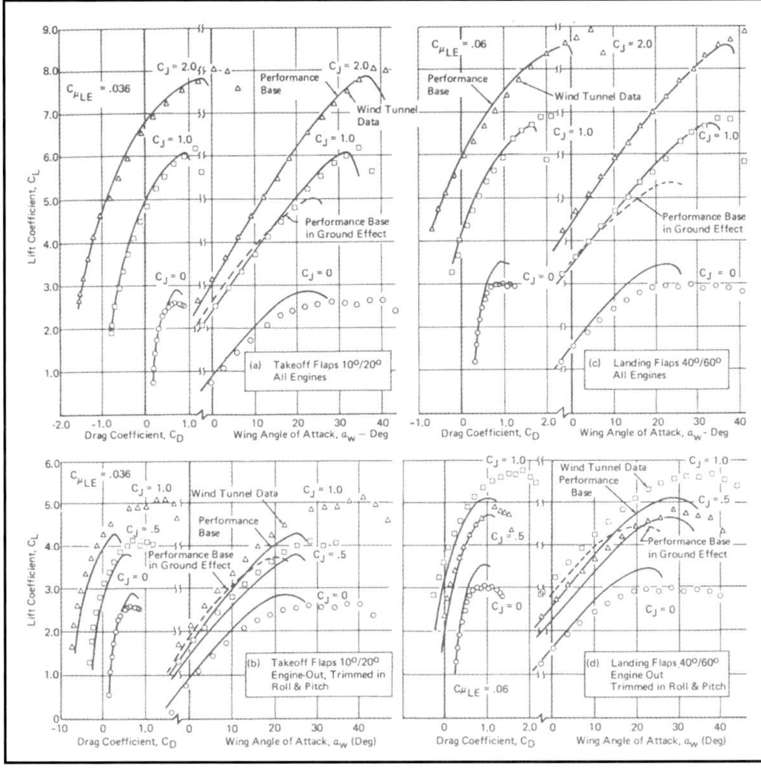

Left: Figure A-08: Basic wind-tunnel data submitted in the proposal. These data were adjusted for geometry differences between the wind tunnel model and the AMST proposal configuration to obtain the basis for the performance calculations. *Courtesy of the Boeing Company*

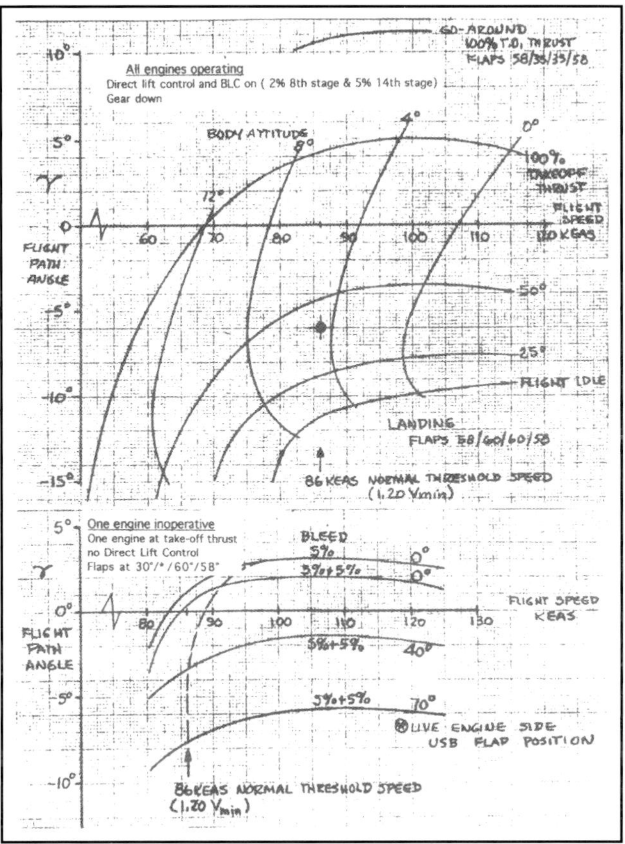

Above: Figure A-09: Landing and go-around performance was estimated from wind tunnel data: 160,000 pounds of gross weight, sea level, 59°F. *Courtesy of the Boeing Company*

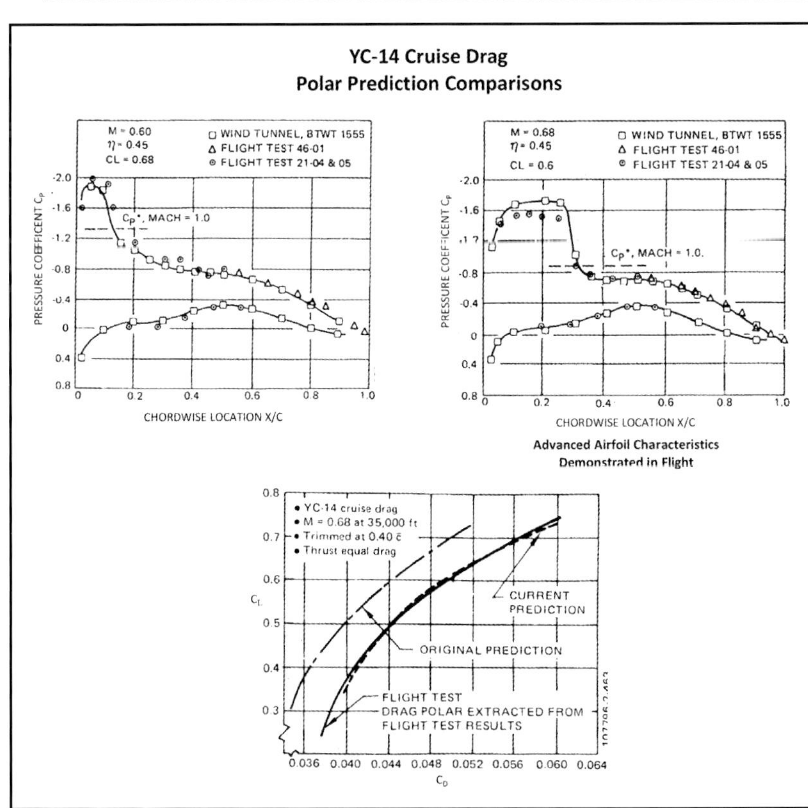

Left: Figure A-10: Flight test / wind tunnel test comparisons. Pressure distributions on the YC-14 wing were measured both in flight and in the wind tunnel, and this figure shows the good correlation obtained. It appears that the wing was operating as designed and was not the source of excess drag as postulated in the Air Force Flight Test Report. The error in drag prediction was due mostly to inadequate wind tunnel testing at cruise speed during YC-14 development, since all emphasis at the time was on STOL flight. These very expensive wind tunnel tests involved duplicating engine gross thrust, using airflow to simulate the jet exhaust. The gross thrust force is much greater than the airplane drag, since no ram engine drag is included (it must be put in by calculation), and it must be measured extremely carefully in order to get good results. Also, many special tests must be made to get mounting-interference effects. Cost and schedule pressures prohibited paying adequate attention to these details for the YC-14. Subsequent refined testing done for the C-14 proposal produced a drag "prediction" based on wind tunnel data much closer to the flight test results. *Courtesy of the Boeing Company*

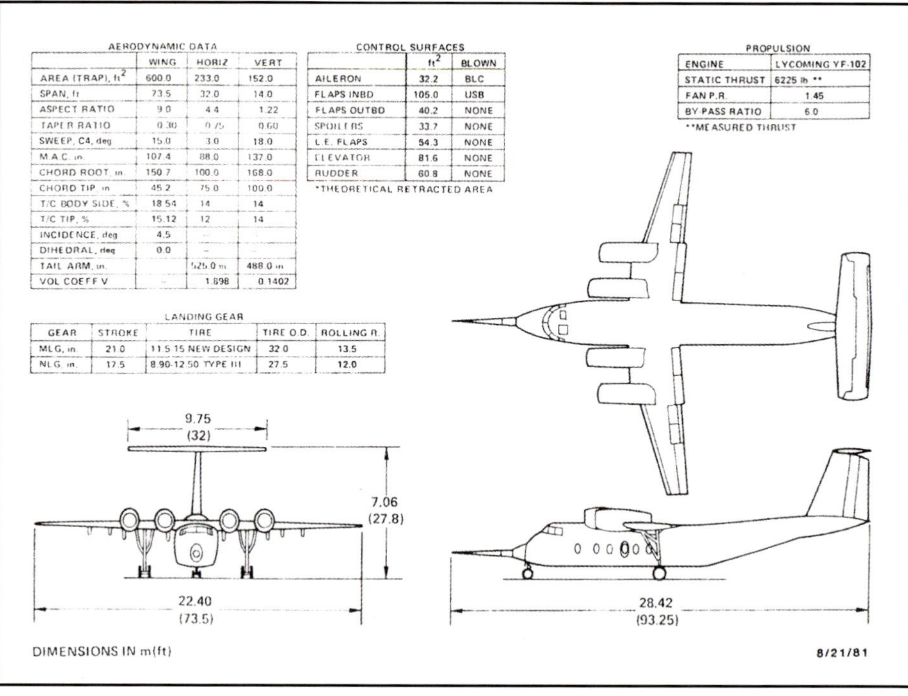

AERODYNAMIC DATA

	WING	HORIZ	VERT
AREA (TRAP), ft^2	600.0	233.0	152.0
SPAN, ft	73.5	32.0	14.0
ASPECT RATIO	9.0	4.4	1.22
TAPER RATIO	0.30	0.75	0.60
SWEEP, C4, deg	15.0	3.0	18.0
M.A.C. in.	107.4	88.0	137.0
CHORD ROOT, in.	150.7	100.0	168.0
CHORD TIP, in	45.2	75.0	100.0
T/C BODY SIDE, %	18.54	14	14
T/C TIP, %	15.12	12	14
INCIDENCE, deg	4.5	–	–
DIHEDRAL, deg	0.0	–	–
TAIL ARM, in.		525.0 in	488.0 in
VOL COEFF V	–	1.898	0.1402

CONTROL SURFACES

	ft^2	BLOWN
AILERON	32.2	BLC
FLAPS INBD	105.0	USB
FLAPS OUTBD	40.2	NONE
SPOILERS	33.7	NONE
L.E. FLAPS	54.3	NONE
ELEVATOR	81.6	NONE
RUDDER	60.8	NONE

*THEORETICAL RETRACTED AREA

PROPULSION

ENGINE	LYCOMING YF-102
STATIC THRUST	6225 lb **
FAN P.R.	1.45
BY-PASS RATIO	6.0

**MEASURED THRUST

LANDING GEAR

GEAR	STROKE	TIRE	TIRE O.D.	ROLLING R.
MLG, in.	21.0	11.5-15 NEW DESIGN	32.0	13.5
NLG, in.	17.5	8.90-12.50 TYPE III	27.5	12.0

Figure A-11: Technical details of the NASA Quiet STOL Research Aircraft (QSRA). *Public domain*

Figure A-12: Boundary-Layer Control (BLC) System

As described in chapter 3 and shown in the diagram on Page 58 and the picture on Page 59, the YC-14 had a typical BLC system where the air for the leading-edge boundary-layer control system was bled from the compressor of the engine. However, its purpose was not to augment the momentum of the basic airflow over the wing. Its purpose was to augment the flow within the boundary layer (that part of the airflow very close to the skin of the wing where it is affected by friction between the air and the wing surface). When the leading-edge and trailing-edge flaps are positioned for landing, the airflow over the top of the wing leading edge is at a very high velocity, creating very low pressures in that location. Just behind that area the airflow starts to slowdown as it goes towards the wing trailing edge, and the pressure rises. The flow in the boundary layer, which has been slowed by friction, does not have the momentum needed to push its airflow against this rising pressure. Therefore, the boundary-layer airflow tends to separate off the wing surface, forcing the free stream flow to do the same, thereby creating a large loss in lift and an increase in drag. The boundary-layer control flow, having a small volume (less than 7 percent of engine compressor flow) but high momentum is injected into the boundary layer in the downstream direction. Through mixing, it gives the boundary-layer flow the momentum it needs to push against the rising free stream pressure. The free stream airflow follows the boundary layer and thereby retains its proper direction parallel to the wing surface, maintaining its high lift and at the same time giving good flow over the ailerons, thereby maintaining their effectiveness. It's the case of a relatively small amount of momentum, injected with great finesse at just the right point, can have an influence on the entire flow on the wing.

Image 1
Free-Flowing Nozzle

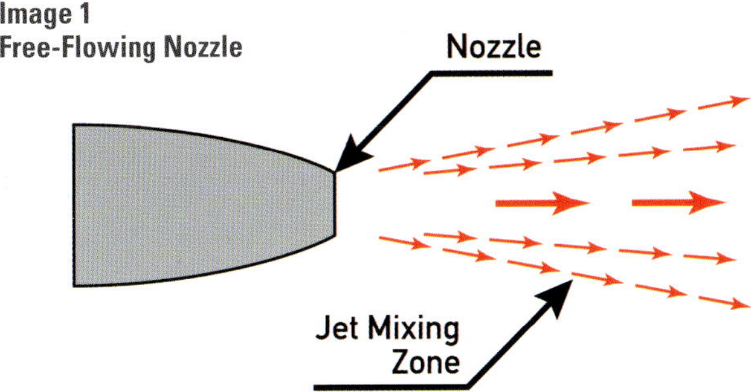

Image 2
Departing Entrained Air Lowers Pressure on Curved Surface

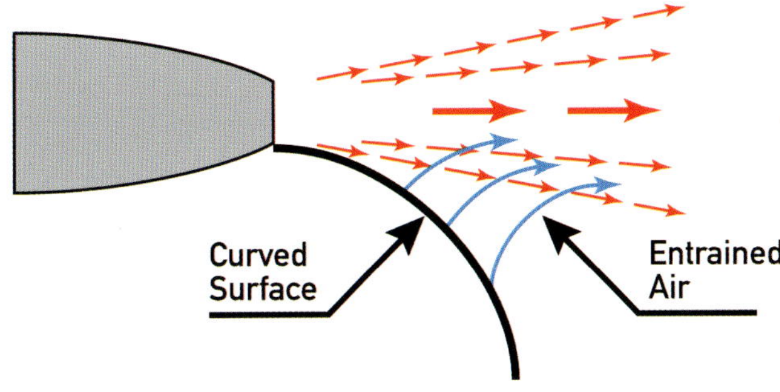

Image 3
Lowered Pressure Causes Jet Flow to Turn

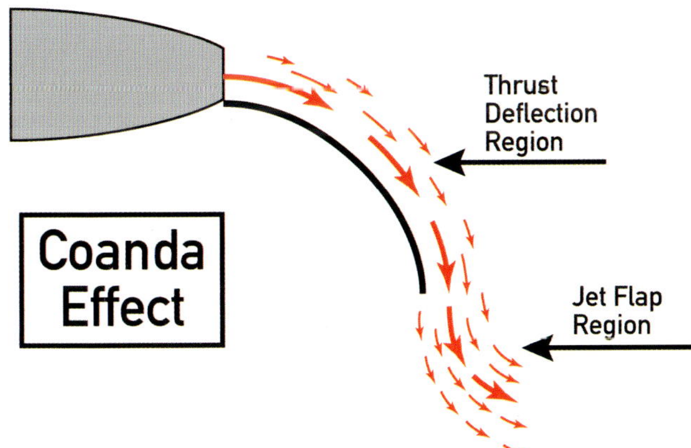

Courtesy of Jennings Heilig

Figure A-13: THE COANDA EFFECT

How The Coanda Effect creates the non-intuitive turning of a jet stream is described here.

Image 1 shows a nozzle exhausting into ambient air. The nozzle flow mixes on its boundary with the ambient air and drags some of this entrained air along with it. The mixing boundary gradually expands in area and slows the nozzle air until it has lost its kinetic energy, which has turned into heat via the mixing of a multitude of vortices. If the ambient air is not static but is moving beside and behind the nozzle, the mixing slows the nozzle flow to the point where its speed is the same as the speed of the ambient flow.

Image 2 shows a curved surface placed along the lower boundary of the jet as it exits the nozzle. Just as shown in image 1 the jet mixes with the ambient air along its boundary. With the curved surface in place the entrainment caused by the mixing lowers the pressure between the jet and the curved surface. Entrainment carries flow away from this mixing area faster than it can be drawn in from both sides of the jet.

Image 3 shows the result of the pressure in the lower mixing area getting so low that the higher pressures above the jet push it down until it nearly parallels the direction of the curved surface. If the jet is thin compared to the radius of the turn of the surface, the flow at the trailing edge nearly matches the angle of the trailing edge surface. If the jet is relatively thick, the turning won't be complete, and the turning of the jet momentum will be less than the turning of the surface. When the nozzle flow reaches the trailing edge of the curved surface, it still may have a great deal of momentum. If the nozzle and curved surface are moving through the ambient air, the jet then acts like a jet flap described by I. M. Davidson (Ref. 1), distorting the ambient flow around the surface (and its associated wing) in a way that augments the lift. In the case of the YC-14, this jet flap effect was such that for every pound of thrust that was deflected the airplane actually showed 2 pounds of upward force.

References and Bibliography

References

1. Davidson, I. M., "The Jet Flap," *Journal of the Royal Aeronautical Society*, Vol. 60, No. 541, 1956, pp. 25–50.

2. Schairer, G. S., "A Designer Looks at V/STOL," paper presented at the NASA Langley Research Center, Hampton, Virginia, 1959 (unpublished).

3. Schairer, G. S., "Looking Ahead in V/STOL." Joint Meeting of the Inst. of the Aeronautical Sciences and The Royal Aeronautical Society, London, Sept. 1961 (unpublished).

4. Wimpress, J. K., "Shortening the Take-off and Landing Field Lengths of High-Speed Aircraft," 26th Meeting of the AGARD Flight Mechanics Panel, June 1965 (unpublished).

5. Wimpress, J. K., "Aerodynamic Technology Applied to Takeoff and Landing," *Annals of the New York Academy of Sciences, International Congress on Subsonic Aeronautics*, Vol. 154, Article 2, Nov. 1968, pp. 962–981.

6. Foody, J. L., "The Air Force/Boeing Advanced Medium STOL Transport Prototype," Society of Automotive Engineers, Preprint No. 730365, Air Transportation Meeting, Miami, FL., April 1973.

7. Kimes, L. J., "YC-14 Engine Installation Features," AIAA paper 74-972, Aug. 1974.

8. Skavdahl, H., Wang, T., and Hirt, W. J., "Nozzle Development for the Upper Surface Blown Jet Flap on the YC-14 Airplane," Society of Automotive Engineers, Preprint No. 740469, Air Transportation Meeting, Dallas, TX., April 1974.

9. Wimpress, J. K., "Upper Surface Blowing Technology as Applied to the YC-14 Airplane," Society of Automotive Engineers, Preprint No. 730916, National Aerospace Engineering and Manufacturing Meeting, Los Angeles, CA., Oct. 1973.

10. May, F. W., and Bean, G. E., "Aerodynamic Design of the Boeing YC-14 Advanced Medium STOL Transport (AMST)," AIAA paper 75-1015, Aug. 1975.

11. Lee, A. H., "YC-14 Flight Control," AIAA paper 75-1027, Aug. 1975.

12. Lee, A. H., "YC-14 Flight Control System Development Experience," Flight Control Criteria Symposium, Naval Postgraduate School, Monterey, CA, July 1978.

13. Spitzer, R. E., "Use of the Flight Simulator in YC-14 Design," Boeing Aerospace Co., Sept. 1975.

14. Ernst, H. L., and Gupta, A., "YC-14 System for Leading Edge Boundary-Layer Control," AIAA paper 74-1278, Oct. 1974.

15. Foster, B. E., "YC-14 Advanced Medium STOL Transport Final Flight Test Report," Boeing Aerospace Co., DC748-10130-1, Oct. 1977.

Bibliography

For convenience, this bibliography is grouped into four areas: YC-14, Coanda Effect, An-71/72/73/74, and Japanese STOL. Those references listed under the YC-14 heading provide descriptive material on the YC-14 beyond that given in the case study text. Those references given under the Coanda Effect heading will provide the reader with some background on the Coanda Effect concept used to enhance the lift of the YC-14 aircraft. Those references that describe Soviet-Russian aircraft utilizing technology, similar to that employed in the YC-14 design, are listed under the An 71/72/73/74 heading. Similarly, Japanese STOL aircraft descriptions are listed under the Japanese STOL heading.

YC-14

"RFPs Issued for Medium STOL Transport," *Aviation Week & Space Technology*, Vol. 96, No. 5, 1972, p. 21.

"USAF Asks Proposals on STOL Engine," *Aviation Week & Space Technology*, Vol. 96, No. 7, 1972, p. 26.

Spitzer, R. E., Rumsey, P.C., and Quigley, H.C., "Use of the Flight Simulator in the Design of a STOL Research Aircraft," AIAA paper 72-762, AIAA 5th Aircraft Design, Flight Test and Operations Meeting, Los Angeles, Aug. 1972.

"Boeing AMST Concept Shown," *Aviation Week & Space Technology*, Vol. 97, No. 19, 1972, p. 13.

Twiss, R. L., "Boeing Reaches Finals of STOL Program," *The Seattle Times*, Nov. 10, 1972, p. A-1.

"Boeing Wins $95.2-million STOL Contract," *Seattle Post-Intelligencer*, Nov. 11, 1972, p. A-1.

"Boeing STOL: 'Great Potential' Seen," *The Seattle Times*, Nov. 11, 1972, p. A-4.

"Boeing Wins Contract for Advanced Plane," *The Renton Record-Chronicle*, Vol. LI, No. 136, Nov. 12, 1972, pp. 1–2.

Twiss, R.L., "Boeing Official Sees Great Future in STOL," *The Seattle Times*, Nov. 19, 1972, p. E3.

"Competitors Picked for Advanced STOL," *Aviation Week & Space Technology*, Vol. 97, No. 21, 1972, pp. 16–17.

"NASA Awards Lockheed Team QUESTOL Design Refinement," *Aviation Week & Space Technology*, Vol. 97, No. 22, 1972, p. 19.

Kolcum, E.H., "Air Cushion Landing Proposed for AMST," *Aviation Week & Space Technology*, Vol. 98, No. 2, 1973, pp. 40–44.

"Boeing Freezes AMST Prototype Design," *Aviation Week & Space Technology*, Vol. 100, No. 11, 1974, pp. 38–41.

"Boeing Contract is Revamped," *The Seattle Times*, May 14, 1974, p. C16.

Tactical Gunship Version of the Boeing YC-14 Advanced Medium STOL Aircraft is Being Studied by the Manufacturer and the Air Force," *Aviation Week & Space Technology* (Industry Observer), Vol.101, No. 9, 1974, p. 13.

"Upper Surface Blowing Configured Rockwell International Aero Commander with United Aircraft of Canada JT15D Engines is Furnishing NASA Langley Research Center Aerodynamic and Noise Data (NASA photo by Robert E. Nye)," *Aviation Week & Space Technology*, Vol. 101, No. 12, 1974, p. 1, cover.

"YC-15 Ready for Fuselage Mating," *Aviation Week & Space Technology*, Vol. 101, No. 17, 1974, p. 36.

"Free-flight (YC-14) Model," *Aviation Week & Space Technology*, Vol. 101, No. 17, 1974, p. 53.

"AMST Adaptability to Transports Studied," *Aviation Week & Space Technology*, Vol. 101, No. 17, 1974, p. 55.

"NASA Refining Present STOL Concepts," *Aviation Week & Space Technology*, Vol. 101, No. 17, 1974, p. 56.

Davenport, F. J., and Hunt, D.N. " Deflection of a Thick Jet by a Convex Surface: A Practical Problem of Powered Lift," AIAA paper 75-167, 13th Aerospace Sciences Meeting, Pasadena, California, Jan. 1975.

"AMST-A Hercules for the 1980s." *Flight International*, Vol. 107, No. 3438, 1975, pp. 147–155.

Elson, B.M., "Eased Pilot Workload Sought in YC-14," *Aviation Week & Space Technology*, Vol. 102, No. 8, 1975, pp. 56–57.

"Boeing AMST (YC-14) at Halfway Mark," *Boeing News*, Vol. 34, No. 12, 1975, p. 3.

"The World Has Waited 43 Years for This Idea. It's Worth Waiting One More. (Boeing YC-14)," *Aviation Week & Space Technology*, Vol. 102, No. 23, 1975, pp. 50–51.

"The Jet That Could Land in the Grand Canyon with a 27,000-pound Payload. (Boeing YC-14)," *Aviation Week & Space Technology*, Vol. 103, No. 1, 1975, pp. 30–31.

"Boeing Seeks Expanded Military Sales," *Aviation Week & Space Technology*. Vol. 103, No. 5, 1975, p. 22.

Kestek, R. E. "YC-14 Digital Flight Control Data Management," AIAA paper 75-1087, AIAA Guidance and Control Conference, Boston, Massachusetts, Aug. 1975.

Curnutt, R. A., and Tomich, E.J., "Electronics Systems Contribution to YC-14 STOL Performance." IEEE EASCON '75 Conference, Sept. 1975.

Twiss, R. L., "Engines for Boeing's New Short-field Transport Test OK," *The Seattle Times*, Feb. 29, 1976, p. C8.

"YC-14 Propulsive Lift System Tested," *Aviation Week & Space Technology*, Vol. 104, No. 10, 1976, p. 47.

"Boeing AMST Entry Nearing Completion," *Aviation Week & Space Technology*, Vol. 104, No. 14, 1976, pp. 44–45.

"YC-14 Answers Multiple Needs as a New-Era Tactical Airplane," *Boeing News*, Vol. 35, No. 14, 1976, p. 3.

Foody, J. J., "YC-14 Status Report," Society of Automotive Engineers, Preprint No. 760539, SAE National Air Transportation Meeting, New York, May 1976.

"Revolutionary YC-14 Debuts Tomorrow at Boeing Field," *Boeing News*, Vol. 35, No. 23, 1976, p. 1.

"Boeing YC-14 Prototype Ready to Compete with Douglas' YC-15," *The Renton Record-Chronicle*, Vol. LV, No. 95, June 13, 1976, p. 8, sec. A.

Pryne, E., "YC-14: Boeing Hopes Ride on its Payload," *The Renton Record-Chronicle*, Vol. LV, No. 101, June 24, 1976, p. 2, sec. A.

"Boeing Readies YC-14 for Flight Test," *Aviation Week & Space Technology*, Vol. 104, No. 25, 1976, p. 22.

"Details of YC-14 Engines, Flaps Shown," *Aviation Week & Space Technology*, Vol. 105, No. 3, 1976, p. 25.

"Lifting Power," *The Seattle Times*, Aug. 10, 1976, p. A3.

Twiss, R. L., "Boeing's Dumpy-Looking Plane is Pretty in Test," *The Seattle Times*, Aug. 10, 1976, p. B-8.

"Beautiful Test for the Ugly YC-14," *Seattle Post-Intelligencer*, Aug. 10, 1976, p. A-6.

"The Payoff," *The Renton Record-Chronicle*, Vol. LV, No. 128, Aug. 11, 1976, pp. 1-2, sec. A.

"YC-14 Makes First Flight; Year of Testing to Follow," *Boeing News*, Vol. 35, No. 32, 1976, p. 1.

"Boeing YC-14 Entry in AMST Competition," *Aviation Week & Space Technology*, Vol. 105, No. 7, 1976, p. 1, cover.

O'Lone, G., "First Flight Launches YC-14 Testing," *Aviation Week & Space Technology*, Vol. 105, No. 7, 1976, pp. 22–23.

"Boeing's AMST Entry Readied for First Flight," *Aviation Week & Space Technology*, Vol. 105, No. 7, 1976, p. 45

"End of YC-14's Perfect First Flight," *Boeing News*, Vol. 35. No. 33, 1976, p. 1.

Twiss, R. L., "YC-14 Performing Well in Early Tests," *The Seattle Times*, Sept. 12, 1976, p. B-8.

"Our Ugly Duckling Just Turned into a Swan. (Boeing YC-14)," *Aviation Week & Space Technology*, Vol. 105, No. 14, 1976, pp. 30–31.

Twiss, R. L., "YC-14 'Boeing's Most Exciting Since B-47," *The Seattle Times*, March 6, 1977, p. C-6.

Fink, D. E, "YC-14 Nearing Joint Test Force Trials," *Aviation Week & Space Technology*, Vol. 105, No. 15, 1976, pp. 41–43.

"Second YC-14 in Flight," *The Renton Record-Chronicle*, Vol. LV, No. 174, 1976, p. 2, sec. A.

Elson, B.M., "USAF YC-14 Prototypes Begin New Flight Test Phase," *Aviation Week & Space Technology*, Vol. 105, No. 22, 1976, pp. 64–65.

"McDonnell Douglas YC-15 (top) and Boeing YC-14. Competitors in the USAF Advanced Medium STOL Transport Program are Shown in Flight Demonstrations at the Paris Air Show (AW&ST photos by Steven G. Hanson)," *Aviation Week & Space Technology*, Vol. 106, No. 25, 1977. p. 1, cover.

"Boeing YC-14 STOL Transport Lifts Off," *Aviation Week & Space Technology*, Vol. 106, No. 25, 1977, p. 17.

"McDonnell Douglas YC-15 STOL Transport," *Aviation Week & Space Technology*, Vol. 106, No. 25, 1977, p. 19.

North, D.M., "YC-14 Designed to Cut Pilot Workload," *Aviation Week & Space Technology*, Vol. 107, No. 3, 1977, pp. 41–47.

Twiss, R.L, "Boeing YC-14 Praised at Paris Air Show," *The Seattle Times*, July 24, 1977, p. B-4.

Martin, D. L. and Gangaas, G., "Testing of the YC-14 Digital Flight Control System Software," AIAA paper 77-1077, ALAA Guidance and Control Conference, Hollywood, Florida, Aug., 1977.

"New Soviet Cargo Aircraft Tested," *Aviation Week & Space Technology*, Vol. 108, No. 2, 1978, p. 29.

"Boeing, McDonnell Douglas Eye Continued AMST Development," *Aviation Week & Space Technology*, Vol. 108, No. 3, 1978, p. 29.

"In the Long Run, the Best Decision for the Short Haul (Boeing YC-14)," *Aviation Week & Space Technology*, Vol. 108, No. 6, 1978, pp. 44–45.

Riddle, D. W., Innis, R.C., Martin, J. L., and Cochrane, J. A, "Powered-Lift Takeoff Performance Characteristics Determined from Flight Test of the Quiet Short-Haul Research Aircraft (QSRA)," AIAA paper 81-2409, AIAA/SETP/SFTE/SAE/IEEE/ITEA 1st Flight Testing Conference, Las Vegas, Nevada, Nov. 1981.

"McPherson Wins Flight Award," *Boeing News*, Vol. 40, No. 46, 1981, p. 1.

Poisson-Quinton, P., "The Jet Flap Story: An Opportunity for Wing/Propulsion Integration," The Royal Aeronautical Society, 22nd Lanchester Memorial Lecture, June 1982.

Pace, S., "Pumping Iron at Mach .7," *Airpower*, Vol. 18, No. 2, 1988, pp. 34–51.

"The YC-14: A Plane 'Ahead of Its Time," *Boeing News*, Vol. 50, No. 14, 1991, p. C.

Coanda Effect

Stine, G. H., "Coanda Effect." (Letters to the Editor), *Aviation Week & Space Technology*, Vol. 98, No. 1, 1973, p. 64.

Stine, G. H., "The Rises and Falls of Henri-Marie Coanda," *Air and Space*, Vol. 4, No. 3, 1989, pp. 90–95.

Reba, I., "Applications of the Coanda Effect," *Scientific American*, Vol. 214, No. 6, 1966, pp. 84–92.

Guzzardi, W. Jr., "Cutting Russia's Harvest of US Technology," *Fortune*, Vol. 107, No. 11, 1983, pp. 102–112.

An 71/72/73/74

"New Soviet Cargo Aircraft Tested," *Aviation Week & Space Technology*, Vol. 108, No. 2, 1978, p. 29.

"An-72 Aerodynamic Features Shown," *Aviation Week & Space Technology*, Vol. 108, No. 4, 1978, p. 30.

Wetmore, W. C., "An-72 STOL Prototype Debuts in West," *Aviation Week & Space Technology*, Vol. 110, No. 25, 1979, pp. 20–22.

"Soviet Designers Shown with An-72 Transport," *Aviation Week & Space Technology*, Vol. 115, No. 23, 1981, p. 43.

"Soviet Claim World Records for Antonov An-72 Transport," *Aviation Week & Space Technology*, Vol. 119, No. 26, 1983, p. 11.

"USSR An-72 Displays Aerobatic Maneuverability," *Aviation Week & Space Technology*, Vol. 121, No. 11, 1984, p. 31.

"Soviet An-72 Transport Flies at Farnborough Air Show," *Aviation Week & Space Technology*, Vol. 121, No. 13, 1984, p. 58.

"Soviet Display Helicopter, Transport," *Aviation Week & Space Technology*, Vol. 122, No. 15, 1984, pp. 64–65.

"Soviet An-74 at Paris Air Show (AW&ST photo by Robin Adshead)," *Aviation Week & Space Technology*, Vol. 126, No. 25, 1987, p. 1, cover.

Fricker, J., "Russian AWACS Programs Face Funding Problems," *Aviation Week & Space Technology*, Vol. 143, No. 23, 1995, pp. 89–92.

Japanese STOL

O'Lone, R., "Japan's STOL Highlights Air Show," *Aviation Week & Space Technology*, Vol. 119, No. 19, 1983, pp. 16–18.

"Japan's STOL Uses Blown Flaps for Lift," *Aviation Week & Space Technology*, Vol. 119, No. 21, 1983, p. 16.

"Japan's STOL Transport at Gifu Air Show (AW&ST photo by Shisel Kuwabara)," *Aviation Week & Space Technology*, Vol. 119, No. 26, 1983, p. 1, cover.

"STOL Program Ends (Industry Observer)," *Aviation Week & Space Technology*, Vol. 134, No. 14, 1991, p. 11.